THE POINT OF LAW

DATA PROTECTION ACT EXPLAINED

(Third Edition)

PIERS LEIGH-POLLITT & JAMES MULLOCK

London: The Stationery Office

Applications for reproduction should be made in writing to The Stationery Office Limited, St Crispins, Duke Street, Norwich NR3 1PD.

The information contained in this publication is believed to be correct at the time of manufacture. Whilst care has been taken to ensure that the information is accurate, neither the publisher nor the authors can accept responsibility for any errors or ommissions or for changes to the details given. Every effort has been made to trace copyright holders and to obtain permission for the use of copyright material. The publishers will gladly receive any information enabling them to rectify any errors or omissions in subsequent editions.

Piers Leigh-Pollitt and James Mullock have asserted their moral rights under the Copyright, Design and Patents Act 1988, to be identified as the authors of this work.

A CIP catalogue record for this book is available from the British Library
A Library of Congress CIP catalogue record has been applied for

First edition © Osborne Clarke 1999
Second edition © Osborne Clarke 2000
Third edition © Osborne Clarke 2001

ISBN 0 11 702754 5

Printed in the United Kingdom for The Stationery Office by Albert Gait Ltd, Grimsby.
TJ005245 C10 09/01 9385 14819

CONTENTS

The Data Protection Act 1998, Explained

The "Data Protection Act 1998, Explained" was written by Piers Leigh-Pollitt and James Mullock of Osborne Clarke, a firm of solicitors with offices in Bristol, London, Thames Valley, Barcelona, Brussels, Cologne, Copenhagen, Frankfurt, Helsinki, Madrid, Palo Alto, Paris, Rotterdam and Tallinn.

Piers Leigh-Pollitt is a solicitor in Osborne Clarke's Thames Valley Employment team, which provides a full breadth of contentious and non-contentious employment law advice to a range of commercial clients.

James Mullock is a partner in Osborne Clarke's London IT & Telecoms team and specialises in providing commercial legal advice to users and suppliers of technology services and products.

OSBORNE CLARKE UK OFFICES:

Osborne Clarke
London

Hillgate House
26 Old Bailey
London EC4M 7HS

Tel: 020 7809 1000
Fax: 020 7809 1005

Osborne Clarke
Thames Valley

Apex Plaza
Forbury Road
Reading RG1 1AX

Tel: 0118 925 2000
Fax: 0118 925 0038

Osborne Clarke
Bristol

50 Queen Charlotte Street
Bristol BS1 4HE

Tel: 0117 923 0220
Fax: 0117 927 9209

Web Site: http://www.osborneclarke.com

Disclaimer

This publication is intended to provide a brief commentary on the Data Protection Act 1998 and should not be relied upon by any party without taking further legal advice.

Additions to the third edition of this book

After much delay, the Data Protection Act 1998 ("the 1998 Act" or "the Act") finally came into force on 1 March 2000. The first edition of this text was written at a time when there was merely speculation about how some aspects of the 1998 Act would operate and before a number of other pieces of legislation affecting data privacy had been introduced in the UK. This new edition expands upon the previous two editions by providing the following additional information and commentary on:

- the Regulation of Investigatory Powers Act 2000 and the Lawful Business Practice Regulations 2000;
- the Freedom of Information Act 2000;
- the forthcoming Code of Practice on *The use of personal data in employer/employee relationships*;
- employee monitoring and setting up a monitoring programme;
- important new provisions relating to direct marketing;
- significant changes to the procedure for obtaining information about a worker's criminal records;
- up-dated information on cross-border data flows and the "safe harbour" agreement between the EU and the USA;
- additional practical guidance on "best practice" to ensure compliance with the 1998 Act;
- new regulations introduced to target communications providers.

Introduction

The aim of this book is to explain how the requirements of the 1998 Act affects those who use information about individuals.

The reader will be given a full understanding of the practical implications of the 1998 Act by means of comprehensive annotations to its provisions drawn from relevant experience from the Data Protection Act 1984 (the "1984 Act"), published guidance and personal analysis.

Unlike the 1984 Act, the 1998 Act imposes a number of obligations which must be satisfied before obtaining, recording or holding personal information. Criminal convictions and fines are the deterrents by which the 1998 Act will punish complacent organisations. This is in addition to the call on management time and bad publicity which may result from a data protection infringement.

As the importance of information to business and the expansion of the information industry both grow, the number of people whose working lives will be affected by the 1998 Act is bound to increase.

In particular, organisations should ensure that their marketing, personnel and IT departments have a working knowledge of the ways in which the 1998 Act governs their use of personal information.

The 1998 Act provides individuals whose personal information is processed by another person or company with more extensive rights than they have enjoyed previously. Individuals most likely to benefit from such rights are customers, employees and marketing contacts of a business.

Organisations will need to evaluate whether individuals genuinely have the right to access the information they seek. Exemptions and transitional provisions may apply in certain circumstances and organisations should be as much aware of their rights to restrict access as to the obligation to facilitate it.

The structure of this guide

The next section of this chapter *("the 1998 Act - an overview")* summarises the major provisions of the 1998 Act. It is intended as an introduction to the requirements with which organisations must comply. We recommend that those new to this legislation refer first to this overview. The following section *("Other UK Data Privacy Legislation and Codes of Practice")* introduces the reader to some of the other UK laws which regulate the use of data.

The introduction is concluded with a section *("Practical Application of the Acts")* which gives an overview of the types of policies and procedures which businesses could consider introducing to assist their compliance with the Acts. This section also includes a list of useful contact details, and a table and a series of flow diagrams which explain the 1998 Act's transitional provisions and certain rights granted to individuals under it.

There then follows a copy of the 1998 Act, with explanatory annotations which will also avoid the need to cross refer to other sections of the 1998 Act or to certain guidance notes published to the Commissioner.

Use of the term the "Commissioner" in this book is a reference to the position which, under the 1984 Act was known as the Data Protection Registrar. This title is changed to the Information Commissioner by virtue of section 6 of the 1998 Act. As, at the time of writing, the current Commissioner is Elizabeth France, all references made to the Commissioner in the annotations to the 1998 Act are in the feminine. Please note that the 1998 Act refers to the Commissioner in the masculine.

The 1998 Act – an overview

Does the 1998 Act affect you?

The 1998 Act applies to the *processing of data* which are deemed to be *personal data*, unless certain exemptions apply (see the overview on the Act's transitional provisions below, as well as Part IV, Schs 8, 13 and 14 of the Act).

All of the above terms set out in italics are defined at section 1(1) of the 1998 Act. Our commentary at that section explains more fully what those terms mean. However, in order to understand the terminology used in this overview, these key definitions are explained in broad terms below.

Data – this term covers not only information *processed* or which is intended to be *processed* by means of automatic devices (such as IT systems), but also information recorded on what the 1998 Act calls *relevant filing systems*.

Relevant filing systems – these refer to any structured set of information which is organised either by reference to individuals or by criteria relating to individuals so that specific details about a particular person may easily be selected from that system.

An example may assist. Mr Ostrich is a property surveyor and one of a number of people who have written to Mr Buzzard in connection with a proposed property purchase. A jumbled file of letters connected to the purchase kept by Mr Buzzard which includes correspondence sent by Mr Ostrich would not constitute a relevant filing system. This is because the file is neither structured nor organised in line with the definition in the 1998 Act. However, were the file to be re-arranged so that the correspondence were grouped by reference to the writer of each letter (for example, by name or occupation) then the file would become a relevant filing system.

Personal Data – this relates to *data* from which it is possible to identify a living individual, either directly from that information or from additional information which is in (or likely to come into) the possession of anyone *processing* that *data*.

The words "likely to come into the possession" were not included in the 1984 Act's definition of personal data. The Office of the Information Commissioner ("OIC") has verbally expressed its opinion to the authors that these words should be interpreted very broadly, to the extent they could be taken to mean "might conceivably". Whether the courts take this view remains to be seen, but the addition of the words is very significant since they mean that the 1998 Act may now apply to the use of information which does not on its own identify an individual such as a customer reference number, a post code or a telephone number.

The definition also specifically includes any expression of opinion and (unlike the 1984 Act) any indication of the intentions of the data user in respect of an individual. Personnel records will now therefore potentially be accessible to employees unless certain exemptions apply (for example, the exemptions covering management forecasts/planning, confidential references and negotiations - see Sch 7).

Processing – this term covers almost any conceivable use of *data*, from the moment the *data* are obtained, to the method of recording, retrieving, disclosing and destroying the *data*. The definition is far broader than that included in the 1984 Act. When added to the fact that the 1998 Act covers some manually recorded data, this means that many more uses of personal information are now subject to data protection legislation.

Finally, those who determine the manner in which processing is carried out are known as *"Data Controllers"*.

Do you need to notify the OIC that you are processing personal data?

Most businesses will be obliged to notify the OIC of the fact that they are processing personal data[1]. Failure to do so is a criminal offence, so it is important for all businesses, including small start-up companies, to address this issue from the outset. There are some exemptions from the requirement to notify and the OIC has produced a helpful, step-by-step publication to assist[2], available on the Commissioner's website[3].

Further commentary about notification is provided at s.16.

Timetable for the introduction of the 1998 Act – the transitional provisions

The European Directive[4] which the 1998 Act has been drafted to implement required member states to have introduced its provisions into their local laws by *24 October 1998*.

Although the 1998 Act had received Royal Assent by that date, it did not in fact become law until 1 March 2000.

Nevertheless as the 1998 Act was drafted on the assumption that it would be in force on 24 October 1998 that date remains key to its application, and particularly to the transitional provisions contained in Schedules 8 and 13. These provisions excuse the processing of certain types of data from having to comply with specified provisions of

1 The Data Protection (Notification and Notification Fees) Regulations 2000 (SI 2000/188)
2 Notification Exemptions: A Self-Assessment Guide (also published as part of Notification Handbook: A complete guide to notification)
3 See "Useful contact details" for website address
4 Directive 95/46/EC

the 1998 Act for three and nine year periods (depending on the category of data) from 24 October 1998.

The transitional provisions only apply to "processing which was already under way immediately before 24 October 1998"[5]. Analysis of what this might mean and the extent of the exemptions available are set out in the commentary to Schedules 8 and 13 and in the table and flow charts which can be found at Annex 1 to this introduction.

Interpretation of the 1998 Act

Authoritative interpretation of the 1998 Act will come primarily from the courts and, in some cases, from the Commissioner.

The parliamentary debates which finalised the wording of the 1998 Act may also provide guidance as to how it will be interpreted. In places such debates have been referred to in this book.

Very useful for anyone trying to understand UK data protection legislation are the two sets of guidance notes prepared by the Commissioner which, separately, explain her interpretation of the 1984 Act and the 1998 Act. Such guidance notes and access to all current UK data protection registrations can be found on the OIC website (details at the end of this introduction). In addition, the OIC has also published a draft Code of Practice entitled "The use of personal data in employer/employee relationships". At the time of writing, this Code remains in draft form, having provoked a great deal of interest (largely from employers) during the consultation phase. This Code will be examined in greater depth below.

Reference to the "Guidelines" in this book is to version 1 of "The Data Protection Act 1998, an Introduction" published in October 1998 by the Information Commissioner. Whilst the Guidelines are likely to be persuasive in any court deciding upon a data protection issue, it should be noted that they do not constitute a legally binding interpretation of the 1998 Act.

As stated above, the impetus for the 1998 Act derives from an EC Directive. The wording of the Directive will be significant in considering how the 1998 Act will be interpreted. Indeed, under European Union law, if there is a conflict between the wording of the Directive and that of the 1998 Act, individuals (but not companies) will be able to require that the Directive's provisions prevail.

Processing personal data – the major provisions of the 1998 Act explained

As with the 1984 Act, the 1998 Act grants individuals rights in relation to the processing by others of their personal data (see Part II of the Act), whilst requiring data controllers not to process personal data without complying with eight data protection principles (see Sch 1).

---

5   Sch 8, para. 1

However, unlike the 1984 Act, the 1998 Act expands the rights granted to individuals in relation to processing of their personal data. The 1998 Act also imposes new obligations upon data controllers by means of the data protection principles (specifically the first and eighth principles, both of which contain major new requirements).

Although the 1998 Act may on first glance look very similar in its layout to the 1984 Act, the devil is really in the detail.

A brief summary of these major changes is provided below, together with a cross reference to the relevant sections and schedules of the 1998 Act. The new requirements listed below are not intended to provide an exhaustive list of major changes introduced by the 1998 Act.

The first principle (see Sch 1, Part II, paras.1-4 and Schs 2 & 3) - this requires personal data to be processed "fairly and lawfully"[6]. Anyone processing data will be deemed to have done so fairly if they have supplied or made readily available to relevant data subjects the following details (which are referred to as the "fair processing information" in the Guidelines[7]):

1. the identity of the data controller and, if necessary, the identity of any representative appointed by it for the purposes of the 1998 Act;

2. the purpose(s) for which the data subject's personal data are or are intended to be processed; and

3. any other information which in the circumstances should be given to the data subject to ensure that processing is conducted fairly.

This information must be supplied or made available, so far as is possible, when the data are first processed (see Sch 1, Part II, para 2). The 1998 Act waives the requirement to disclose the fair processing information in certain circumstances (see Sch 1, Part II, para 3) - most notably if the disclosure would involve a disproportionate effort when compared with the benefit derived by a data subject in being provided with that information.

A second requirement which must be complied with before a data controller's processing of personal data will be considered "fair and lawful" is that at least one of the conditions of Schedule 2 must have been met. In relation to the processing of what the 1998 Act defines as *"sensitive personal data"* (see s.2), data controllers must also satisfy at least one of the conditions of Schedule 3.

Consent is often the key to fair and lawful processing, as one of the Schedule 2 conditions is that the data subject has consented to the processing. A similar Schedule 3 condition is that the data subject has given his/her "explicit consent" to the processing of sensitive personal data. This is obviously a more exacting test for data controllers to meet, and further consideration of this is given in the commentary at

---

6   Sch 1, Part I, para. 1
7   Guidelines, Chapter 3, para 1.11

Schedule 3.

In many cases such consent could be obtained via an appropriately worded form, setting out the fair processing information and asking data subjects to signify their consent to specific processing. To comply with the 1998 Act, such forms (which may be drafted in a "tick box" format) should be prominently included in any communication sent to a data subject. For the same reason, they should also only be included in communications which the data subject is obliged to return to the data controller. In other words, consent should never be inferred from an individual's failure to return a communication containing a request for their consent.

In considering how to comply with the first principle in the context of personal data obtained via the Internet, the inclusion of relevant fair processing information in a web site privacy policy which is referred to in a tick box consent form is now well advised. Such a policy could, for example, detail any proposed marketing activities which will be undertaken using a web site user's personal data, whether the site makes use of cookies or other similar information gathering devices or techniques, and who should be contacted to obtain further details about the web site operator's processing activities.

Employers should, in relation to their employees' personal data, consider detailing relevant fair processing information in a format freely available to those employees (for example an employment privacy policy). They should also consider how they will ensure that any processing of employee personal data will be deemed to have met at least one of the conditions of Schedule 2 and, if relevant, Schedule 3. Employment contracts may need to be amended to facilitate this. Further commentary regarding employment privacy policies is set out at the final section of this Introductory chapter under the heading "Information security and the need for employment policies and procedures". Whilst on the subject of privacy policies, the reader's attention is also drawn to the commentary on the British Standards Institutes Policy 7799 set out at Schedule 1, Part II para 10 of the Act.

Annex II to this introduction sets out a flow diagram which details factors relevant to successful compliance with the 1998 Act. This should be considered by data processors when they obtain personal data from individuals.

The Information Commissioner and the National Consumer Council have devised the "information padlock" symbol ♂ which, it is hoped, will be readily used by organisations which process personal data. In time, individuals will come to instantly recognise it as a sign that their personal data are being collected. It is not a kitemark which gives any assurances to data subjects that the collection of their data is guaranteed to comply with the 1998 Act; however, it will alert individuals to the fact that their data are about to be processed. This should prompt individuals to satisfy themselves that they are happy for their data to be collected for particular purposes. In a leaflet entitled "Be open...", published by the OIC, it states that "the information padlock" signpost should be:

"...clearly positioned at any point where information is requested - this could be within any medium, such as an advertisement coupon, application form or internet site. If an option box is used, the signpost should be placed next to it.

Wherever the signpost appears an explanation of why the information is requested should be detailed, or directions given to where such an explanation is provided."

Electronic copies of the signpost can be downloaded from the Commissioner's website www.dataprotection.gov.uk.

The sixth principle (see Part II of the Act) - The 1998 Act gives data subjects the following rights:

1. to be provided with:

    - information as to whether or not their personal data are being processed;
    - details about the data (i.e. a description of the data, the purpose(s) of processing and the likely or actual recipients of the data); and
    - a copy of all personal data of which he or she is the subject (s.7 and 8);

2. to prevent processing likely to cause damage or distress (s.10);

3. to prevent direct marketing (s.11);

4. to require a data controller not to make a decision based solely on automated means which significantly affects him or her (s.12);

5. to receive compensation from a data controller for its breach of the 1998 Act (provided, in most cases, that the data subject can demonstrate that the breach has caused the data subject financial loss) (s.13); and

6. to have inaccurate personal data blocked, erased, or destroyed (s.14).

Further information may be obtained from the commentary alongside the section numbers mentioned above.

Set out at Annex III to this introduction are two flow diagrams which summarise arguably the most significant rights mentioned above, i.e. the right to access personal data, and the right for data subjects to have disclosed to them the information which constitutes their personal data.

The flow diagram at Annex IV also explains the operation of the other data subject rights mentioned above. Both flow diagrams are prepared from a data controller's point of view.

The eighth principle (see Sch 1, Part II, paras 13-15 and Sch 4) - this states that any transfer of personal data to a destination outside the European Economic Area (the "EEA")[8] will be prohibited unless:

---

8   At the time of writing the EEA consists of the following countries: The EU Member States (Austria, Belgium, Denmark, Finland, France, Germany, Greece, Ireland, Italy, Luxembourg, The Netherlands, Portugal, Spain, Sweden, United Kingdom) and Iceland, Norway and Liechtenstein

- the destination country/territory ensures that there will be an adequate level of security for the information transferred;

- the individual concerned consents to the transfer being made;

- the transfer is necessary either to perform a contract between the data controller and the data subject, or to conclude a contract between the data controller and another party where the contract is in the data subject's interests;

- the transfer is necessary for reasons of substantial public interest, or is made in connection with legal advice, legal proceedings, or defending legal rights;

- the transfer is necessary to protect the vital interests of the data subject;

- the personal data transferred are on a public register (provided that conditions governing use or access to that register are complied with by the person to whom the data are or may be disclosed after the transfer); or

- the transfer is made subject to a contract approved by the Commissioner or the transfer has been approved by the Commissioner.

Again, consent for specific transfers could be obtained from data subjects (subject to the same guidance given above in relation to how consent can be obtained).

With regard to the first bullet point above, at the time of writing, the Commissioner has published details of thirteen countries[9] which she considers *are likely* to have an "adequate level of security" (basically because they have implemented data privacy laws, or because the European Commission is near to completing negotiations with those countries regarding their data privacy legislation). It is anticipated that full details of countries which the Commissioner considers to provide an adequate level of security will be posted on her office's website (www.dataprotection.gov.uk.) At the time of writing the European Commission has adopted a "Decision" to the effect that Switzerland and Hungary provide adequate protection for personal data transferred to those countries from the EU. The United States of America is a special case. Where personal data are transferred to a member of a so called "Safe Harbour" programme it is deemed to achieve adequate security. Fuller details of these programmes and further guidance given by the Commissioner as to what constitutes adequate security can be found at the commentary to Sch 1, Part II para s.13-15 of the Act. It is interesting to follow the progress of data protection legislation in the USA, where legislators have responded positively to the perceived areas of chief concern: health and medical information and children's data. The result has been the implementation of two statutes, The Health Insurance Portability and Accountability Act and the Children's Online Privacy Protection Act. It remains to be seen whether similar legislation, particularly regarding the use of children's personal data, will be introduced here[10].

---

9   The countries are Australia, Canada, Guernsey, Hong Kong, The Isle of Man, Israel,
     Japan, Jersey, New Zealand, Poland, The Slovak Republic, Slovenia and Taiwan.
10   NB of note is the Direct Marketing Association's "Code of Practice for Commercial
     Communications to Children On-Line"

With regard to the last bullet point above, at the time of writing contracts to facilitate compliance with the eighth principle still await approval from the European Parliament. Two separate pro-forma contracts produced by the Confederation of British Industry and the International Chamber of Commerce have been considered and may in the future be deemed suitable to be signed by a transferor and transferee of personal data outside the EEA. The European Commission has published a set of model clauses[12], and these await approval from the European Parliament, which may take place by late summer 2001.

Other UK Data Privacy Legislation and Codes of Practice

Overview

Having introduced the Directive which required the UK and the other European Union member states to implement the Act, the European Commission did not rest on its laurels in respect of data privacy legislation. A raft of further laws has been put up for implementation and the UK Government has taken the opportunity to pass additional new legislation to govern uses of data. The result has been that the UK is now seen by many as a heavily regulated territory when it comes to the use of personal data.

The following sections seek to introduce the reader to some of these additional laws. Much of the legislation overlaps with the provisions of the 1998 Act and the authors have sought to explain what the practical implications of this will be.

The Telecommunications (Data Protection and Privacy) Regulations 1999 (SI 1999/2093)[13] (the "Telecoms Regulations") and Directive 97/66/EC (the "Telecoms Data Protection Directive")

The Telecoms Regulations form a separate piece of legislation to the 1998 Act which (in their entirety) also came into force on 1 March 2000. They will not be relevant to all readers as they implement certain provisions of the Telecoms Data Protection Directive[14].

The Telecoms Data Protection Directive originally specifically targeted data protection issues arising from the supply and use of telecommunications products and services, although its scope has since been broadened to cover electronic commerce services and technologies. Like the 1998 Act, it should have been implemented by Member States by 24 October 1998 (save for one of its provisions). Although this

---

12   see Draft version of Commission Decision on "Standard Contractual Clauses under article 26(4) of Directive 95/46/EC for the transfer of personal data to processors established in third countries" dated 1 July 2001.
13   As amended by SI 2000/157.
14   Directive 97/66/EC

deadline was not met by Member States, some of its provisions relating to direct marketing activities using certain cold calling and junk faxing techniques (discussed below) were introduced on 1 May 1999.

The aim of this section is to provide an introduction to the Telecoms Regulations and the Telecoms Data Protection Directive. This introduction is not in any way intended to provide a comprehensive summary, and each respective piece of legislation should be researched further if considered relevant.

The Telecoms Regulations (as amended) contain provisions:

- prohibiting the use of automated calling systems for direct marketing purposes without the consent of the call's recipient;

- prohibiting the unsolicited use of fax and telephone communications and, from 24 October 2001, e-mail and conventional mail communications for direct marketing purposes to corporate recipients and individuals without prior consent;

- requiring technical and organisational measures to be taken by communications service providers to ensure security of communications;

- requiring communications service providers to erase or make anonymous, within a certain period, details of customer traffic data where such details are not required for billing purposes or not used to market its own products (with a customer's consent);

- obliging communications operators to issue non-itemised bills to corporate or individual users who request such a service;

- requiring communications operators to restrict access to personal data processed by them to those who have a need to know which is connected to the provision of the operator's products or services;

- obliging communications operators to enable their customers to block caller line identification information except where such information is requested by others in order to trace malicious communications, or where required by the emergency services;

- requiring communications operators to enable customers free of charge to prevent communications from being automatically forwarded to them;

- relating to the publishing of printed or electronic user directory information.

- regulating the use of mobile and satellite data as to the geographic location of a user

For non-communications operators, the requirements of the first and second bullet points above will have significance. The first point to note is that these provisions may be enforced by both individuals and companies, sole traders or partnerships. The prohibitions apply to cold telephone calls, SMS messages, junk faxes, junk mail and junk emails sent for direct marketing purposes. Agencies run by the Direct Marketing Association have been established to list publicly available details of parties who do not wish to receive direct marketing communications or materials by each of these formats (the Fax, Mailing and Telephone Preference Services). For example, anyone faxing advertisements to an individual or business whose fax number is listed with the Fax Preferece Service is in direct breach of the Telecoms Regulations and can become the subject of enforcement proceedings by the OIC. Contact details for the Fax, Mailing and Telephone Preference Services can be found at the end of this introduction.

The Telecoms Data Protection Directive contains a further prohibition upon legally unauthorised listening, taping, storage and surveillance or interception of communications without the consent of all parties to that communication unless such activities are conducted in order to evidence a legitimate business transaction. This provision has been implemented by virtue of the Lawful Business Practice Regulations 2000 (see below).

It should also be borne in mind that under the Human Rights Act 1998, the "right to privacy" (particularly with regard to public sector employees) is extended into the workplace. It is therefore vital for businesses to notify employees of the legitimate reasons for monitoring emails and internet activity (i.e. to prevent and detect "flame mails", harassment, discrimination, defamation, visits to inappropriate websites, and so on). Employers should address such issues in their e-mail and internet policies.

Regulation of Investigatory Powers Act 2000 ("RIPA")

Introduction and legislative background: RIPA came into force on 24 October 2000. It aims to ensure that any monitoring of communications is carried out in compliance with the Telecoms Data Protection Directive, and the European Convention on Human Rights and also sets out how law enforcement agencies may gain access to information controlled by communication providers. Section 1(3) RIPA introduces a new privacy right by creating a new tort. Any interception of a communication in the UK by, or with the express or implied consent of, a person having the right to control the operation or use of a private telecommunication system is actionable if it is without lawful authority.

RIPA's provisions do not cover the use of private networks not attached to a public communication system. Most business telephone and e-mail communications will make use of a public telephone network. Accordingly, as an employer will have the right to control the operation or use of its networks, RIPA's provisions have clear potential to affect their ability to read e-mails and other communications in their own systems, such as voice-mails and other messages for monitoring.

There are both criminal penalties and civil remedies in respect of breaches of RIPA, and the tort mentioned above is actionable by the sender, the recipient, or the intended recipient. In practice, RIPA gives both the sender and the intended recipient of an e-mail intercepted by an employer the right to damages.

There will be no right to this if interception has lawful authority. In this instance, interception has lawful authority in two situations:

- if the interception has, or the person intercepting has reasonable grounds for believing it has, the consent of the sender **and** the intended recipient of the communication (section 3(1) RIPA);

- if it is authorised by regulations introduced by the Secretary of State (section 4(2) RIPA). Those regulations have been introduced by way of the Telecommunications (Lawful Business Practice) (Interception of Communication) Regulations ("the Lawful Business Regulations").

The Telecommunications (Lawful Business Practice) (Interception of Communications) Regulations (the "Lawful Business Regulations") 2000 SI 2000/2699

The Lawful Business Regulations specify the circumstances in which both private businesses and public authorities may lawfully intercept communications. They came into force on 24 October 2000.

What do the Lawful Business Regulations provide?

The Lawful Business Regulations authorise certain interceptions of telecommunication communications which would otherwise be prohibited by section 1 of RIPA.

In an employment context, the interception has to be by or at the request of an employer in connection with the employer's business and using that business's own telecommunications system.

The Lawful Business Regulations provide that interceptions are authorised for **monitoring or recording** electronic communications without consent in the following circumstances:

- in the interests of national security (though this can only be achieved by public authorities);

- to prevent or detect crime (including protecting the network against viruses or hackers, combating or investigating fraud);

- to investigate or detect unauthorised use of telecommunication systems (such as monitoring to ensure that employees do not breach company policy on the use of the e-mail system or the internet);

- to ensure the effective operation of the system (e.g. monitoring to guard against viruses or hackers);

- to provide evidence of the communications in order to establish the existence of facts or ascertaining compliance with practices or procedures of the business (e.g. evidence of a commercial transaction, audit, debt recovery, dispute resolution);

- to ascertain compliance with regulatory or self-regulatory practices or procedures which are relevant to the business (e.g. monitoring to check that the business complies with internal or external regulatory rules or guidelines);

- quality control and staff training.

The Lawful Business Regulations also authorise businesses to monitor **but not record** electronic communications without consent as follows:

- (for charitable bodies) to monitor communications to confidential anonymous counselling or support helplines;

- to determine whether communications are relevant to the business (eg. to check voice-mail and e-mails while staff are absent).

Interceptions are authorised only if the business has made reasonable efforts to inform the user of the system that they may be intercepted. In its explanatory notes to the Lawful Business Regulations, the DTI comments that "the persons who use a system are the people who make direct use of it. Someone who calls from outside, or who receives a call outside, using another system is not a user of the system on which the interception is made". Although the DTI's observations do not have legal force, the clear message is that organisations must concentrate their efforts on informing their staff, contractors and other internal users if they plan to undertake any form of surveillance.

The easiest way to inform employees or contractors that their e-mails may be intercepted is to include this in a well publicised e-mail policy.

How do the Lawful Business Regulations link in with the 1998 Act?

The consultation paper for the Lawful Business Regulations states that RIPA and the regulations "in no way prejudice the rules on the processing of personal data laid out in the Data Protection Act 1998". So even though the regulations provide certain exemptions from the requirement to obtain consent, consent may still need to be obtained unless another condition from Schedule 2 or Schedule 3 (where relevant) of the 1998 Act applies[15].

The 1998 Act requires data controllers to follow the "fair processing code" as set out in the first principle[16]. This means having to provide (or make readily available) to the persons whose calls and e-mails are being intercepted the following information:

- the identity of the data controller (eg the employer);

- the reasons for the interception (eg to provide evidence of a commercial transaction); and

- any further information to ensure the processing is fair (eg if the employer had some other reason for monitoring or recording the call which would not be obvious to the person making or receiving the call).

---

15 See notes to Schedule 2 (relating to sensitive personal data and personal data) and Schedule 3 (relating to sensitive personal data only) for further details.

16 See above, under *Processing personal data – the major provisions of the 1998 Act explained*, together with the notes to Schedule 1, Part II, para 1.

Other than where processing (which includes both monitoring and recording of e-mails and telephone calls) is being carried out to safeguard national security or for the prevention or detection of crime, data controllers will still have to comply with the "fair processing code".

Furthermore, they will have to ensure that one of the Schedule 2 conditions is fulfilled (for ordinary personal data) and that a further condition from Schedule 3 is fulfilled (for sensitive personal data) in order to comply with the first data protection principle.

Note that, under the 1998 Act, unless businesses are recording sensitive personal data, it is unlikely that they will need to get the actual consent of the caller; the caller simply needs to be informed that the recording will take place and the reasons for making the recording.

Unless the Lawful Business Regulations apply then, in accordance with section 3(1) RIPA, businesses will need to have reasonable grounds for believing that correspondents have consented to the interception before the interception can be carried out.

The Freedom of Information Act 2000

The Freedom of Information Act 2000, which received Royal Assent on 30 November 2000 gives a general right of access to information held by public authorities (subject to various exemptions) and obliges such authorities to adopt schemes to publish certain information. It was introduced to replace a code of practice[17] which required government departments and other public authorities to make specified information available to the public, and to release certain data in response to requests. Like the Data Protection Act it is enforced by the Commissioner. The term public authorities would include, for example, National Health Service bodies, schools and colleges, the police and other companies owned by the Crown or a public authority. Interesting aspects of the Freedom of Information Act to note include that:

- where information is exempt from disclosure a public duty is imposed on authorities to detail why, in its view, public interest in disclosure outweighs public interest in maintaining a relevant exemption;

- the information which section 1 of the act gives a right of access to is generally seen as being broader than the definition of "data" in the 1998 Act. For example, manual records held in *any* system not just a relevant filing system are covered and are therefore accessible;

- timescales within which access requests must be complied with vary from the 1998 Act - in certain situations a limit of 20 working days is imposed; and

- if the applicant is the subject of the personal information requested by him or her then the provisions of the 1998 Act will also apply to that application.

---

17   The Code of Practice on Access to Government Information

Draft Code of Practice: The use of personal data in employer/employee relationships (the "Code")

Introduction: At the time of writing this third edition, the Code has still yet to be finalised although most recent indications suggest it should be published in Autumn 2001. After consultation on the draft Code earlier this year (2001), the OIC decided that it needed more input from employees. About 90% of responses initially came from employers and organisations representing employers, with one observer commenting wryly that some of the submissions were "longer than the code itself"[18]! Employers' arguments are for the need to monitor e-mail and internet use to stop the distribution of defamatory, pornographic or offensive material for which they could be vicariously liable. Countering those arguments are the concerns of the individual, whose privacy is undoubtedly compromised by such activities.

The OIC is keen to reach a consensus and steer a course between the Lawful Business Regulations, which are largely permissive of workplace surveillance, and the 1998 Act and the Human Rights Act 1998, which are more concerned with protecting individuals' rights to privacy.

The draft Code is divided into two parts: Part I sets out the standards that must be met to ensure compliance with the Code, while Part II sets out the interpretation of the 1998 Act on which the standards are based. Part I covers a broad range of subjects, under the following headings:

- Managing Data Protection;
- Recruitment;
- Employment Records;
- Access and Disclosure;
- Contract and Agency Staff;
- Employee Monitoring;
- Medical Testing;
- Discipline and Dismissal;
- Retention of Records/Former Employees.

Understandably, perhaps, press attention has been concentrated on the controversial "employee monitoring" section, which covers covert and non-covert monitoring of telephones, e-mail, internet access, video and audio, vehicle and public record information. Some of these will be looked at briefly below, but full details can be obtained from the draft Code, available from the Commissioner's website. It is stressed that the draft Code is subject to change and that, even when it is published in its final form, it will be regularly reviewed to take account of "changes in the law, developments in the interpretation of data protection and related legislation, increased availability and use of technology and the evolution of good employment practice".[19]

18 Iain Bourne, Strategic Policy manager at the OIC
19 See page 2, Introduction to the draft Code

Legal status of the Code

The Code is issued by the Commissioner in accordance with her powers under section 51(3)(b) of the 1998 Act. Like all codes of practice, it will not have direct legal effect, but the Commissioner has stated that she "will take into account the extent to which an employer has complied with [the] Code when determining whether there has been a breach of the Principles and, if there has, whether formal action is appropriate."[20]

Employee monitoring

The draft Code has some useful guidance on general principles of employee monitoring, as well as specific guidance on different types of monitoring activities.

Employers should firstly establish the specific business purpose for which the monitoring is to be introduced and make a written record of this purpose. They should assess the impact of the monitoring on the privacy of staff, and only introduce monitoring once they have established that the benefits are not disproportionate to the adverse impact. Trade unions or other employee representatives should be consulted before any assessment is concluded.

Employers are urged always to consider the least intrusive method of surveillance to achieve the business needs, and adopt that method. Targeting is also important (provided it is carried out in a non-discriminatory way), because where an identifiable risk is posed by only a few people, it is unlikely that monitoring of all staff will be justified.

Informing staff and others who will be affected by the monitoring is crucial, unless the employer is seeking to prevent or detect a crime, and such a disclosure would undermine the prospects of success.

What does the draft Code have to say about...

... monitoring or recording e-mail messages?

As with all types of surveillance, the Commissioner is keen to emphasise the need on the part of employers to consider whether "the adverse impact of monitoring is out of proportion to the benefits."[21] The watchword is "proportionality" - employers should not carry out intrusive surveillance on all members of staff where less intrusive methods would achieve the same ends, or where suspected miscreants could be targeted. For example, it may be possible, if the employer's concern is about timewasting, simply to check e-mail traffic data, rather than checking the content of e-mails.

Before checking e-mail content, the employer should consider whether a check on the subject matter of the e-mail will achieve the same ends. The draft Code also warns

---

20   See page 2, Introduction to the draft Code
21   Page 31, draft Code

employers not to "open e-mails that are clearly personal."[22] It is the authors' view that matters may not always be so clear-cut. Employers who have a reason to mistrust a particular member of staff (for example, because they have a reason to suspect that he or she may be leaving and taking with them confidential information to set up a rival business) often want to open all e-mails of the targeted employee because they cannot be sure that an innocent sounding subject heading is quite as harmless as it appears. Clear policy drafting is required to ensure that employees are aware of the circumstances in which their communications may be monitored or recorded.

The need to detect computer viruses will not justify opening incoming e-mails. Instead, automated monitoring and detecting processes should be used.

Where staff are absent and the employer needs to gain access to their e-mails, the onus is on the employer to ensure that its employees are fully aware of this. Interestingly, however, the Commissioner recognises that if, when checking e-mails for this purpose, it becomes apparent that the employee has been doing something which amounts to gross misconduct or a criminal offence, the employer is free to use that information for the new purpose. In other words, the employer can contact the police/institute disciplinary proceedings as appropriate, depending on the seriousness of the misconduct uncovered.

...monitoring internet access?

The draft Code requires employers to be very clear to employees as to the limits of acceptable internet use. For example, it states that "a simple ban on access to "pornography" is not sufficiently clear",[23] although it does not suggest how this could be made any clearer.

As with monitoring e-mail use and traffic data, the draft Code suggests that if timewasting is the employer's concern, there is no need to monitor sites visited by a particular employee - a record of the time spent on the internet will suffice.

Where technical means can be used, these are preferred to more intrusive methods of monitoring behaviour. For example, software applications are available that, it is claimed, can recognise excessive skin tones in an image, and thereby prevent the display of pornographic material.

The draft Code warns employers to take account of the "ease with which websites can be visited unwittingly through unintended responses of search engines, unclear hypertext links, misleading banner advertising or miskeying."[24] As with any employee disciplinary issue, it is important that the employer does not leap to conclusions, but instead keeps an open mind while the investigation/disciplinary proceedings are carried out.

---

22   Page 31, draft Code
23   Page 32, draft Code
24   Page 33, draft Code

If employees are allowed to use the employer's system to access the internet for personal reasons, the draft Code states that, where possible, no record is kept in the system of the sites they have visited or the content they have viewed. If that is not technically possible, it should be made clear to employees what is retained and for how long.

... *the use of CCTV surveillance?*

Closed Circuit television (CCTV) is one of the most widely used surveillance techniques in the UK. Many businesses have opted to use this form of surveillance, primarily for security reasons. In effect this also provides a means to monitor employees. Other uses cited by employers are to monitor health and safety and day to day management issues such as use of car parking spaces.

In the UK, there is no specific legislation which regulates the use of CCTV in the workplace, although the Commissioner issued a voluntary Code of Practice for CCTV users in its current form in July 2000 ("CCTV Code"). The CCTV Code is mainly concerned with the use of surveillance equipment in places to which the public have access rather than by employers to monitor their employees' behaviour.

The Code urges employers to consider less intrusive ways of addressing safety or security risks, before embarking on routine monitoring. Employees need to be made aware of the cameras and the reasons for them. If people other than employees, such as visitors, are likely to be caught by CCTV monitoring they too must be made aware that it is in operation and the purposes for which the information will be used.

The importance of following the CCTV Code cannot be overstated. Criminals could walk free from court if organisations fail to warn them that CCTV systems are operating. Without warning signs posted at relevant locations, any evidence gathered could be inadmissible.[25]

Particular care should be exercised when employees have a reasonable expectation of privacy, and CCTV should not be installed in cloakrooms, vehicles or to monitor individuals in their private offices. If monitoring in such locations is justified (ie in order to detect a suspected crime), the police should be involved.

...*telephone monitoring and recording?*

Employers may have genuine business reasons for monitoring or recording employees' telephone conversations at work, such as assessing employee performance, meeting quality standards or recording details of financial transactions. In particular in the financial service sector where there has been rapid growth in the number of call-centres, monitoring telephone calls is regularly used to maintain standards and customer satisfaction.

Until recently, employers were allowed to monitor all calls made on an internal telecommunications network including calls outside the workplace, provided the

---

25   See Privacy & Data Protection Volume 1 Issue 5 April/May 2001.

interception took place on the non-public side of the network. Such interception was also permitted regardless of the consent or knowledge of either party to the telephone conversation. The 1997 European Court of Human Rights case of *Halford v United Kingdom* highlighted that the legislation in the UK at the time was far from adequate, and in due course the Telecoms Data Protection Directive[26] was introduced. This required member states to implement domestic legislation by the year 2000 to ensure the confidentiality of telephones calls and other communications. The UK's answer was the introduction of RIPA. The draft Code also contributes guidance on telephone monitoring and recording in the workplace.

The draft Code urges employers to use an itemised call record where this will achieve the business aim - such a record will identify timewasting and the costs of personal calls, which will usually be all that the employer seeks to establish, thereby making the need for monitoring redundant. If monitoring has to be carried out, it should be strictly limited and targeted.

The draft Code also requires those making calls to or receiving calls from the organisation, as well as employees, to be made aware of any monitoring and the purpose behind it, unless this is obvious. If there is no better way of achieving this, the draft Code states, the employer should instruct employees to inform callers that their calls may be recorded and why.

Following the recommendations in the OFTEL Guidelines published in August 1999, the draft Code requires employers who carry out monitoring to provide some lines at work, whether by the use of dedicated lines, payphones or otherwise, which employees can use for private calls, confident that calls made from them will not be recorded or monitored.

Key concepts in setting up a monitoring programme

1. Consider all the genuine business reasons behind setting up a monitoring system. For example, is the monitoring being carried out to address time-wasting, discrimination, harassment or bullying, or loss of trade secrets?

2. Enter into consultation with trade unions or employee representatives on how best to implement the business needs. Also consider how to deal with questions on what happens if you monitor for one particular reason, e.g. prevention of crime, but you also uncover some other act of misconduct. In these circumstances, the Code says that if the misconduct is something no reasonable employer would ignore, use of the information is permissible.

3. Acknowledge to the trade union or employee representatives that the information collected through monitoring can be misleading, misinterpreted or even deliberately falsified. Also acknowledge that such information can also be inaccurate because of equipment malfunction. Reassure the representatives that, if

---

26 Directive 97/66 introduced via SI 1999/2093 (as amended by 2000/157) - see later section in this Introduction headed Other UK Data Privacy Legislation

the information is to be used in a way that might have an adverse impact on employees, the information will be presented to them and they will be given the opportunity to challenge or explain it before it is used.

4. Consider how the monitoring can be carried out with the least intrusion:

   (a) If the business reason for monitoring is to address possible time-wasting, low productivity and costs of calls/internet use, then there is no need to have a dedicated monitoring programme. By reviewing e-mail traffic data, time spent on the internet, itemised call records, the business aim can be achieved.

   (b) On the other hand, if the aim is the detection of discrimination, harassment or bullying, or the dissemination of offensive material, reviewing data traffic and subject headings will not necessarily help. Software applications should be used where possible to reveal such antisocial behaviour.

   (c) Where possible, target only those people you reasonably suspect of being guilty of certain misconduct, rather than all employees. However, care should be taken in assessing the criteria for selecting the few to be monitored to minimise the risk of claims of discrimination.

5. The monitoring method and the business reason for it should both be documented.

6. Note that there are exceptional circumstances where there is no need to notify staff that monitoring is taking place. Such circumstances are where the monitoring is to prevent or detect a crime, or when to inform staff would defeat the purpose for which the monitoring was introduced.

7. Devise a monitoring policy or procedure (hopefully with the support of trade union or employee representatives) which fairly balances the need to protect legitimate business interests while not adversely impacting on the privacy of employees.

Publish the policy or procedure to all employees and take on board any constructive feedback.

Practical Application of the Act

Information security and the need for employment policies and procedures

It can be extremely beneficial for an organisation to invest the time and energy into producing policies and procedures which are tailored to the particular organisation. The advantages of having such policies are that all employees can then know their rights and obligations. If employees materially breach any of the policies, they can be dealt with by way of the disciplinary procedure. Likewise, if they feel that their rights have been infringed, they can issue a grievance against the person who has committed the alleged infringement. In the realm of information security, the following should be considered:

- Data protection policy;

- E-mail, internet and IT security policy;

- Whistleblowing policy.

Employees should be asked to read and sign their agreement to the principles contained in the policies, the main points of which will be covered below.

Data protection policy

- Why worry about data protection?

- How is it likely to affect most employees?

- Explain the basic terminology (data, data subject, processing etc).

- How are personal data collected within the organisation?

- For what purposes and by whom are employee personal data processed?

- How employee personal data should be updated.

- What are the data protection principles?

- Responsibilities for collection, storage, correcting data, security, archiving etc.

- Subject access rights - what are they and how can they be exercised?

- How to deal with complaints from customers.

- Obligations which must be met before using customer information for purposes unrelated to contractual obligations owed to those customers eg. marketing.

- Worked examples.

E-mail, internet and IT security policy

- Three main elements:

  - to regulate legitimate business use
  - to specify misuse
  - to allow monitoring in order to regulate legitimate use

- Explain the purpose of the policy: to ensure the system can operate efficiently and without the organisation being exposed to any potential liability, and to obtain employee consent to any monitoring deemed reasonably necessary by the organisation.

- Set out a list of "do's" and "don'ts", eg:

  - Do:
    - use and frequently change passwords
    - set screen savers with a password
    - use warnings and disclaimers in external e-mails

- ensure data protection principles are applied to e-mail usage. Mass sending of unsolicited e-mails (known as "spamming") constitutes a breach of the first principle if the recipients' details were not obtained fairly.

- Don't:
  - send out abusive, discriminatory or defamatory e-mails
  - send out "private and confidential" messages by e-mail without the prior consent of the recipient
  - send out e-mails which communicate sensitive or confidential information about another person
  - create e-mail congestion by sending out trivial messages
  - visit internet sites which are not related to your work.

- Link in with the disciplinary procedure so that employees are clear about the sort of infringements which might lead to disciplinary sanctions (eg the downloading of pornography may be a matter of gross misconduct entitling the organisation to dismiss).

Whistleblowing policy

- What is whistleblowing? It is the common term for alerting a figure of authority about the wrongdoings of another person.

- It is covered by the Public Interest Disclosure Act 1998 ("PIDA").

- Why have a policy? In order to ensure, so far as possible, that employees will feel able to alert the company (rather than an external body, such as the media) about potential fraud or other criminal or illegal activity (etc). If there is no whistleblowing policy, a whistleblower may succeed in a claim that they should be given protection under PIDA for making a disclosure to the media, with all the potential damage this could cause. Also, it is far better to uncover a fraud in the early stages, which is more likely to happen if employees feel that their concerns will be treated seriously.

- How can this be achieved? By providing the correct environment - eg allowing employees to disclose such details without fear of recrimination to the Human Resources Department or a manager outside the whistleblower's department.

Useful Contact Details

Office of the Information Commissioner ("OIC")
Wycliffe House
Water Lane
Wilmslow
Cheshire
SK9 5AF

To notify call: 01625 545740
Information line: 01625 545745
Fax: 01625 524510
DX: 20819 Wilmslow
Email: mail@dataprotection.gov.uk
Website: www.dataprotection.gov.uk

Privacy Laws & Business
Raebarn House
5th Floor
100 Northolt Road
Harrow
Middlesex
HA2 0BX

Tel: 020 8423 1300
Email: info@privacylaws.com
Website: www.privacylaws.com

The Fax, Mailing and Telephone Preference Services are all run by:
The Direct Marketing Association
Haymarket House
1 Oxendon Street
London
SW1Y 4EE.
Tel: 020 7321 2525

Fax Preference Service
Tel: 020 7766 4422

Mailing Preference Service
Tel: 020 7766 4410

Telephone Preference Service
Tel: 020 7766 4420

E-mail Preference Service –
contact
www.dma.org.uk
for details

Criminal Records Bureau
www.crb.gov.uk

The Table and Flow Diagrams

ANNEX I - THE TRANSITIONAL PROVISIONS (SCHEDULE 8)

Type of processing	Exempt from
Eligible manual data[1] (except accessible records)[2]	data protection principles, Parts II and III of the Act *until 24/10/01*
Eligible manual data which were also held immediately before 24/10/98 plus accessible records	1st principle (but not paras 2 & 3 of the fair processing code[3]), 2nd to 5th principles, s.14 (1) to (3) *until 24/10/07*
Accessible records	principles, Parts II and III (but not s.7, s.12A[4], s.15)
Eligible manual data in respect of which: 1. information relates to financial standing of data subject; and 2. data controller is a credit reference agency	principles, Parts II and III (but not s.7, S.12A, s.15)
Processing not by reference to the data subject	the whole Act *until 24/10/01*
Payroll info, unincorporated members' clubs, mailing lists	principles, Parts II & III *until 24/10/01*
Back up data	s.7
Eligible automated data[5]	paras 2 & 3 of the fair processing code[3] and the requirements of Sch 2 & 3 (1st principle), Sch 1 Pt II para 12 (7th principle), 8th principle, s.7.1(b) & (d), 10, 12, 13 (with some exceptions) *until 24/10/01*
Data processed solely for historical research after 23/10/01	
Eligible manual data processed in compliance with the relevant conditions[6]	paras 2 & 3 of the fair processing code,[3] 2nd to 5th principles and s.14(1)-(3) *indefinitely*
Eligible automated data	sch 2 & 3 (1st principle) *indefinitely*
Eligible automated data processed in compliance with the relevant conditions[6] and not by reference to the data subject	paras 2 & 3 of the fair processing code and Sch 2 & 3 (1st principle), 2nd to 5th principles, s.14(1)-(3) *indefinitely*

[1] Eligible manual data - i.e. the data must have been subject to processing which was under way immediately before 24/10/98 - for further details, see notes to Sch 8, para 1(1).

[2] Accessible records - see s.68.

[3] Fair processing code - i.e. paras 1-4 of Sch 1 Part II.

[4] S.12A - see Sch 13.

[5] Eligible automated data - i.e. eligible data which are not eligible manual data.

[6] "relevant conditions" - see s.33.

TRANSITIONAL PROVISIONS

SCHEDULE 8

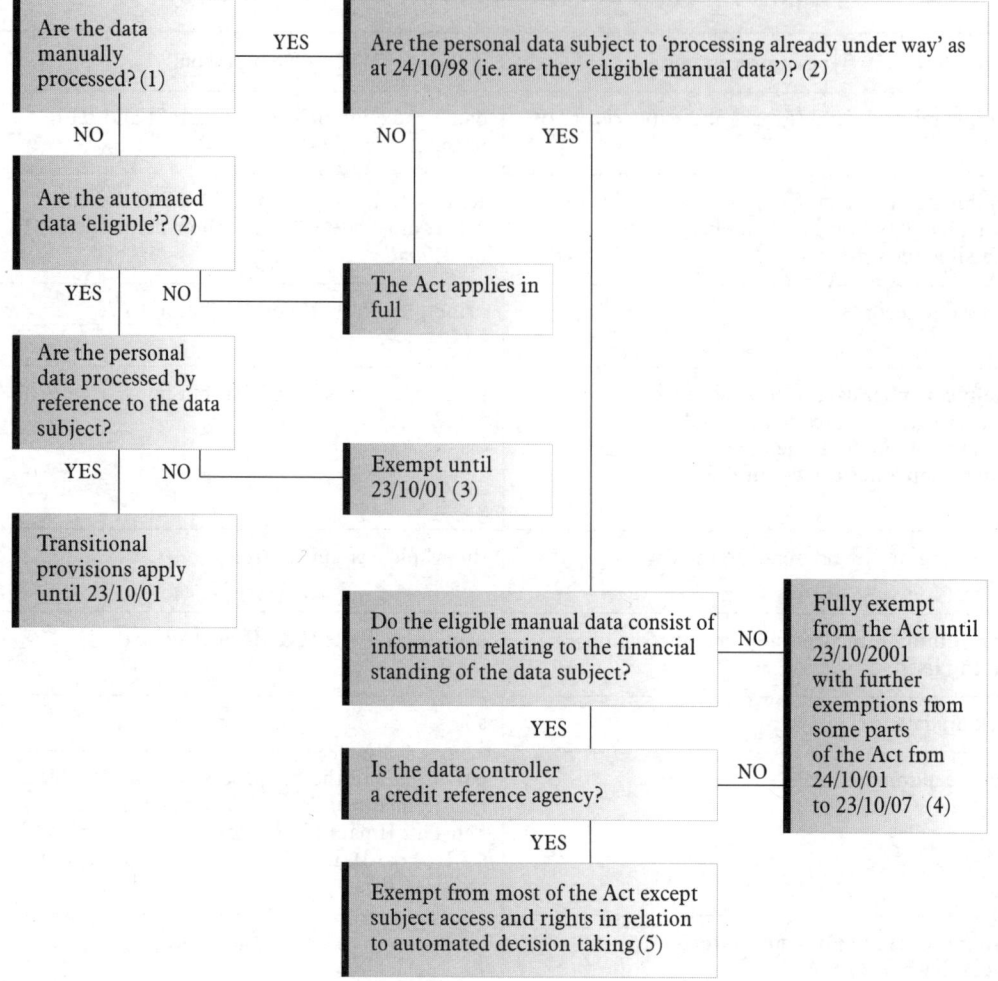

Notes

(1) Also consider exemptions which provide further opportunities for exemptions:

  (a) Schedule 7 - Miscellaneous (including confidential references made by data controller, management forecasts, negotiations with data subject);
  (b) s3 "Special purposes" - journalistic, artistic, literary.

(2) Was processing carried out for the same purpose before 24/10/98? Were the categories of data the same before 24/10/98? Are data disclosed to the same type of recipients as was the case prior to 24/10/98? Are data stored in the same way as they were before 24/10/98? If the answers to all of these are "yes", processing is likely to have already been under way before 24/10/98.

(3) See Sch 8, para 13 for details.

(4) See Sch 8, part III for details.

(5) See Sch 8, para 4 for details.

ANNEX II
OBTAINING PERSONAL DATA FROM DATA SUBJECTS:
INITIAL FACTORS TO CONSIDER

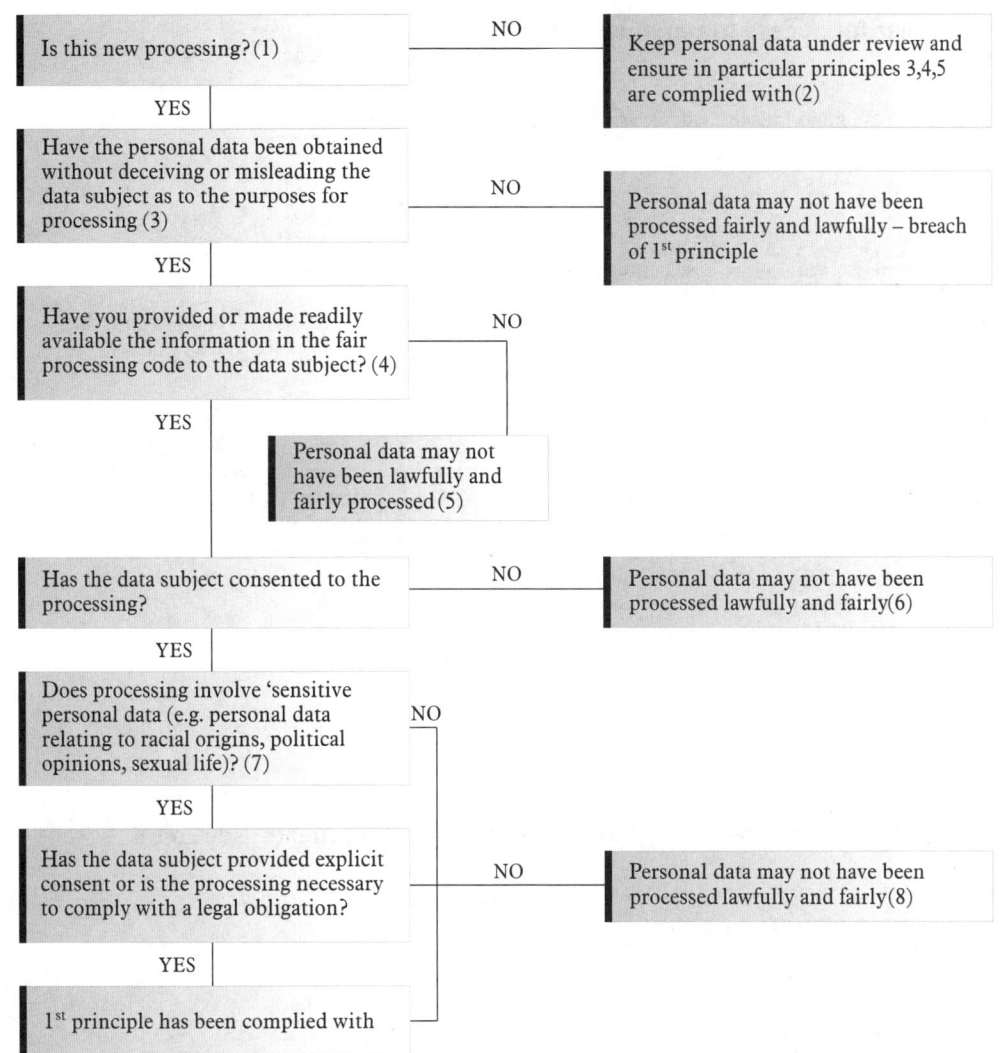

Notes

(1) See Schedule 8 for details. See also flowchart "Transitional Provisions" in Annex 1.

(2) See Sch 1 for details.

(3) 1st principle - fair processing code - Schedule 1, part II, paragraph 1.

(4) 1st principle - fair processing code - Schedule 1, part II, paragraphs 2 and 4.

(5) See Schedule 1 part II, paragraph 3 - exemptions relating to the requirement to produce this information.

(6) But consider other Schedule 2 conditions which may apply.

(7) See Section 2 and Schedule 3.

(8) But consider other Schedule 3 conditions which may apply.

ANNEX **III**

RIGHTS OF DATA SUBJECT

1. Request for access to personal data - Section 7

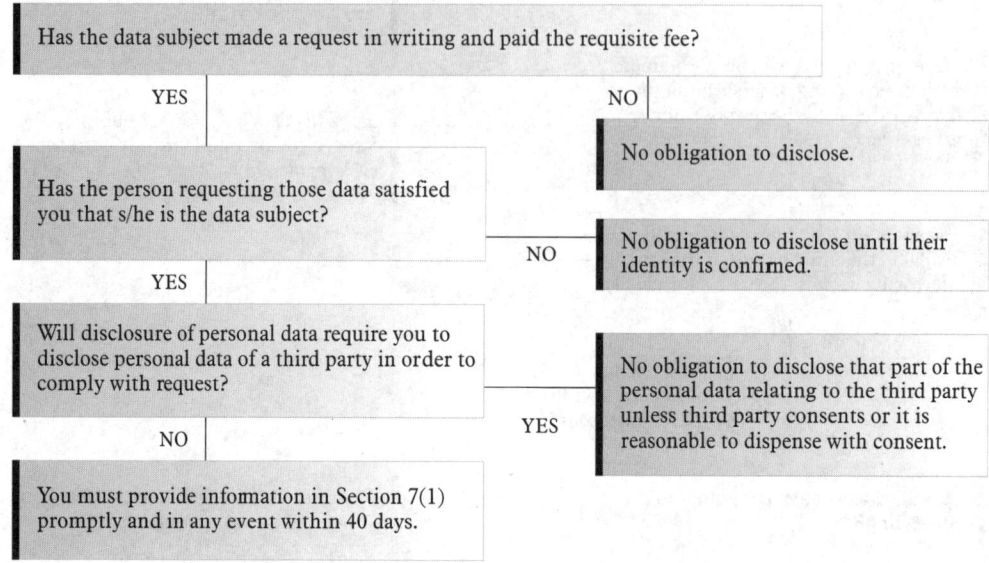

2. Method of providing information contained in a request - Section 8

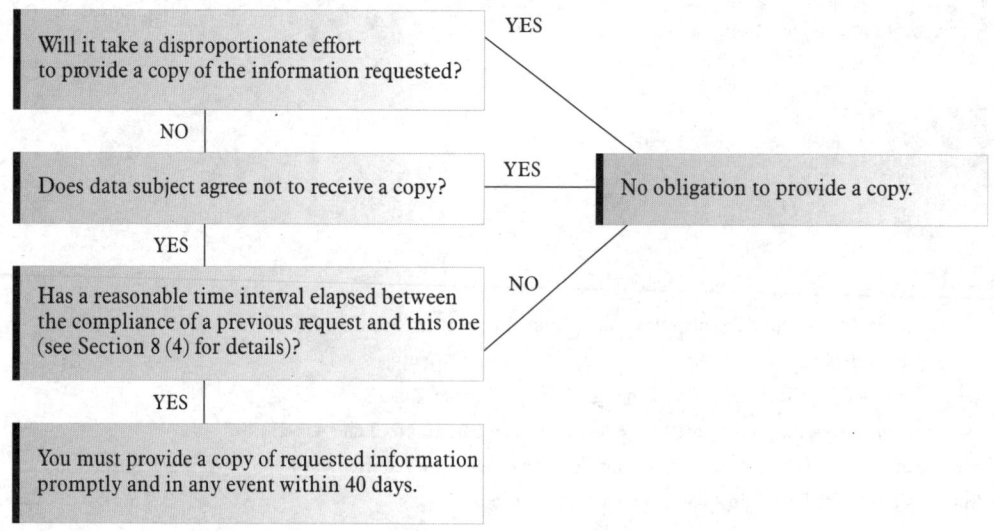

ANNEX IV: RIGHT TO OBJECT

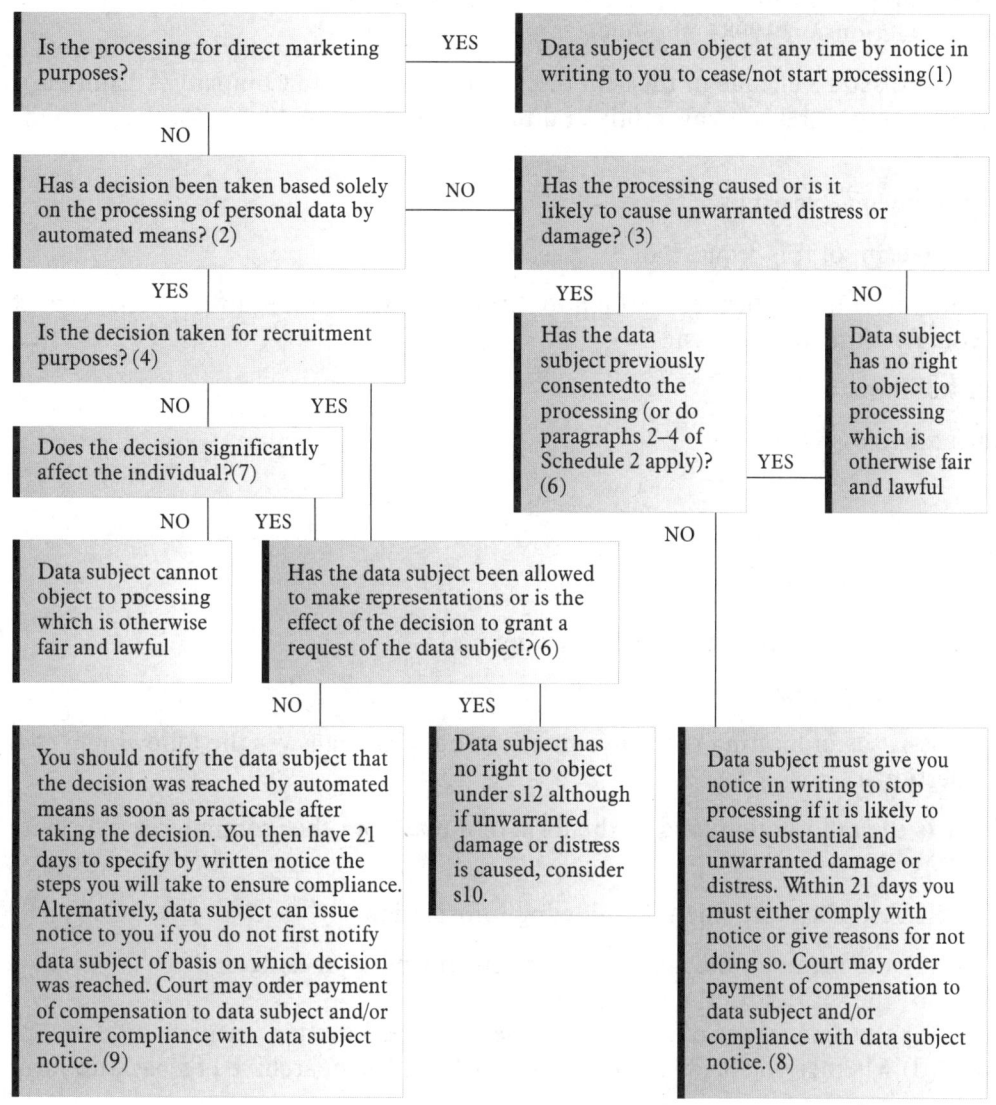

Notes

(1)	s11	(4)	s12(6)	(7)	s12(1)
(2)	s12(1)	(5)	s10(2)	(8)	s10(3) & (4)
(3)	s10	(6)	s12(7)	(9)	s12(1) & (3)

ANNEX V: SAMPLE DATA SUBJECT ACCESS REQUEST FORM

You should complete this form if you want us to supply you with a copy of personal data which we hold about you. You are entitled to receive this information under the Data Protection Act 1998 ("the Act").

You should send a cheque in the sum of £10 made payable to Company A Limited. We will endeavour to respond promptly and in any event within 40 days of the latest of the following:

- your cheque clearing; or

- our receipt of this request; or

- our receipt of any further information from you which is required to enable us to comply with your request.

Your full name:

Your address:

Your date of birth:

[Other identifying feature - eg account details]

1. What information do you seek? Please provided a general description.

2. To assist us in locating the above information, please answer the following questions:

   2.1 Is the information held in the form of e-mails or other computerised format? Yes/No

   If Yes, please provide the following information:

   (a) the names of the authors and recipients of the messages;
   (b) the subjects of the e-mails;
   (c) the dates/range of dates when the messages have been sent;
   (d) whether you believe the e-mails are "live" or in archived or back-up form; and
   (e) any other information which may assist us in our search.[27]

   2.2 Is the information held in manual files? Yes/No

   If Yes, please provide the following information:

   (a) who do you believe holds the manual file about you (eg your team leader, the Human Resources Department)?
   (b) from/to what dates should we search?

3. Have you made an identical or similar request within the past 12 months? If so, when?

4. If you want to know answers to the following, please tick the boxes:

- Why we are processing your personal data   □

- To whom your personal data are disclosed   □

- The source of your personal data   □

If the information you request is of a confidential nature, we may contact you and ask you to provide further information to verify your identity. If we are not satisfied that you are who you say you are, we reserve the right to refuse to grant your request.

If the information you request reveals details directly or indirectly about another person, we will have to seek the consent of that person before we can let you see that information. In certain circumstances we may not be able to disclose the information to you, in which case you will be informed promptly and given full reasons for that decision.

Please note that, while in most cases we will be happy to provide you with copies of the information you request, we nevertheless reserve the right, in accordance with section 8(2) of the Act, not to provide you with copies of the information requested if to do so would take "disproportionate effort".

I confirm that I have read and understood the terms of this subject access form.

Signed ....

Dated ....

Please return this form to: The Data Protection Officer, Company A Limited, [address].

If you have any queries, please call our Data Protection Officer on: [telephone number].

If, when you have received the requested information, you believe that:

- the information is inaccurate or out of date; or

- we should no longer be holding that information; or

- we are using your information for a purpose of which you were unaware; or

- we may have passed inaccurate information about you to someone else;

then you should notify our Data Protection Officer at once, giving your reasons. The Data Protection Officer will then review the information and may amend your personal data in accordance with your wishes. Alternatively, the Data Protection Officer may notify you, giving reasons, as to why he believes the information which he holds about you is in fact accurate and relevant and is being processed for fair and lawful purposes.

Data Protection Act 1998

1998 c. 29

An Act to make new provision for the regulation of the processing of information relating to individuals, including the obtaining, holding, use or disclosure of such information.

[16th July 1998]

Be it enacted by the Queen's most Excellent Majesty, by and with the advice and consent of the Lords Spiritual and Temporal, and Commons, in this present Parliament assembled, and by the authority of the same, as follows:-

PART I

PRELIMINARY

1.– (1) In this Act, unless the context otherwise requires-

"data" means information which-

(a) is being processed by means of equipment operating automatically in response to instructions given for that purpose,

> **S.1(1)**
>
> *(a) - "processed": see definition of "processing" below.*
>
> *"automatically": information held on computer or other sophisticated automated systems. For example, document imaging systems and video surveillance equipment are covered. Operators of CCTV equipment are therefore required to alert people to the fact that the cameras are in operation. For further information, refer to the notes at section 51(3)(b).*

(b) is recorded with the intention that it should be processed by means of such equipment,

> *(b) "intention": even before the information is input into a computer, it has the status of "data" if the intention is to process it in that way. For example, if a data controller receives an unsolicited paper CV and intends to scan it into a computer, that CV will be "data" from the moment of the intention to do so.*

(c) is recorded as part of a relevant filing system or with the intention that it should form part of a relevant filing system, or

(c) "relevant filing system": i.e. manual data of a specific type. See relevant section of (d) below for definition.

(d) does not fall within paragraph (a), (b) or (c) but forms part of an accessible record as defined by section 68;

(d) "accessible record": i.e. a health record, an educational record or an accessible public record. This paragraph was added in the last parliamentary stages of the Bill. It was recognised that such manual records may not fall within paragraphs (a) to (c), resulting in a move to ensure rights of access to information contained in those records.

"data controller" means, subject to subsection (4), a person who (either alone or jointly or in common with other persons) determines the purposes for which and the manner in which any personal data are, or are to be, processed;

"data controller": in an employment context, this person is likely to be the employer. This definition is similar to the "data user" under the 1984 Act, but, owing to the wider definition of "processing" and the fact that certain manual records will now come within the scope of the Act, many more individuals and organisations will be caught within this new definition.

"jointly": where two data controllers act together in determining the purposes and manner of processing.

"in common": where a pool of personal data is shared and each controller acts independently of the other.

"data processor", in relation to personal data, means any person (other than an employee of the data controller) who processes the data on behalf of the data controller;

"data processor": this is similar to the definition of "computer bureau" in the 1984 Act, although it will have a wider application because of the wider definition of "processing". It will include a person who collects and stores data on behalf of the controller, such as an associated company of the controller. It will not include employees of the data controller. For example, if Company A outsources its payroll functions to Company B, Company B will be the "data processor" and Company A the "data controller". It is essential in these circumstances that the relationship between Company A and B is documented in the manner set out in Sch 1, Part II, paras 11-12.

"data subject" means an individual who is the subject of personal data;

"data subject": note that this term cannot apply to a company, only to an individual.

"personal data" means data which relate to a living individual who can be identified-

(a) from those data, or
(b) from those data and other information which is in the possession of, or is likely to come into the possession of, the data controller,

and includes any expression of opinion about the individual and any indication of the intentions of the data controller or any other person in respect of the individual;

"personal data":

Only personal data are caught by the Act, so data which have no bearing on living individuals (e.g. data about companies or the deceased) are outside the scope of the Act. Personal data can be extremely wide ranging and may include such things as mailing lists, photographs scanned onto a computer, soundtracks, DNA profiles of individuals and fingerprints.

"and any information": for example, if the data controller has a code book which interprets data, that will be covered too.

"likely to come into the possession of...". It is uncertain how this will be interpreted. The Commissioner will look at the facts of each case to determine whether there is a likelihood that data or other information will come into the data controller's possession. There is a greater likelihood of this happening if such information is already held by an associated company of the data controller.

"indication of the intentions of the data controller or any other person...": *this is a new provision which did not appear in the 1984 Act. This may include a record on an employee's personnel file of the intention of his manager to move him to a different department. Notable exemptions apply (e.g. management forecasts/ management planning, confidential references, negotiations - see Sch 7).*

"processing", in relation to information or data, means obtaining, recording or holding the information or data or carrying out any operation or set of operations on the information or data, including-

(a) organisation, adaptation or alteration of the information or data,

(b) retrieval, consultation or use of the information or data,

(c) disclosure of the information or data by transmission, dissemination or otherwise making available, or

(d) alignment, combination, blocking, erasure or destruction of the information or data;

"processing":

This is defined in very much wider terms than it was in the 1984 Act. It is difficult to imagine any activity involving data which is not covered by this definition. Those who read manual files, send e-mails or destroy unwanted data, will have undertaken activities caught within the definition. Data controllers need not make any active changes to the data for processing to have occurred; simply by storing it, they will have carried out "processing".

No longer does processing need to be done by reference to the data subject to be covered by the Act. This means that data which are stored by reference to something other than the data subjects (e.g. minutes of a committee meeting stored by reference to that particular committee) will be covered. Search facilities will have to be put in place to cope with potential requests from data subjects (see s.7).

No longer is there a wordprocessing exemption. Documents held on a computer just for text preparation will now be covered by the Act (See, however, the transitional provisions in Sch 8).

"relevant filing system" means any set of information relating to individuals to the extent that, although the information is not processed by means of equipment operating automatically in response to instructions given for that purpose, the set is structured, either by reference to individuals or by reference to criteria relating to individuals, in such a way that specific information relating to a particular individual is readily accessible.

"relevant filing system":

Arguably the most significant new measure contained in the Act is in relation to certain types of manual records, which are covered within the scope of data protection legislation for the first time. For the definition to apply to the manual record, three criteria must be met:

- *there must be a structured set of information;*

- *the structure must be either by reference to individuals or criteria relating to individuals;*

- *specific information about individuals must be readily accessible.*

The Guidelines state that "non-automated information may be found in a variety of different media, e.g. paper files, rollerdex, non-automated microfiche"[28]. Highly structured files, such as card indexes are also likely to be included within the definition.

"set of information": the data must be a set of information with a common theme. Examples given in the Guidelines are to a set of employees or customers. The set need not be physically held in the same file or office, but must be grouped together by "prefix codes, or by attaching an identifying sticker within a file or files" which shows that the information is part of a larger set[29].

"structured": in the preamble to the EC Directive[30] it specifically states that "this Directive covers only filing systems, not unstructured files"[31]. Much commentary has been produced about what is likely to constitute a "structured" set of information. During the Act's passage through parliament, Lord Williams of Mostyn (then Parliamentary Under-Secretary of State to the Home Office) gave the example of a personnel file with his name on the front:

"Let us assume that the file contains every piece of paper or other document about me which the personnel section has collected over the course of my career; and those papers are held in the file in date order, with no means of readily identifying specific information about me except by looking at every document. The Government's clear intention is that such files should not be caught. We want to catch only those records from which specific information about individuals can be readily extracted"[32].

---

28   *Guidelines, Chapter 2, para 1.3*

29   *Guidelines, Chapter 2, para 1.3*

30   *Directive 95/46/EC*

31   *para 27*

32   *House of Lords, 16 March 1998*

This seems to suggest that the more disorganised the filing system, the more likely the data controller will be able to avoid the implications of the Act. It remains to be seen how the courts will interpret this definition. It would appear somewhat unfair that a data controller can circumvent the Act by having a haphazard filing system, although that may well be the effect of this definition.

"...or by reference to criteria relating to individuals": if the set is not structured by reference to the individual, it must be by reference to criteria relating to that individual. Examples given in the Guidelines are: age, sickness record, type of job, credit history, shopping habits, entitlement to particular benefits, or membership of particular organisations[33].

"specific information": the Guidelines suggest[34] that information is specific if it is the sort of information which the data controller envisaged he would be likely to use in the course of his relationship with the individual. Therefore, while certain information may be "specific" (such as appraisals or sickness records), other information may not be.

"readily accessible": without a specific definition of this term, the ordinary dictionary meaning must be relied upon. A test which is suggested in the Guidelines is to see whether the information is "generally accessible at any time to one or more people within the data controller's organisation in connection with the day to day operation of that organisation"[35]. Taking the example of the average employee's personnel file, even where the file is only structured by means of the chronological order of the documentation, it is suggested that anybody searching for a particular piece of information will have little difficulty in finding it, particularly if the person searching is usually responsible for adding to and updating personnel files.

The Guidelines emphasise the fact that the Commissioner cannot categorically state which types of files will or will not be covered by this definition. The final decision in cases of dispute will rest with the courts. The Commissioner has advised data controllers who are in any doubt to undertake a risk assessment and where there is a risk of prejudice, to err on the side of caution and introduce measures to ensure compliance with the Act.

Data controllers should note that transitional relief is available for certain manual records until 23 October 2001. Partial relief is available in certain circumstances from 24 October 2001 until 23 October 2007. See Sch 8.

---

33 Guidelines Chapter 2, para 1.3

34 Guidelines Chapter 2, para 1.3

35 Guidelines Chapter 2, para 1.3

> *If the Commissioner and the data controller disagree about the status of manual information (i.e. whether it falls within the definition of "relevant filing system" or not), the Commissioner will allow the data controller to make representations before deciding whether to take enforcement action. Even if the Commissioner decides not to take such action, an individual who is affected by the data controller's action may nevertheless take action him/herself through the courts.*

(2) In this Act, unless the context otherwise requires-

    (a) "obtaining" or "recording", in relation to personal data, includes obtaining or recording the information to be contained in the data, and

    (b) "using" or "disclosing", in relation to personal data, includes using or disclosing the information contained in the data.

(3) In determining for the purposes of this Act whether any information is recorded with the intention-

    (a) that it should be processed by means of equipment operating automatically in response to instructions given for that purpose, or

    (b) that it should form part of a relevant filing system,

it is immaterial that it is intended to be so processed or to form part of such a system only after being transferred to a country or territory outside the European Economic Area.

(4) Where personal data are processed only for purposes for which they are required by or under any enactment to be processed, the person on whom the obligation to process the data is imposed by or under that enactment is for the purposes of this Act the data controller.

> **S.1(4)** - *Processing only by virtue of an enactment: the data controller nevertheless has the responsibility to ensure that processing is done lawfully and fairly and in accordance with the data protection principles See Sch 1.*

2. In this Act

"sensitive personal data" means personal data consisting of information as to-

> **S.2** - *Sensitive personal data*
>
> *More onerous conditions apply when the data controller is processing sensitive personal data (see Sch 3).*

(a) the racial or ethnic origin of the data subject,

(b) his political opinions,

(c) his religious beliefs or other beliefs of a similar nature,

S.2(c) - *"beliefs of a similar nature": Article 8(1) of the Directive[36] refers to "religious or philosophical beliefs". The Government considered that including a reference to philosophical beliefs was inappropriate because of the "ambiguity of the expression"[37]. The wording "beliefs of a similar nature" is designed to capture such beliefs as humanism and atheism.*

36   *Directive 95/46/EC*
37   *Geoff Hoon MP, (Parliamentary Secretary, Lord Chancellor's Department), speaking on 12 May 1998 in the House of Commons Standing Committee D.*

(d) whether he is a member of a trade union (within the meaning of the Trade Union and Labour Relations (Consolidation) Act 1992),

(e) his physical or mental health or condition,

(f) his sexual life,

(g) the commission or alleged commission by him of any offence, or

(h) any proceedings for any offence committed or alleged to have been committed by him, the disposal of such proceedings or the sentence of any court in such proceedings.

S.2(g) & (h) - *see also s.56.*

3. In this Act

"the special purposes" means any one or more of the following-

(a) the purposes of journalism,

(b) artistic purposes, and

(c) literary purposes.

S.3 - *Special purposes*

Where personal data are processed for the purposes of journalism or for artistic or literary purposes, they will come under this category (see s.32).

4.– (1) References in this Act to the data protection principles are to the principles set out in Part I of Schedule 1.

S.4 - *Data protection principles*

The principles form the fundamental core of the Act, and all processing must be done with careful consideration of the principles (see Sch 1).

(2) Those principles are to be interpreted in accordance with Part II of Schedule 1.

(3) Schedule 2 (which applies to all personal data) and Schedule 3 (which applies only to sensitive personal data) set out conditions applying for the purposes of the first principle; and Schedule 4 sets out cases in which the eighth principle does not apply.

(4) Subject to section 27(1), it shall be the duty of a data controller to comply with the data protection principles in relation to all personal data with respect to which he is the data controller.

S.4(4) - *S.27(1) relates to exemptions from data protection principles and other provisions of the Act.*

5.– (1) Except as otherwise provided by or under section 54, this Act applies to a data controller in respect of any data only if-

S.5(1) - *S.54: Secondary legislation has been passed to enable closer co-operation between the Commissioner and international supervisory authorities[38]. Except as provided by or under that section, the Act is limited to the applications described in this section.*

38   *The Data Protection (Interntaional Co-operation) Order 2000 (SI 2000/190)*

   (a) the data controller is established in the United Kingdom and the data are processed in the context of that establishment, or

   (b) the data controller is established neither in the United Kingdom nor in any other EEA State but uses equipment in the United Kingdom for processing the data otherwise than for the purposes of transit through the United Kingdom.

> **S.5(1)(b)** - *There may be instances where a foreign (and non-EEA) company has data processed in the UK. For example, where a foreign company has a UK subsidiary which processes personal data on behalf of the foreign company, that processing will be caught. In such a case, that company will have to abide by the Act (unless the reason for processing such data is for transit through the UK only (i.e. the data will be held only for so long as to enable it to be transmitted outside the UK)).*

(2) A data controller falling within subsection (1)(b) must nominate for the purposes of this Act a representative established in the United Kingdom.

> **S.5(2)** - *This was introduced at a late stage in the parliamentary process. It is required by the Directive and its purpose is to provide a point of contact to whom data subjects can turn if they have problems with the processing in question.*

(3) For the purposes of subsections (1) and (2), each of the following is to be treated as established in the United Kingdom-

(a) an individual who is ordinarily resident in the United Kingdom,

(b) a body incorporated under the law of, or of any part of, the United Kingdom,

(c) a partnership or other unincorporated association formed under the law of any part of the United Kingdom, and

(d) any person who does not fall within paragraph (a), (b) or (c) but maintains in the United Kingdom-

(i) an office, branch or agency through which he carries on any activity, or

(ii) a regular practice;

> **S.5(3)(d)** - *"office, branch or agency": an American company could place advertisements in UK trade journals but so long as it does not have an office, branch or agency in the UK, it will not be subject to the Act, unless the practice of placing such advertisements amounts to a "regular practice".*
>
> *"EEA State" means any of the 15 member states of the EU plus Iceland, Liechtenstein and Norway.*

and the reference to establishment in any other EEA State has a corresponding meaning.

The Data Protection (International Co-operation) Order 2000 provides for, among other things, the extension of the Commissioner's enforcement powers in relation to certain data controllers who are processing data in the UK but to whom the Act does not apply due to s.5. However, such enforcement powers can only be exercised if the supervisory authority in the EEA Member state whose laws apply to the data controller makes a request to the Commissioner. (See commentary at s.54(3))

6.– (1) The office originally established by section 3(1)(a) of the Data Protection Act 1984 as the office of Data Protection Registrar shall continue to exist for the purposes of this Act but shall be known as the office of Information Commissioner; and in this Act the Information Commissioner is referred to as "the Commissioner".

(2) The Commissioner shall be appointed by Her Majesty by Letters Patent.

(3) For the purposes of this Act there shall continue to be a Data Protection Tribunal (in this Act referred to as "the Tribunal").

(4) The Tribunal shall consist of-

(a) a chairman appointed by the Lord Chancellor after consultation with the Lord Advocate,
(b) such number of deputy chairmen so appointed as the Lord Chancellor may determine, and
(c) such number of other members appointed by the Secretary of State as he may determine.

(5) The members of the Tribunal appointed under subsection (4)(a) and (b) shall be-

(a) persons who have a 7 year general qualification, within the meaning of section 71 of the Courts and Legal Services Act 1990,
(b) advocates or solicitors in Scotland of at least 7 years' standing, or
(c) members of the bar of Northern Ireland or solicitors of the Supreme Court of Northern Ireland of at least 7 years' standing.

(6) The members of the Tribunal appointed under subsection (4)(c) shall be-

(a) persons to represent the interests of data subjects, and
(b) persons to represent the interests of data controllers.

(7) Schedule 5 has effect in relation to the Commissioner and the Tribunal.

S.6 - *See also Sch 5.*

PART II

RIGHTS OF DATA SUBJECTS AND OTHERS

7.– (1) Subject to the following provisions of this section and to sections 8 and 9, an individual is entitled-

Part II - Rights of Data Subjects and Others

S 7(1) - This section sets out the rights of individuals to access their personal data.

Note that the Act's transitional provisions exempt until 24/10/01 any manually processed personal data (except accessible records - see s.68 for explanation), processing of which was under way before 24 October 1998 (see Sch 8, Part II, para 2(1)).

The transitional provisions also waive the requirements of ss.7.1(b), (c)(ii) & (d) in relation to machine processed personal data, processing of which was under way before 24 October 1998 (see Sch 8, para 13(d)).

Access requests do not have to be complied with if:

(a)   S.7(1)(b) cannot be complied with without disclosing information relating to another individual and that other individual does not consent to disclosing information about him/her and it is not reasonable to dispense with such consent (see s.7(4)-(6));

(b)   the data controller has previously complied with an access request from the data subject and the data subject is making an identical or similar request (see s.8(3) and (4)); or

(c)   insufficient information to identify a data subject has been supplied to the data controller (see s.7(3)).

At the time of writing, there are six "subject access" statutory instruments, which are:

- *The Data Protection (Subject Access) (Fees and Miscellaneous Provisions) Regulations 2000 (SI 2000/191);*

- *The Data Protection (Subject Access Modification) (Health) Order 2000 (SI 2000/413);*

- *The Data Protection (Subject Access Modification) (Education) Order 2000 (SI 2000/414);*

- *The Data Protection (Subject Access Modification) (Social Work) Order 2000 (SI 2000/415);*

- *The Data Protection (Miscellaneous Subject Access Exemptions) Order 2000 (SI 2000/419); and*

- *The Data Protection (miscellaneous subject Access Exemptions) (Amendment) Order 2000 (SI 2000/1865).*

The four orders (SIs 413, 414, 415 and 419, which in future will be referred to as "the subject access orders") all modify s. 7 in some way. SIs 413 and 414 provide, in relation to health and education records respectively, for an exemption from the requirement to allow data subject access where to do so would "be likely to cause serious harm to the physical or mental health or condition of the data subject or any other person". Before deciding whether the exemption applies in relation to SI 413, a data controller who is not a health professional is obliged to consult the health professional responsible for the clinical care of the data subject.

SI 414 further stipulates that, even where the above exemption does not apply, there will be an exemption from s. 7 "to the extent to which the application of that section would not be in the best interests of that data subject" where the record in question consists of information "as to whether a data subject is or has been the subject of or may be at risk of child abuse."

SI 415 provides for a slightly less extensive exemption in relation to personal data processed by local authorities under their social services remit; in such cases, s. 7(1)(a) is not exempt, although if applying sections 7(1)(b) to (d) "would be likely to prejudice the carrying out of social work by reason of the fact that serious harm to the physical or mental health or condition of the data subject or any other person would be likely to be caused", there will be no need to comply with those sections.

SI 419 exempts from s.7 personal data where its disclosure is prohibited or restricted by law in order to safeguard the interests of the data subject or some other individual. The personal data which are the subject of this Order are:

- *human fertilisation and embryology information in the UK;*

- *information contained in adoption and parental order records and reports;*

- *statements and records of the special education needs of children in England and Wales; and*

- *(in Scotland only), information provide by the principal reporter for the purposes of a children's hearing.*

SI 1865 makes a slight amendment to SI 419.

(a) to be informed by any data controller whether personal data of which that individual is the data subject are being processed by or on behalf of that data controller,

(b) if that is the case, to be given by the data controller a description of-
    (i) the personal data of which that individual is the data subject,
    (ii) the purposes for which they are being or are to be processed, and

(iii) the recipients or classes of recipients to whom they are or may be disclosed,
(c) to have communicated to him in an intelligible form-
    (i) the information constituting any personal data of which that individual is the data subject, and
    (ii) any information available to the data controller as to the source of those data, and

S.7(1)(c) - *Information must be supplied in a permanent form except where that is not possible, would involve a disproportionate effort or unless the data subject agrees otherwise (see s.8(2)(a) & (b)).*

It should be noted that the "disproportionate effort" argument only operates with regard to providing copies of the requested data. Even if it takes disproportionate effort to comply with a data subject request, a data controller must still comply by using a different means. On a different, but related, matter, a data controller can resist providing information in accordance with the "fair processing code" if to do so would take "disproportionate effort". See Sch 1 part II para 3.

The use of the words "intelligible form" means that relevant parts of the information may need to be explained or decoded.

See s.7(8) & s.7(10) for timescale within which requests must be actioned.

(d) where the processing by automatic means of personal data of which that individual is the data subject for the purpose of evaluating matters relating to him such as, for example, his performance at work, his creditworthiness, his reliability or his conduct, has constituted or is likely to constitute the sole basis for any decision significantly affecting him, to be informed by the data controller of the logic involved in that decision-taking.

S.7(1)(d) - *Note the provisions of s.8(5) relating to the application of this provision where trade secrets are involved.*

(2) A data controller is not obliged to supply any information under subsection (1) unless he has received-

(a) a request in writing, and

S.7(2)(a) - *The Guidelines state that e-mail data subject requests will be valid[39].*

---

39   *Guidelines, Chapter 4, para 1.1*

(b) except in prescribed cases, such fee (not exceeding the prescribed maximum) as he may require.

S.7(2)(b) - *The maximum fee for most subject access requests is £10.[40]*

Where:

- *the data controller is a credit reference agency, the maximum charge that can be levied against a data subject who seeks information relating to his or her financial standing is £2 per request;*

- *a data subject requests access to his or her educational records (within the meaning of Sch 11), a scale of maximum charges (ranging from £1 to £50) may be levied per request if a copy is to be provided, depending on the number of pages comprising the copy (eg the maximum charge of £1 applies to fewer than 20 pages, and the maximum charge of £50 applies to 500 or more pages). Note that if no copy is to be provided, no fee can be levied;*

- *a data subject requests access to his or her health records (within the meaning of s. 68) which are not exclusively automated or intended for automation, there is a transitional provision which applies to requests made before 24 October 2001. Where a permanent copy is to be provided, the maximum fee which may be charged is £50. Note that if no copy is to be provided, no fee can be levied in respect of information solely contained in a health record where that record has at least partially been created in the 40 days prior to the request.*

---

[40]   *The Data Protection (Subject Access) (Fees and Miscellaneous Provisions) Regulations 2000 (SI 2000/191).*

---

(3) A data controller is not obliged to comply with a request under this section unless he is supplied with such information as he may reasonably require in order to satisfy himself as to the identity of the person making the request and to locate the information which that person seeks.

---

s.7(3)

*Identity of the person making the request: it is important for data controllers **not** to accede to a subject access request before they are satisfied as to the identity of the person making the request. It is likely that the seventh data protection principle (relating to security issues) will be infringed if the information is provided to someone who fraudulently claims to be the data subject.*

Locating the data: this provision allows data controllers to require data subjects to assist them in their search. The Commissioner has stated that "in most cases an open-ended request will not satisfy this provision".[41] See the introduction, Annex V, for the sort of information that data controllers may seek from data subjects to enable them to locate the data.

---

41 *See "Subject access to personal data contained in e-mails, compliance advice, which can be found on the Commissioner's website*

(4) Where a data controller cannot comply with the request without disclosing information relating to another individual who can be identified from that information, he is not obliged to comply with the request unless-

(a) the other individual has consented to the disclosure of the information to the person making the request, or

(b) it is reasonable in all the circumstances to comply with the request without the consent of the other individual.

S.7(4) - *This is the provision which sets out a data controller's obligations if compliance with an access request would involve disclosing information relating to another person.*

Note also, if a data controller reasonably believes that other information may come into the data subject's hands which, when taken with the disclosed information, would identify another person, then s.7(4) may also be applied (see s.8(7)).

S.7(4)(b) - *see s.7(6) for factors to consider when determining when it is reasonable to dispense with consent.*

Health, education and social work records

The subject access orders (see entry at s. 7(1)) provide additional wording to be inserted at s. 7(4) in relation to access to health, education and social work records. In the case of SI 414 and 415, the additional wording which is inserted after paragraph (b) is:

"or

(c) the other individual is a relevant person".

A definition is provided of "relevant person" in SI 414, which is inserted after s. 7(11) as:

"(12) A person is a relevant person for the purposes of subsection (4)(c) if he:

(a) is a person referred to in paragraph 4(a) or (b) or paragraph 8(a) or (b) of Schedule 11;

(b) *is employed by an education authority (within the meaning of paragraph 6 of Schedule 11) in pursuance of its functions relating to education and the information relates to him, or he supplied the information in his capacity as such an employee; or*

(c) *is the person making the request."*

The definition of "relevant person" in SI 415 is in broadly similar terms.

The amendment to s. 7(4) in respect of SI 413 is slightly different, although the principle is the same, so the equivalent of the "relevant person" is "a health professional who has compiled or contributed to the health record or has been involved in the care of the data subject in his capacity as a health professional".

*What this means in essence is that a data controller cannot refuse to allow a data subject access to health, education or social work records pertaining to that data subject on the grounds that to do so would also reveal the identity of a health professional, teacher or social worker **unless** providing such access would give rise to the likelihood of serious harm to such persons.*

(5) In subsection (4) the reference to information relating to another individual includes a reference to information identifying that individual as the source of the information sought by the request; and that subsection is not to be construed as excusing a data controller from communicating so much of the information sought by the request as can be communicated without disclosing the identity of the other individual concerned, whether by the omission of names or other identifying particulars or otherwise.

s.7(5) - *Note that, even where a third party's details appear in the information which is the subject of the access request, the data controller cannot simply refuse to disclose the requested information. Instead, the data controller should block out those parts of the information which relate to the third party (assuming the third party refuses to consent to the disclosure and it is not reasonable to dispense with consent).*

(6) In determining for the purposes of subsection (4)(b) whether it is reasonable in all the circumstances to comply with the request without the consent of the other individual concerned, regard shall be had, in particular, to-

(a) any duty of confidentiality owed to the other individual,

(b) any steps taken by the data controller with a view to seeking the consent of the other individual,

(c) whether the other individual is capable of giving consent, and

(d) any express refusal of consent by the other individual.

---

s.7(6) - *This is frequently a problem which occurs in employment contexts. An employee may wish to see a copy of some minutes of a meeting which he or she attended, along with other employees. Although disclosing the minutes will result in the disclosure of third party data, it would seem reasonable to dispense with the consent of those other attendees, assuming that the person making the request knows their identities and was present when all discussions took place.*

---

(7) An individual making a request under this section may, in such cases as may be prescribed, specify that his request is limited to personal data of any prescribed description.

(8) Subject to subsection (4), a data controller shall comply with a request under this section promptly and in any event before the end of the prescribed period beginning with the relevant day.

S.7(8) - *Data controllers must comply with subject access requests promptly on their receipt of a written request identifying the data subject and containing sufficient detail to locate the requested information, and the fee. At the latest, most requests must be complied with within 40 days of receipt (see s.7(10)).*

As data controllers must respond "promptly" to data subject requests they should not assume in every case that they have 40 days to respond.

In certain specified cases, "the prescribed period" is under 40 days (see s.7(10)).

---

(9) If a court is satisfied on the application of any person who has made a request under the foregoing provisions of this section that the data controller in question has failed to comply with the request in contravention of those provisions, the court may order him to comply with the request.

S.7(9) - *Data controllers are permitted a defence to such an application in relation to processing for journalistic, artistic or literary purposes (see s.32(4)).*

The subject access orders (see commentary at s.7(1)) all contain the identical amendment to this section, so that in relation to SIs 413, 414 and 415 it shall read:

"(9) If a court is satisfied on the application of -

(a) any person who has made a request under the foregoing provisions of this section, or

(b) any other person to whom serious harm to his physical or mental health or condition would be likely to be caused by compliance with any such request in contravention of those provisions,

that the data controller in question is about to comply with or has failed to comply with the request in contravention of those provisions, the court may order him not to comply or, as the case may be, to comply with the request."

The reference to "this section" in 9(a) is to be taken to include "this Order".

The significance of this amendment is that it provides a safeguard to people whose safety is likely to be threatened if a subject access request is permitted, by enabling them to apply for a court order to prevent compliance with such request.

(10) In this section-

"prescribed" means prescribed by the Secretary of State by regulations;

"the prescribed maximum" means such amount as may be prescribed;

"the prescribed period" means forty days or such other period as may be prescribed;

"the relevant day", in relation to a request under this section, means the day on which the data controller receives the request or, if later, the first day on which the data controller has both the required fee and the information referred to in subsection (3).

S.7(10) - *Subject access requests must be complied with promptly and in any event (in most cases) within 40 days of a subject access request. The data subject must make the request in writing identifying themselves, and providing sufficient detail to locate the requested information, and the requisite fee.*

The "prescribed period" is under 40 days in the following cases[42]:

- *subject access requests where the data controller is a credit reference agency and where the request is limited to personal data relevant to an individual's financial standing - 7 working days;*

- *subject access requests in relation to educational records - 15 school days[43].*

---

42   *The Data Protection (Subject Access) (Fees and Miscellaneous Provisions) Regulations 2000 (SI 2000/191).*
43   *within the meaning of s.579(1) Education Act 1996.*

(11) Different amounts or periods may be prescribed under this section in relation to different cases.

8.– (1) The Secretary of State may by regulations provide that, in such cases as may be prescribed, a request for information under any provision of subsection (1) of section 7 is to be treated as extending also to information under other provisions of that subsection.

> **s.8** - *A request for information under* any *provision of s. 7(1)(a), (b) or (c) is treated as extending also to information under* all other *provisions of s. 7(1)(a), (b) or (c). However, data subjects have to expressly ask for the logic involved in automatic decision-taking to be provided with that information (s. 7(1)(d)). Similarly, if they do make a request for information under s. 7(1)(d), there is no need to provide information under s. 7(1)(a), (b) or (c) unless it is expressly requested.*[44]
>
> ---
>
> 44   *The Data Protection (Subject Access) (Fees and Miscellaneous Provisions) Regulations 2000 (SI 2000/191).*

(2) The obligation imposed by section 7(1)(c)(i) must be complied with by supplying the data subject with a copy of the information in permanent form unless-

(a) the supply of such a copy is not possible or would involve disproportionate effort, or

(b) the data subject agrees otherwise;

and where any of the information referred to in section 7(1)(c)(i) is expressed in terms which are not intelligible without explanation the copy must be accompanied by an explanation of those terms.

(3) Where a data controller has previously complied with a request made under section 7 by an individual, the data controller is not obliged to comply with a subsequent identical or similar request under that section by that individual unless a reasonable interval has elapsed between compliance with the previous request and the making of the current request.

(4) In determining for the purposes of subsection (3) whether requests under section 7 are made at reasonable intervals, regard shall be had to the nature of the data, the purpose for which the data are processed and the frequency with which the data are altered.

(5) Section 7(1)(d) is not to be regarded as requiring the provision of information as to the logic involved in any decision-taking if, and to the extent that, the information constitutes a trade secret.

(6) The information to be supplied pursuant to a request under section 7 must be supplied by reference to the data in question at the time when the request is received, except that it may take account of any amendment or deletion made

between that time and the time when the information is supplied, being an amendment or deletion that would have been made regardless of the receipt of the request.

S.8(6) - *In other words, in some circumstances the information supplied to the data subject may differ from that held by the data controller at the time of supply.*

However, the Guidelines note that only what could be considered routine amendments and deletions may be made to the information between the date of a request and the date of the reply.[45] Otherwise, data controllers could be tempted to discard any material that they did not wish to disclose to the individual between the date of the request and the date of the response.

---

45   *Guidelines, Chapter 4, para 1.2*

(7) For the purposes of section 7(4) and (5) another individual can be identified from the information being disclosed if he can be identified from that information, or from that and any other information which, in the reasonable belief of the data controller, is likely to be in, or to come into, the possession of the data subject making the request.

Subject access requests - when can they be refused?
In summary, subject access requests can be legitimately refused in the following circumstances:

• *where to comply would necessitate disclosing information relating to another individual (unless that individual has consented to the disclosure or it is reasonable in all the circumstances to dispense with that consent) - s.7(6);*

• *where the data controller has recently complied with an identical or similar request - s.8(3); or*

• *where the data subject has provided the data controller with insufficient information (having been asked to do so) to identify himself as the data subject - s.7(3).*

Also, depending on the nature of the processing, subject access requests can be legitimately refused in the following circumstances:

• *where there is exemption from the "subject information provisions" (as defined in s.27(2)) in Part IV (ss. 27 to 39); or*

• *where the miscellaneous exemptions in Schedule 7 so stipulate (eg confidential references, management forecasts etc).*

> *Also, copies of the information requested need not be provided where to do so would necessitate "disproportionate effort" (**s.8(2)**).*

9.– (1) Where the data controller is a credit reference agency, section 7 has effect subject to the provisions of this section.

(2) An individual making a request under section 7 may limit his request to personal data relevant to his financial standing, and shall be taken to have so limited his request unless the request shows a contrary intention.

(3) Where the data controller receives a request under section 7 in a case where personal data of which the individual making the request is the data subject are being processed by or on behalf of the data controller, the obligation to supply information under that section includes an obligation to give the individual making the request a statement, in such form as may be prescribed by the Secretary of State by regulations, of the individual's rights-

> **S.9(3)** - *The regulations referred to here are the Consumer Credit (Credit Reference Agency) Regulations 2000 (SI 2000/290).*

(a) under section 159 of the Consumer Credit Act 1974 , and

> **S.9(3)(a)** - *Section 159 of the Consumer Credit Act 1974: Credit reference agencies are obliged to disclose information which they hold about consumers, upon receipt of a written request and the prescribed fee. If the consumer then considers that an entry in his file is incorrect and that inaccuracy is likely to prejudice him, he can give notice to the agency requiring it to rectify the error. If there is a dispute between the agency and the consumer, either one may apply to the Commissioner, upon payment of a fee, to make such order as the Commissioner sees fit.*
>
> *Note that ss.158-160 of the Consumer Credit Act 1974 are amended by virtue of s.62 of the Act.*

(b) to the extent required by the prescribed form, under this Act.

The OIC has published a leaflet entitled "No credit" which provides information about the role of credit reference agencies, the purpose of credit scoring systems, and the rights of data subjects to see and amend their files. Copies of the leaflet are available from :

No Credit
PO Box 99
Nelson
BB9 8GS
Tel: 0870 44 21 211.

On 30 March 2000, the Finance & Leasing Association published a revised edition of its Guide to Credit Scoring, to take account of the change in legislation. The guide is produced by the credit industry and credit reference agencies for the use of those in the industry who make decisions about consumer credit.

Note s.7(10) – credit reference agencies and subject access requests (relating to the individual's financial standing) which must be complied with within 7 days, not the usual 40.

10.– (1) Subject to subsection (2), an individual is entitled at any time by notice in writing to a data controller to require the data controller at the end of such period as is reasonable in the circumstances to cease, or not to begin, processing, or processing for a specified purpose or in a specified manner, any personal data in respect of which he is the data subject, on the ground that, for specified reasons-

(a) the processing of those data or their processing for that purpose or in that manner is causing or is likely to cause substantial damage or substantial distress to him or to another, and

(b) that damage or distress is or would be unwarranted.

(2) Subsection (1) does not apply-

(a) in a case where any of the conditions in paragraphs 1 to 4 of Schedule 2 is met, or

(b) in such other cases as may be prescribed by the Secretary of State by order.

S.10(2) - *The right to prevent processing because it is likely to cause unwarranted damage or distress is withdrawn if any of the so-called "lawful processing" conditions have been met, i.e.:*

1.   the data subject consented to the processing, or

2.   the processing is necessary:

> (a) *for the performance of a contract involving the data subject; or*
>
> (b) *for the taking of steps at the request of the data subject so he/she can decide whether to enter a contract; or*
>
> (c) *for the data controller to comply with a legal obligation (other than a contractual obligation); and/or*
>
> (d) *to protect the data subject's vital interests.*
>
> *Unless the Secretary of State orders otherwise, this exemption does not apply in relation to sensitive personal data. At the time of writing, no such order has been made.*

(3) The data controller must within twenty-one days of receiving a notice under subsection (1) ("the data subject notice") give the individual who gave it a written notice-

(a) stating that he has complied or intends to comply with the data subject notice, or

(b) stating his reasons for regarding the data subject notice as to any extent unjustified and the extent (if any) to which he has complied or intends to comply with it.

(4) If a court is satisfied, on the application of any person who has given a notice under subsection (1) which appears to the court to be justified (or to be justified to any extent), that the data controller in question has failed to comply with the notice, the court may order him to take such steps for complying with the notice (or for complying with it to that extent) as the court thinks fit.

> **S.10(4)** - *Note the provisions of s.32(4) in relation to staying proceedings where processing is for one of the "special purposes".*

(5) The failure by a data subject to exercise the right conferred by subsection (1) or section 11(1) does not affect any other right conferred on him by this Part.

> **S.10(5)** - *Note: the transitional provisions waive the requirements of ss.10 & 11 in relation to machine processed personal data in respect of which processing was under way before 24 October 1998 (see Sch 8, para 13(e)).*

11.– (1) An individual is entitled at any time by notice in writing to a data controller to require the data controller at the end of such period as is reasonable in the circumstances to cease, or not to begin, processing for the purposes of direct marketing personal data in respect of which he is the data subject.

> **S.11(1)** - *This is a significant new right which permits individuals to prevent, for example, the inclusion of their personal details on a mailing list for junk mail. Significantly, even where their consent has previously been given, they are entitled to withdraw such consent at any time by notice in writing. This contrasts with data subjects' rights under s.10, under which previous consent is a bar to prevention of future processing.*
>
> *This right should be considered in conjunction with the Telecommunications (Data Protection and Privacy) Regulations 1999 SI 1999/2093[46] ("the Telecoms Regulations") which set out rules relating to the use of telephone, fax, e-mail and mail in direct marketing (see also the Introduction under "Other UK Data Privacy Legislation" for further commentary on the Telecommunications Regulations). If a data controller wishes to send unsolicited direct marketing communications to another business or individual, it must either have the consent of the company or individual concerned or should check the fax/telephone number, e-mail or mail address against the relevant list being operated by the Preference Service. Businesses which engage in such direct marketing would be well advised to regularly clean their marketing databases against these Preference Services Lists. See the Introduction – Useful Contact details for contact details for the Preference Services.*
>
> ---
>
> *46 As amended by SI 2000/157*

(2) If the court is satisfied, on the application of any person who has given a notice under subsection (1), that the data controller has failed to comply with the notice, the court may order him to take such steps for complying with the notice as the court thinks fit.

(3) In this section "direct marketing" means the communication (by whatever means) of any advertising or marketing material which is directed to particular individuals.

> **S.11(3)**
>
> *It would appear that generalised banner advertisements, which surround text on a website, will not fall within this category, since the marketing is not directed to particular individuals. Where an advertisement is selected to be shown to a particular user based on any of his or her personal data this would not be the case.*

12.– (1) An individual is entitled at any time, by notice in writing to any data controller, to require the data controller to ensure that no decision taken by or on behalf of the data controller which significantly affects that individual is based solely on the processing by automatic means of personal data in respect of which that individual is the data subject for the purpose of evaluating matters relating to him such as, for example, his performance at work, his creditworthiness, his reliability or his conduct.

S.12(1) - *This right may be summarised as follows:*

Individuals may require data controllers (by issuing them with a notice) to ensure that automated decisions involving their personal data are not the sole basis by which decisions which significantly affect them are made.

(Note, however, the exemptions at s.12(4)-(7).

An automated decision in relation to an individual is one "which significantly affects that individual [and which] is based solely on the processing by automatic means...". In a study[46] commissioned by the (then) Data Protection Registrar, the Personnel Policy Research Unit (PPRU) considered the word "solely" in this context. Ultimately it will be a matter for the courts to decide, but the study suggested that if the human involvement in the decision-making process was "purely cosmetic" and, if taken in isolation, would provide insufficient results, then the processing will be governed by section 12.

There are numerous types of automated decisions which can be taken, including:

- *decisions about whether to award credit to an applicant;*

- *the use of software which automatically scans CVs and shortlists those which meet pre-determined criteria;*

- *some psychometric tests;*

- *performance tests (eg a checkout operative whose performance is judged by the computer which scans the number of items processed over a given time).*

An example of an automated decision having far-reaching consequences was reported in a recent article in the Times.[47] The headline read "Computer sacks "star" employee over quiz failure", which firmly suggests that no human input was involved at all! Indeed, the dismissed employee, Mr Filer, commented that "it is a strange way to run a company - the machines seem to be taking over from the people." According to the report, Mr Filer was working for a DIY store and had so impressed his boss that he was offered promotion before the results of a 10 minute automated telephone interview had come through. When he was informed that he

---

46   *"The Uses and Misuses of Personal Data in Employer/Employee Relationships" - PPRU Study Report (January 1999).*
47   *The Times, 20 April 2001.*

> *had failed the interview he lost his job without any right of appeal. Unfortunately, the employer stuck rigidly to company policy, without allowing Mr Filer to make representations regarding his performance in the test.*
>
> *There are two possible approaches available to data controllers who make use of automated decisions. The first is that they accept that the decision is an automated one and notify the affected individual under s.12(2) that a decision was taken on that basis. This may then precipitate a procedure which requires the data controller to reconsider the decision. The second approach is to consider whether the decision is an "exempt" decision under s.12(6) (see notes to s.12(5)).*

(2) Where, in a case where no notice under subsection (1) has effect, a decision which significantly affects an individual is based solely on such processing as is mentioned in subsection (1)-

    (a) the data controller must as soon as reasonably practicable notify the individual that the decision was taken on that basis, and

> **S.12(2)(a)** - *The practical effect of this is that organisations which make use of automated decision-taking will have to notify all the data subjects who are likely to be significantly affected by such decisions. They cannot delay in telling the data subjects of the way in which the decision was reached and, it is suggested, should also inform the data subjects of their right to appeal against the decision (under s.12(2)(b)).*

    (b) the individual is entitled, within twenty-one days of receiving that notification from the data controller, by notice in writing to require the data controller to reconsider the decision or to take a new decision otherwise than on that basis.

(3) The data controller must, within twenty-one days of receiving a notice under subsection (2)(b) ("the data subject notice") give the individual a written notice specifying the steps that he intends to take to comply with the data subject notice.

(4) A notice under subsection (1) does not have effect in relation to an exempt decision; and nothing in subsection (2) applies to an exempt decision.

> **S.12(4)** - *i.e. a notice to reconsider a decision does not need to be complied with where ss.12(6) and 12(7) apply or as ordered by the Secretary of State.*

(5) In subsection (4) "exempt decision" means any decision-

(a) in respect of which the condition in subsection (6) and the condition in subsection (7) are met, or

(b) which is made in such other circumstances as may be prescribed by the Secretary of State by order.

Exempt decisions

Note that both a condition from s.12(6) and 12(7) must apply for a decision to be "exempt". The advantage of this, from the data controller's viewpoint, is that the s.12(1) notice does not apply, nor does the time-consuming s.12(2) procedure apply, if the decision is classified as "exempt". In the employment context, the use of an automatic CV scanner could result in a decision "taken in the course of steps taken...for the purpose of considering whether to enter into a contract with the data subject" (s.12(6)(a)(i)), and if the job applicant is successful, "the effect of the decision is to grant a request of the data subject" (s.12(7)a)). If the job applicant is unsuccessful, however, the employer would have to rely on s.12(7)(b) for the decision to be exempt, ie he would have to take steps to "safeguard the legitimate interests of the data subject (for example, by allowing him to make representations)".

S.12(5) *- nb under the Act's subject access provisions, access requests for the logic behind automated decisions requiring disclosure do not need to be complied with where to do so would require the disclosure of trade secrets (see s.8(5)).*

(6) The condition in this subsection is that the decision-

(a) is taken in the course of steps taken-

(i) for the purpose of considering whether to enter into a contract with the data subject,

(ii) with a view to entering into such a contract, or

(iii) in the course of performing such a contract, or

(b) is authorised or required by or under any enactment.

S.12(6) *- Note that under s.12(6)(a)(iii), a performance appraisal which is taken on automated grounds can be an exempt decision, so long as the employee's "legitimate interests" are safeguarded (s.12(7)(b)). Therefore, an employee whose performance is criticised must be given the opportunity to make representations (which, if necessary, must be investigated) before the automated decision is relied upon as determinative of his or her performance.*

(7) The condition in this subsection is that either-

(a) the effect of the decision is to grant a request of the data subject, or

(b) steps have been taken to safeguard the legitimate interests of the data subject (for example, by allowing him to make representations).

(8) If a court is satisfied on the application of a data subject that a person taking a decision in respect of him ("the responsible person") has failed to comply with subsection (1) or (2)(b), the court may order the responsible person to reconsider the decision, or to take a new decision which is not based solely on such processing as is mentioned in subsection (1).

(9) An order under subsection (8) shall not affect the rights of any person other than the data subject and the responsible person.

S.12(9) - *In s.12, "responsible person" means the data subject.*

Note: the transitional provisions waive the requirements of s.12 in relation to machine processed personal data in respect of which processing was under way before 24 October 1998 (see Sch 8, para 13(f)).

Note also: Schedule 13 introduces an additional section (numbered s.12A) relating to data subject's rights in relation to exempt manual data.

13.– (1) An individual who suffers damage by reason of any contravention by a data controller of any of the requirements of this Act is entitled to compensation from the data controller for that damage.

S.13(1) - *The entitlement to compensation only arises on damage being suffered UNLESS a contravention of the Act causes distress in relation to processing conducted for one of the "special purposes" (see below). Note that anybody who suffers damage by reason of a contravention of the Act can claim compensation from the data controller; this right is not restricted to data subjects.*

---

(2) An individual who suffers distress by reason of any contravention by a data controller of any of the requirements of this Act is entitled to compensation from the data controller for that distress if-

(a) the individual also suffers damage by reason of the contravention, or

(b) the contravention relates to the processing of personal data for the special purposes.

> **S.13(2)(b)** - *The entitlement to compensation for distress exists only where damage can also be shown (unless the "special purposes" apply). The "special purposes" are journalism, artistic or literary purposes (see s.32).*

(3) In proceedings brought against a person by virtue of this section it is a defence to prove that he had taken such care as in all the circumstances was reasonably required to comply with the requirement concerned.

> **S.13(3)** - *Data controllers are allowed to ask that proceedings for compensation be stayed if special purpose material is only processed so that it can be published. This is provided that data are only being processed for a special purpose, and so long as they have not been published by the data controller prior to the day before the compensation claim (see s.32(4)).*
>
> *This (s.32(4)) defence is also available in relation to s.14.*
>
> *Note: some parts of s.13 will not apply for machine processed personal data in respect of which processing was under way before 24 October 1998 (see Sch 8, para 13(g)).*

14.– (1) If a court is satisfied on the application of a data subject that personal data of which the applicant is the subject are inaccurate, the court may order the data controller to rectify, block, erase or destroy those data and any other personal data in respect of which he is the data controller and which contain an expression of opinion which appears to the court to be based on the inaccurate data.

(2) Subsection (1) applies whether or not the data accurately record information received or obtained by the data controller from the data subject or a third party but where the data accurately record such information, then-

(a) if the requirements mentioned in paragraph 7 of Part II of Schedule 1 have been complied with, the court may, instead of making an order under subsection (1), make an order requiring the data to be supplemented by such statement of the true facts relating to the matters dealt with by the data as the court may approve, and

> **S.14(2)(a)** - *If a data subject supplies inaccurate information to a data controller, and the data controller has complied with the bullet points below, then instead of requiring inaccurate data to be rectified, blocked, erased or destroyed a court may instead require a statement of truth to be added to the data.*

> *The data controller:*
>
> • *must have taken reasonable steps to ensure the data's accuracy; and*
>
> • *if it has been informed by the data subject that he/she thinks the data are inaccurate, a note of this must be placed on the data.*

    (b) if all or any of those requirements have not been complied with, the court may, instead of making an order under that subsection, make such order as it thinks fit for securing compliance with those requirements with or without a further order requiring the data to be supplemented by such a statement as is mentioned in paragraph (a).

(3) Where the court-

    (a) makes an order under subsection (1), or

    (b) is satisfied on the application of a data subject that personal data of which he was the data subject and which have been rectified, blocked, erased or destroyed were inaccurate,

it may, where it considers it reasonably practicable, order the data controller to notify third parties to whom the data have been disclosed of the rectification, blocking, erasure or destruction.

(4) If a court is satisfied on the application of a data subject-

    (a) that he has suffered damage by reason of any contravention by a data controller of any of the requirements of this Act in respect of any personal data, in circumstances entitling him to compensation under section 13, and

    (b) that there is a substantial risk of further contravention in respect of those data in such circumstances,

the court may order the rectification, blocking, erasure or destruction of any of those data.

(5) Where the court makes an order under subsection (4) it may, where it considers it reasonably practicable, order the data controller to notify third parties to whom the data have been disclosed of the rectification, blocking, erasure or destruction.

(6) In determining whether it is reasonably practicable to require such notification as is mentioned in subsection (3) or (5) the court shall have regard, in particular, to the number of persons who would have to be notified.

S.14(6) - *Sch 13, para 1 introduces a similar right to that granted by s.14 in relation to manual records (excluding manually recorded historical research) benefiting from the transitional period's exemptions (see Sch 13 (1).*

15.– (1) The jurisdiction conferred by sections 7 to 14 is exercisable by the High Court or a county court or, in Scotland, by the Court of Session or the sheriff.

(2) For the purpose of determining any question whether an applicant under subsection (9) of section 7 is entitled to the information which he seeks (including any question whether any relevant data are exempt from that section by virtue of Part IV) a court may require the information constituting any data processed by or on behalf of the data controller and any information as to the logic involved in any decision-taking as mentioned in section 7(1)(d) to be made available for its own inspection but shall not, pending the determination of that question in the applicant's favour, require the information sought by the applicant to be disclosed to him or his representatives whether by discovery (or, in Scotland, recovery) or otherwise.

PART III

NOTIFICATION BY DATA CONTROLLERS

16.– (1) In this Part "the registrable particulars", in relation to a data controller, means-

(a) his name and address,

(b) if he has nominated a representative for the purposes of this Act, the name and address of the representative,

(c) a description of the personal data being or to be processed by or on behalf of the data controller and of the category or categories of data subject to which they relate,

(d) a description of the purpose or purposes for which the data are being or are to be processed,

(e) a description of any recipient or recipients to whom the data controller intends or may wish to disclose the data,

(f) the names, or a description of, any countries or territories outside the European Economic Area to which the data controller directly or indirectly transfers, or intends or may wish directly or indirectly to transfer, the data, and

(g) in any case where-

(i) personal data are being, or are intended to be, processed in circumstances in which the prohibition in subsection (1) of section 17 is excluded by subsection (2) or (3) of that section, and

(ii) the notification does not extend to those data,

a statement of that fact.

S.16(1) - *The Notification Regulations[48] provide for an overhaul of the old registration system. The system is now called "notification" with the intention being to simplify the procedure. There are fewer standard purposes, data subject categories and data classes than there were under the registration system. The process of notification has been made easier since it can now be done on-line, using a straightforward, step-by-step process.*

The OIC has published a "Notification Handbook" which provides a comprehensive guide to the notification process. It also provides detailed guidance in "Notification Exemptions – a self assessment guide" for data controllers who believe that they may be exempt from having to notify (see s.17(4)).

The details to be provided under the notification process include the registrable particulars shown above plus a general description of security measures to be taken against unauthorised or unlawful processing, accidental loss, damage or destruction of personal data (see s.18(2)(b)).

It now costs data controllers £35 per year to submit their notification, which lasts for just one year, rather than three years under the previous system.

Failure to notify when required is a criminal offence (s. 21(1)).

Changes to notification

The Notification Regulations also oblige data controllers who have notified the Commissioner of their processing activities to notify the Commissioner promptly of any changes to matters which have been previously notified. Regulation 12 requires data controllers to supply such information "as soon as practicable and in any event within a period of 28 days from the date on which the entry or, as the case may be, the general description [of measures to be taken to comply with the seventh data protection principle], becomes inaccurate or incomplete." This is modified by Regulation 13, which provides that the duty under Regulation 12 varies according to whether or not the change in processing affects data which are subject to processing which was already under way immediately before 24 October 1998. If the change does relate to such data, the data controller has to provide different (and more extensive) information to the Commissioner than if the change relates to newer processing.

The Guidelines state that anyone already registered under the 1984 Act, or applying to be so registered (or indeed appealing against refusal of such registration) will not be required to re-register under the Act until either their registration expires or 24 October 2001, whichever is the earlier[49](see Sch 14, para 2).

---

48 *The Data Protection (Notification and Notification Fees) Regulations 2000 (SI 2000/188).*
49 *Guidelines, Chapter 8, para 2.1*

(2) In this Part-

"fees regulations" means regulations made by the Secretary of State under section 18(5) or 19(4) or (7);

"notification regulations" means regulations made by the Secretary of State under the other provisions of this Part;

"prescribed", except where used in relation to fees regulations, means prescribed by notification regulations.

(3) For the purposes of this Part, so far as it relates to the addresses of data controllers-

(a) the address of a registered company is that of its registered office, and
(b) the address of a person (other than a registered company) carrying on a business is that of his principal place of business in the United Kingdom.

17.– (1) Subject to the following provisions of this section, personal data must not be processed unless an entry in respect of the data controller is included in the register maintained by the Commissioner under section 19 (or is treated by notification regulations made by virtue of section 19(3) as being so included).

(2) Except where the processing is assessable processing for the purposes of section 22, subsection (1) does not apply in relation to personal data consisting of information which falls neither within paragraph (a) of the definition of "data" in section 1(1) nor within paragraph (b) of that definition.

S.17(2) - *"assessable processing": processing which is likely to cause substantial damage/distress to data subjects or significantly prejudice their rights and freedoms (see s.22(1)).*

(3) If it appears to the Secretary of State that processing of a particular description is unlikely to prejudice the rights and freedoms of data subjects, notification regulations may provide that, in such cases as may be prescribed, subsection (1) is not to apply in relation to processing of that description.

(4) Subsection (1) does not apply in relation to any processing whose sole purpose is the maintenance of a public register.

S.17(4) - *The Notification Regulations also detail the exemptions from notification. The OIC has also produced a guide[50] which is available on the Commissioner's website. Data controllers who are unsure of whether they need to notify can work through nine questions to enable them to find out.*

Exemptions are available for:

- *non-automated processing;*

- *processing for personal, family or household affairs (including recreational purposes);*

- *some not for profit organisations[51];*

- *maintenance of a public register;*

- *if processing of personal data is limited to:*

- *staff administration;*

- *advertising, marketing and public relations;*

- *accounts and records (other than where personal data have been processed by or obtained from a credit reference agency).*

See notes at s.22 and s.24(1) which may nevertheless require the provision of certain information even if the above exemptions apply.

It is also worth noting that the exemption from the requirement to notify does not, unlike the 1984 Act, provide an exemption from compliance with the Act. So, for example, a data controller who only processes employee data for staff administration purposes must nevertheless ensure that information about the nature of the processing is made readily available to staff.

---

50   *Notification Exemptions: A Self-Assessment Guide.*
51   *See questions 8 and 9 of Notification Exemptions: A Self-Assessment Guide for more details.*

18.– (1) Any data controller who wishes to be included in the register maintained under section 19 shall give a notification to the Commissioner under this section.

(2) A notification under this section must specify in accordance with notification regulations-

   (a) the registrable particulars, and
   (b) a general description of measures to be taken for the purpose of complying with the seventh data protection principle.

S.18(2)(b) - *Details are required of the security measures to be taken against unauthorised/unlawful processing, accidental loss, damage or destruction of personal data. The notification procedure requires data controllers to answer questions relating to the measures they may have taken, such as whether efforts have been made to comply with British Standard Code of Practice for information security management (BS7799).*

(3) Notification regulations made by virtue of subsection (2) may provide for the determination by the Commissioner, in accordance with any requirements of the regulations, of the form in which the registrable particulars and the description mentioned in subsection (2)(b) are to be specified, including in particular the detail required for the purposes of section 16(1)(c), (d), (e) and (f) and subsection (2)(b).

(4) Notification regulations may make provision as to the giving of notification-

(a) by partnerships, or

(b) in other cases where two or more persons are the data controllers in respect of any personal data.

(5) The notification must be accompanied by such fee as may be prescribed by fees regulations.

(6) Notification regulations may provide for any fee paid under subsection (5) or section 19(4) to be refunded in prescribed circumstances.

19.– (1) The Commissioner shall-

(a) maintain a register of persons who have given notification under section 18, and

(b) make an entry in the register in pursuance of each notification received by him under that section from a person in respect of whom no entry as data controller was for the time being included in the register.

S.19(1) - *By Regulation 10 of the Notification Regulations, the Commissioner is required to provide a data controller who has supplied its notification details to the Commissioner with a notice confirming the register entry promptly and in any event within 28 days of notification.*

(2) Each entry in the register shall consist of-

(a) the registrable particulars notified under section 18 or, as the case requires, those particulars as amended in pursuance of section 20(4), and

(b) such other information as the Commissioner may be authorised or required by notification regulations to include in the register.

S.19(2) - *Regulation 11 of the Notification Regulations provides that:*

"In addition to the matters mentioned in section 19(2)(a) of the Act, the Commissioner may include in a register entry -

> *(a) a registration number issued by the Commissioner in respect of that entry;*

> *(b) the date on which the entry is treated... as having been included in pursuance of a notification under section 18 of the Act;*

> *(c) the date on which the entry falls or may fall to be removed by virtue of regulations 14 or 15 below; and*

> *(d) information additional to the registrable particulars for the purpose of assisting persons consulting the register to communicate with any data controller to whom the entry relates concerning matters relating to the processing of personal data."*

Regulation 14 of the Notification Regulations provides that, other than in transitional circumstances (set out in Regulation 15), the annual fee for retention of a register entry is £35. Regulation 15 provides that where a data controller is currently registered under the 1984 Act, that registration will continue until either its expiry of 24 October 2001, whichever is sooner.

---

(3) Notification regulations may make provision as to the time as from which any entry in respect of a data controller is to be treated for the purposes of section 17 as having been made in the register.

(4) No entry shall be retained in the register for more than the relevant time except on payment of such fee as may be prescribed by fees regulations.

S.19(4) - *Registrations will need to be renewed annually. This requirement is more onerous than that under the 1984 Act which required a renewal every 3 years.*

---

(5) In subsection (4) "the relevant time" means twelve months or such other period as may be prescribed by notification regulations; and different periods may be prescribed in relation to different cases.

(6) The Commissioner-

    (a) shall provide facilities for making the information contained in the entries in the register available for inspection (in visible and legible form) by members of the public at all reasonable hours and free of charge, and

    (b) may provide such other facilities for making the information contained in those entries available to the public free of charge as he considers appropriate.

(7) The Commissioner shall, on payment of such fee, if any, as may be prescribed by fees regulations, supply any member of the public with a duly certified copy in writing of the particulars contained in any entry made in the register.

> **S.19(7)** - *The Data Protection (Fees under section 19(7)) Regulations 2000 (SI 2000/187) stipulates that the fee for providing a certified copy of a register entry is £2.*

20.– (1) For the purpose specified in subsection (2), notification regulations shall include provision imposing on every person in respect of whom an entry as a data controller is for the time being included in the register maintained under section 19 a duty to notify to the Commissioner, in such circumstances and at such time or times and in such form as may be prescribed, such matters relating to the registrable particulars and measures taken as mentioned in section 18(2)(b) as may be prescribed.

(2) The purpose referred to in subsection (1) is that of ensuring, so far as practicable, that at any time-

    (a) the entries in the register maintained under section 19 contain current names and addresses and describe the current practice or intentions of the data controller with respect to the processing of personal data, and

    (b) the Commissioner is provided with a general description of measures currently being taken as mentioned in section 18(2)(b).

(3) Subsection (3) of section 18 has effect in relation to notification regulations made by virtue of subsection (1) as it has effect in relation to notification regulations made by virtue of subsection (2) of that section.

(4) On receiving any notification under notification regulations made by virtue of subsection (1), the Commissioner shall make such amendments of the relevant entry in the register maintained under section 19 as are necessary to take account of the notification.

S.20(4) - *By Regulation 10 of the Notification Regulations, the Commissioner is required to provide confirmation of the amendment to the register entry to the data controller promptly and in any event within 28 days of the amendment being sought.*

21.– (1) If section 17(1) is contravened, the data controller is guilty of an offence.

S.21(1) - *Note that failure to register is a strict liability offence.*

In addition to the exemptions explained at s.17 and s.21(3), processing benefiting from the transitional exemptions, or the national security or domestic purposes exemptions, will also not be caught by s.21(1).

However, exemption from the registration obligation will not exempt a data controller from its obligation to respond within 21 days to written requests for its "registrable particulars" (i.e. the information detailed at s.16(1)(a)-(f) (see s.24(1)).

(2) Any person who fails to comply with the duty imposed by notification regulations made by virtue of section 20(1) is guilty of an offence.

(3) It shall be a defence for a person charged with an offence under subsection (2) to show that he exercised all due diligence to comply with the duty.

22.– (1) In this section "assessable processing" means processing which is of a description specified in an order made by the Secretary of State as appearing to him to be particularly likely-

(a) to cause substantial damage or substantial distress to data subjects, or
(b) otherwise significantly to prejudice the rights and freedoms of data subjects.

S.22 - *Processing which was already under way immediately before 24 October 1998 is not assessable processing for the purposes of this section (see Sch 8, para 19).*

S.22(1) - *At the time of writing no such order has been made, although a Home Office consultation paper[52] suggests that three categories (data matching, processing which involves genetic information and processing by private investigators) will be subject to preliminary assessment by the Commissioner.*

---

52   *dated August 1998*

(2) On receiving notification from any data controller under section 18 or under notification regulations made by virtue of section 20 the Commissioner shall consider-

 (a) whether any of the processing to which the notification relates is assessable processing, and

 (b) if so, whether the assessable processing is likely to comply with the provisions of this Act.

S.22(2) - *Regulation 9 of the Notification Regulations provides that where the Commissioner considers that any of the processing to which a notification relates is assessable processing, written notice will be provided to the data controller within 10 days of receipt of the notification. See also s.22(3).*

Note that the Guidelines state that the Commissioner may only consider and prohibit as assessable processing which has actually commenced[53].

---

53   Guidelines, Chapter 7, para 14

---

(3) Subject to subsection (4), the Commissioner shall, within the period of twenty-eight days beginning with the day on which he receives a notification which relates to assessable processing, give a notice to the data controller stating the extent to which the Commissioner is of the opinion that the processing is likely or unlikely to comply with the provisions of this Act.

(4) Before the end of the period referred to in subsection (3) the Commissioner may, by reason of special circumstances, extend that period on one occasion only by notice to the data controller by such further period not exceeding fourteen days as the Commissioner may specify in the notice.

(5) No assessable processing in respect of which a notification has been given to the Commissioner as mentioned in subsection (2) shall be carried on unless either-

 (a) the period of twenty-eight days beginning with the day on which the notification is received by the Commissioner (or, in a case falling within subsection (4), that period as extended under that subsection) has elapsed, or

 (b) before the end of that period (or that period as so extended) the data controller has received a notice from the Commissioner under subsection (3) in respect of the processing.

(6) Where subsection (5) is contravened, the data controller is guilty of an offence.

(7) The Secretary of State may by order amend subsections (3), (4) and (5) by substituting for the number of days for the time being specified there a different number specified in the order.

23.– (1) The Secretary of State may by order-

    (a) make provision under which a data controller may appoint a person to act as a data protection supervisor responsible in particular for monitoring in an independent manner the data controller's compliance with the provisions of this Act, and

> **S.23(1)(a)** - *This would appear to give the Commissioner the power to impose upon a company the appointment of an independent data protection compliance officer. It remains to be seen what exemptions (under s.23(1)(b)) will apply to such supervisors.*

    (b) provide that, in relation to any data controller who has appointed a data protection supervisor in accordance with the provisions of the order and who complies with such conditions as may be specified in the order, the provisions of this Part are to have effect subject to such exemptions or other modifications as may be specified in the order.

(2) An order under this section may-

    (a) impose duties on data protection supervisors in relation to the Commissioner, and

    (b) confer functions on the Commissioner in relation to data protection supervisors.

24.– (1) Subject to subsection (3), where personal data are processed in a case where-

    (a) by virtue of subsection (2) or (3) of section 17, subsection (1) of that section does not apply to the processing, and

    (b) the data controller has not notified the relevant particulars in respect of that processing under section 18,

the data controller must, within twenty-one days of receiving a written request from any person, make the relevant particulars available to that person in writing free of charge.

> **S.24(1)** - *This requires a data controller who is exempt from the requirement to be registered nevertheless to supply details of its "relevant particulars" (see s.24(2)) on 21 days' written notice.*

(2) In this section "the relevant particulars" means the particulars referred to in paragraphs (a) to (f) of section 16(1).

(3) This section has effect subject to any exemption conferred for the purposes of this section by notification regulations.

(4) Any data controller who fails to comply with the duty imposed by subsection (1) is guilty of an offence.

(5) It shall be a defence for a person charged with an offence under subsection (4) to show that he exercised all due diligence to comply with the duty.

25.– (1) As soon as practicable after the passing of this Act, the Commissioner shall submit to the Secretary of State proposals as to the provisions to be included in the first notification regulations.

(2) The Commissioner shall keep under review the working of notification regulations and may from time to time submit to the Secretary of State proposals as to amendments to be made to the regulations.

(3) The Secretary of State may from time to time require the Commissioner to consider any matter relating to notification regulations and to submit to him proposals as to amendments to be made to the regulations in connection with that matter.

(4) Before making any notification regulations, the Secretary of State shall-

(a) consider any proposals made to him by the Commissioner under subsection (1), (2) or (3), and

(b) consult the Commissioner.

26.– (1) Fees regulations prescribing fees for the purposes of any provision of this Part may provide for different fees to be payable in different cases.

(2) In making any fees regulations, the Secretary of State shall have regard to the desirability of securing that the fees payable to the Commissioner are sufficient to offset-

(a) the expenses incurred by the Commissioner and the Tribunal in discharging their functions and any expenses of the Secretary of State in respect of the Commissioner or the Tribunal, and

(b) to the extent that the Secretary of State considers appropriate-

(i) any deficit previously incurred (whether before or after the passing of this Act) in respect of the expenses mentioned in paragraph (a), and

(ii) expenses incurred or to be incurred by the Secretary of State in respect of the inclusion of any officers or staff of the Commissioner in any scheme under section 1 of the Superannuation Act 1972.

PART IV

EXEMPTIONS

27.– (1) References in any of the data protection principles or any provision of Parts II and III to personal data or to the processing of personal data do not include references to data or processing which by virtue of this Part are exempt from that principle or other provision.

(2) In this Part "the subject information provisions" means-

(a) the first data protection principle to the extent to which it requires compliance with paragraph 2 of Part II of Schedule 1, and

(b) section 7.

S.27(2) - *the "subject information provisions" exempt:*

- *paras 2 & 3 of the fair processing code (see para 2, Pt II Sch 1); and*

- *the subject access rights (see s.7).*

(3) In this Part "the non-disclosure provisions" means the provisions specified in subsection (4) to the extent to which they are inconsistent with the disclosure in question.

S.27(3) - *the "non-disclosure provisions" exempt:*

- *the 1st principle (except where compliance with Sch 2 & 3 is required);*

- *the 2nd principle (processing for a specified purpose), 3rd principle (personal data to be adequate and not excessive), 4th principle (accurate and up to date personal data), 5th principle (personal data not to be kept longer than necessary);*

- *s.10 (right to prevent damaging or distressing processing); and*

- *s.14(1)- (3) (right to rectify, block, erase and destroy inaccurate data)*

to the extent to which they are inconsistent with the disclosure in question.

(4) The provisions referred to in subsection (3) are-

(a) the first data protection principle, except to the extent to which it requires compliance with the conditions in Schedules 2 and 3,

(b) the second, third, fourth and fifth data protection principles, and

(c) sections 10 and 14(1) to (3).

(5) Except as provided by this Part, the subject information provisions shall have effect notwithstanding any enactment or rule of law prohibiting or restricting the disclosure, or authorising the withholding, of information.

28.– (1) Personal data are exempt from any of the provisions of-

(a) the data protection principles,

(b) Parts II, III and V, and

> **S.28(1)(b)** - *Part II contains the rights of individuals, Part III relates to notification, Part V covers enforcement provisions and s.55 prohibits unlawful obtaining of personal data.*

    (c) section 55,

if the exemption from that provision is required for the purpose of safeguarding national security.

> **S.28(1)**
>
> *An appeal to the Data Protection Tribunal has, at the time of writing, recently been made by a Mr Robert Henderson, a retired tax inspector. He is appealing against an order from the Home Secretary preventing him from gaining access to his MI5 file, on grounds of national security. Mr Henderson complained about the Secret Service investigating his activities after he allegedly wrote "hate mail" to Tony Blair and his wife Cherie Booth. The case is due to be heard in November 2001. Similarly, the case of Norman Baker, Liberal Democrat MP for Lewes, is, at this time of writing, due to be heard by the Data Protection Tribunal. This case again relates to the refusal of MI5 to provide access to the data subject's MI5 file. While under the 1984 Act, MI5 had a blanket exemption, now data subjects have a right of appeal. The Tribunal will be asked why MI5 will not allow access to those files not under active MI5 consideration and which have no possible link to terrorism or serious crime.*
>
> *This is an interesting area which will no doubt keep the Data Protection Tribunal busy if these two cases favour Mr Henderson or Mr Baker.*[54]
>
> ---
>
> 54   *Acknowledgements to "Privacy & Data Protection", Volume 1 Issue 6, June 2001 where this case was reported*

(2) Subject to subsection (4), a certificate signed by a Minister of the Crown certifying that exemption from all or any of the provisions mentioned in subsection (1) is or at any time was required for the purpose there mentioned in respect of any personal data shall be conclusive evidence of that fact.

> **S.28(2)** - *A certificate of exemption signed by a cabinet minister (or the Lord Advocate) stating that the exemption applies will trigger this exemption.*

(3) A certificate under subsection (2) may identify the personal data to which it applies by means of a general description and may be expressed to have prospective effect.

(4) Any person directly affected by the issuing of a certificate under subsection (2) may appeal to the Tribunal against the certificate.

> **S.28(4)** - *Note that the right to appeal against the issuing of the certificate may be exercised by anyone directly affected, not just the data subject.*
>
> *The practice and procedure of the Data Protection Tribunal in such appeals is governed by The Data Protection Tribunal (National Security Appeals) Rules 2000 (SI 2000/206). See Sch 6 para 7 for more details.*

(5) If on an appeal under subsection (4), the Tribunal finds that, applying the principles applied by the court on an application for judicial review, the Minister did not have reasonable grounds for issuing the certificate, the Tribunal may allow the appeal and quash the certificate.

(6) Where in any proceedings under or by virtue of this Act it is claimed by a data controller that a certificate under subsection (2) which identifies the personal data to which it applies by means of a general description applies to any personal data, any other party to the proceedings may appeal to the Tribunal on the ground that the certificate does not apply to the personal data in question and, subject to any determination under subsection (7), the certificate shall be conclusively presumed so to apply.

(7) On any appeal under subsection (6), the Tribunal may determine that the certificate does not so apply.

(8) A document purporting to be a certificate under subsection (2) shall be received in evidence and deemed to be such a certificate unless the contrary is proved.

(9) A document which purports to be certified by or on behalf of a Minister of the Crown as a true copy of a certificate issued by that Minister under subsection (2) shall in any legal proceedings be evidence (or, in Scotland, sufficient evidence) of that certificate.

(10) The power conferred by subsection (2) on a Minister of the Crown shall not be exercisable except by a Minister who is a member of the Cabinet or by the Attorney General or the Lord Advocate.

(11) No power conferred by any provision of Part V may be exercised in relation to personal data which by virtue of this section are exempt from that provision.

(12) Schedule 6 shall have effect in relation to appeals under subsection (4) or (6) and the proceedings of the Tribunal in respect of any such appeal.

29.– (1) Personal data processed for any of the following purposes-

(a) the prevention or detection of crime,

(b) the apprehension or prosecution of offenders, or

(c) the assessment or collection of any tax or duty or of any imposition of a similar nature,

are exempt from the first data protection principle (except to the extent to which it requires compliance with the conditions in Schedules 2 and 3) and section 7 in any case to the extent to which the application of those provisions to the data would be likely to prejudice any of the matters mentioned in this subsection.

> **S.29(1)** - *There are 4 crime and taxation exemptions.*
>
> *The first exempts the following from applying to processing which may prejudice (a) to (c):*
>
> - *the 1st principle (except the obligation to comply with Sch 2 & 3); and*
>
> - *subject access rights.*

(2) Personal data which-

(a) are processed for the purpose of discharging statutory functions, and

(b) consist of information obtained for such a purpose from a person who had it in his possession for any of the purposes mentioned in subsection (1),

are exempt from the subject information provisions to the same extent as personal data processed for any of the purposes mentioned in that subsection.

> **S.29(2)** - *The second exempts the subject information provisions (see s.27(2)) to the extent that they may prejudice s.29(1)(a) and (b).*

(3) Personal data are exempt from the non-disclosure provisions in any case in which-

(a) the disclosure is for any of the purposes mentioned in subsection (1), and

(b) the application of those provisions in relation to the disclosure would be likely to prejudice any of the matters mentioned in that subsection.

> **S.29(3)** - *The third exempts the non-disclosure provisions (see s.27(3)) in any case where disclosure is made for any of the purposes listed in s.29(1) and those purposes may be prejudiced by such disclosure.*

The term "may be prejudiced" is not defined. The Guidelines (mirroring the opinions of the Registrar in relation to the 1984 Act which contained a similar provision) state that the Commissioner will expect to discover a "substantial chance rather than a mere risk that in a particular case the purposes would be noticeably damaged"[55].

55   *Guidelines Chapter 5, para 2.2.4*

(4) Personal data in respect of which the data controller is a relevant authority and which-

    (a) consist of a classification applied to the data subject as part of a system of risk assessment which is operated by that authority for either of the following purposes-

        (i) the assessment or collection of any tax or duty or any imposition of a similar nature, or

        (ii) the prevention or detection of crime, or apprehension or prosecution of offenders, where the offence concerned involves any unlawful claim for any payment out of, or any unlawful application of, public funds, and

    (b) are processed for either of those purposes,

are exempt from section 7 to the extent to which the exemption is required in the interests of the operation of the system.

(5) In subsection (4)-

"public funds" includes funds provided by any Community institution;

"relevant authority" means-

    (a) a government department,

    (b) a local authority, or

    (c) any other authority administering housing benefit or council tax benefit.

S.29(4) to (5) - *The fourth exemption applies where personal data are processed pursuant to the assessment of possible offences concerning the assessment/collection of taxes or duties or the fraudulent use of public funds if:*

- *the data controller is a government department, local authority or any other authority administering housing or council tax benefit; and*

- *the personal data consist of a classification applied to the data subject as part of a risk assessment system operated for tax or crime prevention/detection purposes*

to the extent that the exemption is necessary in the interests of the operating system.

30.– (1) The Secretary of State may by order exempt from the subject information provisions, or modify those provisions in relation to, personal data consisting of information as to the physical or mental health or condition of the data subject.

> **S.30(1)** - *The Data Protection (Subject Access Modification) (Health) Order 2000 (SI 2000/413) provides certain exemptions from the subject access provisions. See commentary at s.7 for further details.*
>
> *With the introduction of the above mentioned Order, plus the other orders introduced under this section and referred to below, to a certain degree a burden is removed from areas of society which regularly process vast amounts of data. Having said that, the exemptions or modifications are limited to the subject information provisions and the data controllers in the fields of health, education and social work will still have to ensure compliance with other aspects of the Act.*

(2) The Secretary of State may by order exempt from the subject information provisions, or modify those provisions in relation to-

(a) personal data in respect of which the data controller is the proprietor of, or a teacher at, a school, and which consist of information relating to persons who are or have been pupils at the school, or

(b) personal data in respect of which the data controller is an education authority in Scotland, and which consist of information relating to persons who are receiving, or have received, further education provided by the authority.

> **S.30(2)** - *School: under section 4 of the Education Act 1996, a "school" is an institution providing primary and secondary education.*
>
> *The Data Protection (Subject Access Modification) (Education) Order 2000 (SI 2000/414) provides certain exemptions from the subject access provisions. See commentary at s.7 for further details.*

(3) The Secretary of State may by order exempt from the subject information provisions, or modify those provisions in relation to, personal data of such other descriptions as may be specified in the order, being information-

(a) processed by government departments or local authorities or by voluntary organisations or other bodies designated by or under the order, and

(b) appearing to him to be processed in the course of, or for the purposes of, carrying out social work in relation to the data subject or other individuals;

S.30(3)(b) - *"...or other individuals": George Howarth MP (then Parliamentary Under-Secretary of State for the Home Department), commented that "there are other interests involving the wider community that need to be taken into account, such as concern about how the actions or behaviour of an individual might impact on others". He also gave the example of an individual who seeks to do voluntary work with children in care: "Social workers might initially suspect that the person was not suitable but, following investigations, decide that their fears were groundless. If that person asked to see his file and discovered that social workers had had doubts about his suitability, the goodwill needed for voluntary work might disappear. That may appear to be a Big Brother approach, but we cannot be too careful where access to children, voluntary or otherwise is involved."[56]*

The Data Protection (Subject Access Modification) (Social Work) Order 2000 (SI 2000/415) provides certain exemptions from the subject access provisions. See commentary at s.7 for further details.

---

56   *House of Commons Standing Committee D, 21 May 1998*

but the Secretary of State shall not under this subsection confer any exemption or make any modification except so far as he considers that the application to the data of those provisions (or of those provisions without modification) would be likely to prejudice the carrying out of social work.

(4) An order under this section may make different provision in relation to data consisting of information of different descriptions.

s.30(4) - *The orders which have been made under this section are:*

- *The Data Protection (Subject Access Modification) (Health) Order 2000 (SI 2000/413);*

- *The Data Protection (Subject Access Modification) (Education) Order 2000 (SI 2000/414);*

- *The Data Protection (Subject Access Modification) (Social Work) Order 2000 (SI 2000/415).*

For further details, see commentary at s.7.

(5) In this section-

"education authority" and "further education" have the same meaning as in the Education (Scotland) Act 1980 ("the 1980 Act"), and "proprietor"-

(a) in relation to a school in England or Wales, has the same meaning as in the Education Act 1996,

(b) in relation to a school in Scotland, means-

    (i) in the case of a self-governing school, the board of management within the meaning of the Self-Governing Schools etc. (Scotland) Act 1989,

    (ii) in the case of an independent school, the proprietor within the meaning of the 1980 Act,

    (iii) in the case of a grant-aided school, the managers within the meaning of the 1980 Act, and

    (iv) in the case of a public school, the education authority within the meaning of the 1980 Act, and

(c) in relation to a school in Northern Ireland, has the same meaning as in the Education and Libraries (Northern Ireland) Order 1986 and includes, in the case of a controlled school, the Board of Governors of the school.

31.– (1) Personal data processed for the purposes of discharging functions to which this subsection applies are exempt from the subject information provisions in any case to the extent to which the application of those provisions to the data would be likely to prejudice the proper discharge of those functions.

> **S.31(1)** - *This exemption is known in the Guidelines[57] as the "regulatory activity exemption". Exemption from the subject information provisions (see s.27(2)) applies in relation to any of the watchdog functions listed in s.31(2) or of the type described in s.31(4), but only to the extent that such functions or type of regulation would be likely to be prejudiced if the exemption did not apply.*
>
> ---
> 57   *Guidelines Chapter 5, para 2.4.*

(2) Subsection (1) applies to any relevant function which is designed-

(a) for protecting members of the public against-

    (i) financial loss due to dishonesty, malpractice or other seriously improper conduct by, or the unfitness or incompetence of, persons concerned in the provision of banking, insurance, investment or other financial services or in the management of bodies corporate,

    (ii) financial loss due to the conduct of discharged or undischarged bankrupts, or

    (iii) dishonesty, malpractice or other seriously improper conduct by, or the unfitness or incompetence of, persons authorised to carry on any profession or other activity,

(b) for protecting charities against misconduct or mismanagement (whether by trustees or other persons) in their administration,

(c) for protecting the property of charities from loss or misapplication,

(d) for the recovery of the property of charities,

(e) for securing the health, safety and welfare of persons at work, or

(f) for protecting persons other than persons at work against risk to health or safety arising out of or in connection with the actions of persons at work.

(3) In subsection (2) "relevant function" means-

(a) any function conferred on any person by or under any enactment,

(b) any function of the Crown, a Minister of the Crown or a government department, or

(c) any other function which is of a public nature and is exercised in the public interest.

(4) Personal data processed for the purpose of discharging any function which-

(a) is conferred by or under any enactment on-
   (i) the Parliamentary Commissioner for Administration,
   (ii) the Commission for Local Administration in England, the Commission for Local Administration in Wales or the Commissioner for Local Administration in Scotland,
   (iii) the Health Service Commissioner for England, the Health Service Commissioner for Wales or the Health Service Commissioner for Scotland,
   (iv) the Welsh Administration Ombudsman,
   (v) the Assembly Ombudsman for Northern Ireland, or
   (vi) the Northern Ireland Commissioner for Complaints, and

(b) is designed for protecting members of the public against-
   (i) maladministration by public bodies,
   (ii) failures in services provided by public bodies, or
   (iii) a failure of a public body to provide a service which it was a function of the body to provide,

are exempt from the subject information provisions in any case to the extent to which the application of those provisions to the data would be likely to prejudice the proper discharge of that function.

(5) Personal data processed for the purpose of discharging any function which-

(a) is conferred by or under any enactment on the Director General of Fair Trading, and

(b) is designed-
   (i) for protecting members of the public against conduct which may adversely affect their interests by persons carrying on a business,
   (ii) for regulating agreements or conduct which have as their object or effect the prevention, restriction or distortion of competition in connection with any commercial activity, or
   (iii) for regulating conduct on the part of one or more undertakings which amounts to the abuse of a dominant position in a market,

are exempt from the subject information provisions in any case to the extent to which the application of those provisions to the data would be likely to prejudice the proper discharge of that function.

32.– (1) Personal data which are processed only for the special purposes are exempt from any provision to which this subsection relates if-

S.32(1) - *Any of the special purposes (journalistic, literary and artistic purposes) will only qualify for this exemption if all conditions listed at (a) to (c) are present.*

Article 9 of the Directive[58] allows member states to find their own way of providing exemptions or derogations from the Directive's main provisions for processing solely for journalistic purposes or the purposes of artistic or literary expression. The exemptions which apply to this section follow lengthy discussions with media interests to identify the difficulties of reconciling the right of privacy with rules governing freedom of expression.

Because of the wholesale exemptions available to those who can demonstrate that their activities fall within the special purposes, some data controllers who are not conventionally seen, say, as journalists, may try to force the definition to fit their circumstances. Richard Allen MP asked the following question of Geoff Hoon MP: "is it sufficient for a person to define himself as a journalist, artist or litterateur simply because he has amassed a great deal of data that could be put on a web page?"[59] Geoff Hoon confirmed that the medium used was unimportant; if, for example, someone put personal data on a web page for the purposes of journalism, that person would be covered by this section. The merit of the journalism, literature or art is immaterial.

See ss. 44 to 46 and s. 53, which give the Commissioner powers to ensure that processing carried out for the "special purposes" is compliant with the provisions of s.32(1).

---

58   *Directive 95/46/EC.*
59   *House of Commons Standing Committee D, 12 May 1998*

(a) the processing is undertaken with a view to the publication by any person of any journalistic, literary or artistic material,

(b) the data controller reasonably believes that, having regard in particular to the special importance of the public interest in freedom of expression, publication would be in the public interest, and

> **S.32(1)(b)** - *Given the ongoing debate as to the public interest of freedom of the press against the right to privacy, it will be interesting to see how the courts rule upon the term "public interest in freedom of expression". The effect of the introduction of the Human Rights Act 1998 will also need to be considered. (See also s.32(3)).*

    (c) the data controller reasonably believes that, in all the circumstances, compliance with that provision is incompatible with the special purposes.

(2) Subsection (1) relates to the provisions of-

    (a) the data protection principles except the seventh data protection principle,

    (b) section 7,

    (c) section 10,

    (d) section 12, and

    (e) section 14(1) to (3).

> **S.32(2)** - *If all the conditions stipulated in s.32(1) apply, the processing is exempt from the following provisions:*
>
> *(a)   all data protection principles except the seventh (security measures);*
>
> *(b)   s.7 - subject access;*
>
> *(c)   s.10 - right to prevent processing likely to cause damage or distress;*
>
> *(d)   s.12 - rights in relation to automated decision-taking;*
>
> *(dd) s.12A (applicable until 24 October 2007 - see Schedule 13, para 2) - rights in relation to exempt manual data;*
>
> *(e)   s.14(1) to (3) - provisions relating to rectification, blocking, erasure and destruction of inaccurate data.*

(3) In considering for the purposes of subsection (1)(b) whether the belief of a data controller that publication would be in the public interest was or is a reasonable one, regard may be had to his compliance with any code of practice which-

    (a) is relevant to the publication in question, and

    (b) is designated by the Secretary of State by order for the purposes of this subsection.

S.32(3)(b) - *The Data Protection (Designated Codes of Practice) Order 2000 (SI 2000/418) provides that the following are designated codes of practice:*

- *The Code on Fairness and Privacy (issued by the Broadcasting Standards Commission in June 1998);*

- *The ITC Programme Code (issued by the Independent Television Commission in Autumn 1998);*

- *The Code of Practice published by the Press Complaints Commission in December 1997;*

- *The Producers' Guidelines (issued by the BBC in November 1996);*

- *The Programme Code (issued by the Radio Authority in March 1998).*

(4) Where at any time ("the relevant time") in any proceedings against a data controller under section 7(9), 10(4), 12(8) or 14 or by virtue of section 13 the data controller claims, or it appears to the court, that any personal data to which the proceedings relate are being processed-

(a) only for the special purposes, and
(b) with a view to the publication by any person of any journalistic, literary or artistic material which, at the time twenty-four hours immediately before the relevant time, had not previously been published by the data controller,

the court shall stay the proceedings until either of the conditions in subsection (5) is met.

S.32(4) - *Proceedings for:*

- *a breach of the right to a response to a subject access request;*

- *a breach of the right to prevent processing likely to cause unwarranted damage or distress;*

- *a breach of rights in relation to automated decision-making;*

- *a breach of rights in relation to exempt manual data (see s.12A(3), to be found in Sch 13 para 2(b));*

- *compensation for damage or distress; and*

- *the rectification, blocking, erasure and destruction of inaccurate data*

will trigger the availability of the grounds for a stay in court proceedings under this section if the processing being considered fits the criteria set out at s.32 (4)(a)-(b).

(5) Those conditions are-

    (a) that a determination of the Commissioner under section 45 with respect to the data in question takes effect, or

    (b) in a case where the proceedings were stayed on the making of a claim, that the claim is withdrawn.

> **S.32(5)** - *The stay in proceedings will only run until either the claim is withdrawn, or the Commissioner determines that personal data are not being processed:*
>
> *(a) for one of the special purposes, or*
>
> *(b) with a view to the publication of any special purpose material which has not previously been published by the data controller.*
>
> *Determination under s.45: This provides that notice must be given of such determination and that a right of appeal exists against this notice.*

(6) For the purposes of this Act "publish", in relation to journalistic, literary or artistic material, means make available to the public or any section of the public.

> **S.32(6)** - *"publish": this would include placing the data on the internet.*

33.– (1) In this section-

"research purposes" includes statistical or historical purposes;

"the relevant conditions", in relation to any processing of personal data, means the conditions-

    (a) that the data are not processed to support measures or decisions with respect to particular individuals, and

    (b) that the data are not processed in such a way that substantial damage or substantial distress is, or is likely to be, caused to any data subject.

> **S.33(1)(b)** - *Even if the processing is carried out for research purposes, the exemption will not apply if substantial damage or distress is, or is likely to be, caused to the data subject.*

(2) For the purposes of the second data protection principle, the further processing of personal data only for research purposes in compliance with the relevant conditions is not to be regarded as incompatible with the purposes for which they were obtained.

> **S.33(2)** - *So long as the data were originally obtained for one or more specified and lawful purposes, any further processing for research purposes only and in compliance with the relevant conditions set out in s.33(1) will not be regarded as incompatible with the original purpose or purposes for which the data were obtained.*

(3) Personal data which are processed only for research purposes in compliance with the relevant conditions may, notwithstanding the fifth data protection principle, be kept indefinitely.

> **S.33(3)** - *The fifth data protection principle will not apply in relation to personal data processed for research purposes, so data can be held indefinitely.*

(4) Personal data which are processed only for research purposes are exempt from section 7 if-

(a) they are processed in compliance with the relevant conditions, and
(b) the results of the research or any resulting statistics are not made available in a form which identifies data subjects or any of them.

> **S.33(4)** - *S.7 (right of subject access) will not apply, so long as data subjects cannot be identified from the results of research or statistics.*

(5) For the purposes of subsections (2) to (4) personal data are not to be treated as processed otherwise than for research purposes merely because the data are disclosed-

(a) to any person, for research purposes only,
(b) to the data subject or a person acting on his behalf,
(c) at the request, or with the consent, of the data subject or a person acting on his behalf, or
(d) in circumstances in which the person making the disclosure has reasonable grounds for believing that the disclosure falls within paragraph (a), (b) or (c).

S.33(5) - *The exemption will still be available even if certain specified and wide-ranging disclosures are made. This ties in with Sch 8, para 18.*

34. Personal data are exempt from-

(a) the subject information provisions,

(b) the fourth data protection principle and section 14(1) to (3), and

(c) the non-disclosure provisions,

if the data consist of information which the data controller is obliged by or under any enactment to make available to the public, whether by publishing it, by making it available for inspection, or otherwise and whether gratuitously or on payment of a fee.

S.34 - *In relation to information which the data controller is obliged to make available to the public, this exemption applies to:*

- *the subject information provisions (see s.27(2));*

- *the requirement for data to be kept accurate and up to date, and the right to rectify, block, erase and destroy inaccurate personal data; and*

- *the non-disclosure provisions (see s.27(3)).*

Also note that the provisions of s.17(1) excuse those maintaining a public register from having to notify under the Act.

This section provides an exemption which, if fully exploited, could drive a coach and horses through the good intentions of the Act. The Commissioner has made her concerns known in a submission to the Home Office Working Party on Electoral Procedures, entitled "The Sale of the Register of Electors" (published in August 1998). Under s.34, information which is passed on to electoral registration officers (EROs) for electoral purposes may be sold on to a third party without the data subject's knowledge or consent (provided a condition from Schedule 2 (and, in the case of sensitive personal data, Schedule 3) is satisfied). For those individuals who have taken great care to tick opt-out boxes or to register with the Mailing Preference Service, it can be particularly galling if their information is made available in this way.

In the submission referred to above, the Commissioner has said that "it is difficult to see a clear justification" for this exemption so far as it relates to the electoral roll. She points out that there is "no obvious basis in the Directive for exempting the Register from the provisions of Article 10 which deal with the fair obtaining of data from the data subject....Thus it is arguable that compliance with the EU Data Protection Directive requires a change in the law relating to the Register to ensure that personal information is obtained by EROs in accordance with the provisions of Article 10."

In answer to this, the Representation of the People Act 2000, which is now in force, provides for the electoral roll to be split into two registers; the first will be an edited version which will be made available to the public (and will exclude personal data of those who do not wish their details to be made available in this way), while the second, full version, will be used for crime prevention, credit checks and voting purposes. Regulations will in due course deal with this and should go some way to allaying the concerns of those who disliked the way in which the electoral roll was made so readily available. However, some commentators have expressed their concern about the sale of any electoral role information. Swansea Liberal Democrat Councillor Mike Day has said: "If credit reference agencies have access to this sort of information, it could drive people away from registering to vote, further eroding democratic rights."[60]

See also commentary at Sch 1 Part II paragraph 3.

---

60   *Mike Day, quoted in "Privacy & Data Protection", Volume 1, Issue 5 (April/May 2001)*

35.– (1) Personal data are exempt from the non-disclosure provisions where the disclosure is required by or under any enactment, by any rule of law or by the order of a court.

S.35(1) - *See s.27(3) for an explanation of the non-disclosure provisions.*

(2) Personal data are exempt from the non-disclosure provisions where the disclosure is necessary-

(a) for the purpose of, or in connection with, any legal proceedings (including prospective legal proceedings), or

(b) for the purpose of obtaining legal advice,

or is otherwise necessary for the purposes of establishing, exercising or defending legal rights.

36. Personal data processed by an individual only for the purposes of that individual's personal, family or household affairs (including recreational purposes) are exempt from the data protection principles and the provisions of Parts II and III.

37. Schedule 7 (which confers further miscellaneous exemptions) has effect.

38.– (1) The Secretary of State may by order exempt from the subject information provisions personal data consisting of information the disclosure of which is prohibited or restricted by or under any enactment if and to the extent that he considers it necessary for the safeguarding of the interests of the data subject or the rights and freedoms of any other individual that the prohibition or restriction ought to prevail over those provisions.

> **s.38** - *The Data Protection (Miscellaneous Subject Access Exemptions) Order 2000 (SI 2000/419) provides certain exemptions from s.7. See commentary at s.7 for further details.*

(2) The Secretary of State may by order exempt from the non-disclosure provisions any disclosures of personal data made in circumstances specified in the order, if he considers the exemption is necessary for the safeguarding of the interests of the data subject or the rights and freedoms of any other individual.

39. Schedule 8 (which confers transitional exemptions) has effect.

PART V

ENFORCEMENT

40.– (1) If the Commissioner is satisfied that a data controller has contravened or is contravening any of the data protection principles, the Commissioner may serve him with a notice (in this Act referred to as "an enforcement notice") requiring him, for complying with the principle or principles in question, to do either or both of the following-

(a) to take within such time as may be specified in the notice, or to refrain from taking after such time as may be so specified, such steps as are so specified, or

(b) to refrain from processing any personal data, or any personal data of a description specified in the notice, or to refrain from processing them for a purpose so specified or in a manner so specified, after such time as may be so specified.

S.40 - *The Commissioner can take steps to enforce the Act either on her own account or as a result of a complaint by a data subject or by any other person who is directly affected by the processing carried out by a data controller.*

S.40(1) - *Enforcement notices: if the Commissioner believes that any of the data protection principles has been infringed, she can serve the data controller with an enforcement notice. This sets out within a certain time period the steps which the data controller is required to take.*

(2) In deciding whether to serve an enforcement notice, the Commissioner shall consider whether the contravention has caused or is likely to cause any person damage or distress.

S.40(2) - *One of the considerations for the Commissioner in deciding whether to serve such a notice is whether the contravention "has caused or is likely to cause any person damage or distress". Even if the Commissioner decides that there was no damage or distress caused or likely to be caused, it may still be appropriate to serve an enforcement notice[61].*

---

61   For example, see British Gas Trading Limited v Data Protection Registrar 1998

(3) An enforcement notice in respect of a contravention of the fourth data protection principle which requires the data controller to rectify, block, erase or destroy any inaccurate data may also require the data controller to rectify, block, erase or destroy any other data held by him and containing an expression of opinion which appears to the Commissioner to be based on the inaccurate data.

S.40(3) - *Breach of the fourth data protection principle: the enforcement notice can require a data controller to rectify, block, erase or destroy both inaccurate data and any other information containing an expression of opinion based on the inaccurate data.*

(4) An enforcement notice in respect of a contravention of the fourth data protection principle, in the case of data which accurately record information received or obtained by the data controller from the data subject or a third party, may require the data controller either-

(a) to rectify, block, erase or destroy any inaccurate data and any other data held by him and containing an expression of opinion as mentioned in subsection (3), or

(b) to take such steps as are specified in the notice for securing compliance with the requirements specified in paragraph 7 of Part II of Schedule 1 and, if the Commissioner thinks fit, for supplementing the data with such statement of the true facts relating to the matters dealt with by the data as the Commissioner may approve.

> **S.40(4)** - *Data which are inaccurate (or out of date) as a result of wrong information provided by the data subject or a third party: the enforcement notice can require the data controller to:*
>
> * *rectify, block, erase or destroy the inaccurate data and any other information containing an expression of opinion based on the inaccurate data;*
>
> * *take steps to ensure compliance with para 7 of Part II of Sch 1 (this provides that no infringement of the fourth data protection principle will be deemed to have occurred if the data controller has accurately recorded the wrong information provided by the data subject or a third party and (a) the data controller has taken reasonable steps to ensure the accuracy of data; and (b) if the data subject has complained about the inaccuracy of the data, the data indicate that fact);*
>
> * *provide a statement of the true facts relating to the matters dealt with by the data.*

(5) Where-

(a) an enforcement notice requires the data controller to rectify, block, erase or destroy any personal data, or

(b) the Commissioner is satisfied that personal data which have been rectified, blocked, erased or destroyed had been processed in contravention of any of the data protection principles,

an enforcement notice may, if reasonably practicable, require the data controller to notify third parties to whom the data have been disclosed of the rectification, blocking, erasure or destruction; and in determining whether it is reasonably practicable to require such notification regard shall be had, in particular, to the number of persons who would have to be notified.

> **S.40(5)** - *Notification of third parties: the enforcement notice could require the data controller to notify third parties to whom the data have been disclosed of the effects of the notice. This may depend on the number of third parties who would have to be notified.*

(6) An enforcement notice must contain-

   (a) a statement of the data protection principle or principles which the Commissioner is satisfied have been or are being contravened and his reasons for reaching that conclusion, and

   (b) particulars of the rights of appeal conferred by section 48.

> **S.40(6)** - *Contents of notice: it must contain a statement of principle(s) contravened and rights of appeal under section 48.*

(7) Subject to subsection (8), an enforcement notice must not require any of the provisions of the notice to be complied with before the end of the period within which an appeal can be brought against the notice and, if such an appeal is brought, the notice need not be complied with pending the determination or withdrawal of the appeal.

> **S.40(7)** - *Compliance with the notice cannot be required during the period in which an appeal can be brought (unless s.40(8) applies).*

(8) If by reason of special circumstances the Commissioner considers that an enforcement notice should be complied with as a matter of urgency he may include in the notice a statement to that effect and a statement of his reasons for reaching that conclusion; and in that event subsection (7) shall not apply but the notice must not require the provisions of the notice to be complied with before the end of the period of seven days beginning with the day on which the notice is served.

> **S.40(8)** - *If compliance is a matter of urgency, the notice will contain a statement requiring compliance no earlier than 7 days after the notice has been served.*

(9) Notification regulations (as defined by section 16(2)) may make provision as to the effect of the service of an enforcement notice on any entry in the register maintained under section 19 which relates to the person on whom the notice is served.

> **S.40(9)** - *The Data Protection (Notification and Notification fees) Regulations 2000 (SI 2000/188) make no such provision.*

(10) This section has effect subject to section 46(1).

> **S.40(10)** - *Enforcement notices under s.46(1) in respect of processing carried out for the special purposes are treated in a different way (see s.46(1)).*

41.– (1) If the Commissioner considers that all or any of the provisions of an enforcement notice need not be complied with in order to ensure compliance with the data protection principle or principles to which it relates, he may cancel or vary the notice by written notice to the person on whom it was served.

> **S.41(1)** - *Either the Commissioner may consider that part or all of the enforcement notice need not be complied with (s.41(1)) or the data controller may apply for a variation or cancellation of the notice if it can show that circumstances have changed so as to render part or all of the notice unnecessary (s.41(2)). This gives greater flexibility than under the 1984 Act, which allowed only for cancellation, rather than variation, of the notice.*

(2) A person on whom an enforcement notice has been served may, at any time after the expiry of the period during which an appeal can be brought against that notice, apply in writing to the Commissioner for the cancellation or variation of that notice on the ground that, by reason of a change of circumstances, all or any of the provisions of that notice need not be complied with in order to ensure compliance with the data protection principle or principles to which that notice relates.

S.41(2) - *If the Commissioner does not agree that the notice should be cancelled or varied, the data controller can appeal to the Data Protection Tribunal against the notice under s.48(2). This is a significant new right for data controllers, but an appeal will only be successful if a genuine change of circumstances renders compliance with the notice unnecessary.*

42.– (1) A request may be made to the Commissioner by or on behalf of any person who is, or believes himself to be, directly affected by any processing of personal data for an assessment as to whether it is likely or unlikely that the processing has been or is being carried out in compliance with the provisions of this Act.

S.42(1) - *This is a new provision. A data subject (or any other person who believes himself to be directly affected by the processing of personal data) may request an assessment as to whether the data controller has complied with the Act. It may appear alarming to a data controller that someone who may not actually be directly affected by the processing can apply to the Commissioner for an assessment, so long as he believes himself to be so affected.*

(2) On receiving a request under this section, the Commissioner shall make an assessment in such manner as appears to him to be appropriate, unless he has not been supplied with such information as he may reasonably require in order to-

(a) satisfy himself as to the identity of the person making the request, and
(b) enable him to identify the processing in question.

S.42(2) - *The Commissioner will have to satisfy herself as to the identity of the person making the request and ensure that that person can identify the processing which is the cause of complaint.*

(3) The matters to which the Commissioner may have regard in determining in what manner it is appropriate to make an assessment include-

(a) the extent to which the request appears to him to raise a matter of substance,
(b) any undue delay in making the request, and
(c) whether or not the person making the request is entitled to make an application under section 7 in respect of the personal data in question.

S.42(3) - *The Commissioner is obliged to carry out an assessment so long as the information in s.44(2) has been provided, although the manner of the assessment may depend on other factors, such as whether or not the person would be entitled to have access to the data under s.7. If a complaint does not sufficiently concern the Commissioner, she may decide to issue a letter to the complainant saying as much, setting out the reasons for reaching that conclusion. That letter may constitute an "assessment" under this section.*

(4) Where the Commissioner has received a request under this section he shall notify the person who made the request-

    (a) whether he has made an assessment as a result of the request, and

    (b) to the extent that he considers appropriate, having regard in particular to any exemption from section 7 applying in relation to the personal data concerned, of any view formed or action taken as a result of the request.

S.42(4) - *Anybody who makes a request for an assessment is entitled to receive notification from the Commissioner, regardless of whether an assessment is actually made.*

43.– (1) If the Commissioner-

    (a) has received a request under section 42 in respect of any processing of personal data, or

    (b) reasonably requires any information for the purpose of determining whether the data controller has complied or is complying with the data protection principles,

he may serve the data controller with a notice (in this Act referred to as "an information notice") requiring the data controller, within such time as is specified in the notice, to furnish the Commissioner, in such form as may be so specified, with such information relating to the request or to compliance with the principles as is so specified.

S.43(1) - *It may not be possible for the Commissioner to respond to a request for an assessment without further information. This section enables her to gather the required information by issuing a formal notice. Alternatively, quite separate from a s.42 request, the Commissioner may issue an information notice of her own volition in order to see whether the data controller has complied with the Act.*

(2) An information notice must contain-

    (a) in a case falling within subsection (1)(a), a statement that the Commissioner has received a request under section 42 in relation to the specified processing, or

    (b) in a case falling within subsection (1)(b), a statement that the Commissioner regards the specified information as relevant for the purpose of determining whether the data controller has complied, or is complying, with the data protection principles and his reasons for regarding it as relevant for that purpose.

(3) An information notice must also contain particulars of the rights of appeal conferred by section 48.

(4) Subject to subsection (5), the time specified in an information notice shall not expire before the end of the period within which an appeal can be brought against the notice and, if such an appeal is brought, the information need not be furnished pending the determination or withdrawal of the appeal.

> **S.43(4)** - *As with the enforcement notice, compliance with the information notice is not required until the period for bringing an appeal has expired and compliance may be delayed until either the appeal is determined or withdrawn. This is subject to special circumstances set out in s.43(5), when compliance can be required no earlier than 7 days after the date on which notice is served.*

(5) If by reason of special circumstances the Commissioner considers that the information is required as a matter of urgency, he may include in the notice a statement to that effect and a statement of his reasons for reaching that conclusion; and in that event subsection (4) shall not apply, but the notice shall not require the information to be furnished before the end of the period of seven days beginning with the day on which the notice is served.

(6) A person shall not be required by virtue of this section to furnish the Commissioner with any information in respect of-

    (a) any communication between a professional legal adviser and his client in connection with the giving of legal advice to the client with respect to his obligations, liabilities or rights under this Act, or

    (b) any communication between a professional legal adviser and his client, or between such an adviser or his client and any other person, made in connection with or in contemplation of proceedings under or arising out of this Act (including proceedings before the Tribunal) and for the purposes of such proceedings.

(7) In subsection (6) references to the client of a professional legal adviser include references to any person representing such a client.

(8) A person shall not be required by virtue of this section to furnish the Commissioner with any information if the furnishing of that information would, by revealing evidence of the commission of any offence other than an offence under this Act, expose him to proceedings for that offence.

(9) The Commissioner may cancel an information notice by written notice to the person on whom it was served.

> **S.43(9)** - *No variation is permitted; unlike the enforcement notice, the information notice can only be cancelled.*

(10) This section has effect subject to section 46(3).

44.– (1) If the Commissioner-

  (a) has received a request under section 42 in respect of any processing of personal data, or
  (b) has reasonable grounds for suspecting that, in a case in which proceedings have been stayed under section 32, the personal data to which the proceedings relate-
    (i) are not being processed only for the special purposes, or
    (ii) are not being processed with a view to the publication by any person of any journalistic, literary or artistic material which has not previously been published by the data controller,

he may serve the data controller with a notice (in this Act referred to as a "special information notice") requiring the data controller, within such time as is specified in the notice, to furnish the Commissioner, in such form as may be so specified, with such information as is so specified for the purpose specified in subsection (2).

> **S.44(1)** - *In certain circumstances, the Commissioner can serve the data controller with a special information notice. The purpose of such a notice is to see whether the special purposes exemption applies. The Commissioner is not permitted to serve a special information notice of her own volition - either a s.42 request must have been received or there must have been a stay of proceedings under s.32.*
>
> *The special information notice must contain specified information as set out in s.44(3) and (4).*

(2) That purpose is the purpose of ascertaining-

  (a) whether the personal data are being processed only for the special purposes, or

  (b) whether they are being processed with a view to the publication by any person of any journalistic, literary or artistic material which has not previously been published by the data controller.

(3) A special information notice must contain-

  (a) in a case falling within paragraph (a) of subsection (1), a statement that the Commissioner has received a request under section 42 in relation to the specified processing, or

  (b) in a case falling within paragraph (b) of that subsection, a statement of the Commissioner's grounds for suspecting that the personal data are not being processed as mentioned in that paragraph.

(4) A special information notice must also contain particulars of the rights of appeal conferred by section 48.

(5) Subject to subsection (6), the time specified in a special information notice shall not expire before the end of the period within which an appeal can be brought against the notice and, if such an appeal is brought, the information need not be furnished pending the determination or withdrawal of the appeal.

> **S.44(5)** - *Timing: this mirrors the corresponding provisions in respect of enforcement notices and information notices (ss. 40 and 43).*

(6) If by reason of special circumstances the Commissioner considers that the information is required as a matter of urgency, he may include in the notice a statement to that effect and a statement of his reasons for reaching that conclusion; and in that event subsection (5) shall not apply, but the notice shall not require the information to be furnished before the end of the period of seven days beginning with the day on which the notice is served.

(7) A person shall not be required by virtue of this section to furnish the Commissioner with any information in respect of-

  (a) any communication between a professional legal adviser and his client in connection with the giving of legal advice to the client with respect to his obligations, liabilities or rights under this Act, or

  (b) any communication between a professional legal adviser and his client, or between such an adviser or his client and any other person, made in connection with or in contemplation of proceedings under or arising out of this Act (including proceedings before the Tribunal) and for the purposes of such proceedings.

(8) In subsection (7) references to the client of a professional legal adviser include references to any person representing such a client.

(9) A person shall not be required by virtue of this section to furnish the Commissioner with any information if the furnishing of that information would, by revealing evidence of the commission of any offence other than an offence under this Act, expose him to proceedings for that offence.

(10) The Commissioner may cancel a special information notice by written notice to the person on whom it was served.

45.– (1) Where at any time it appears to the Commissioner (whether as a result of the service of a special information notice or otherwise) that any personal data-

(a) are not being processed only for the special purposes, or

(b) are not being processed with a view to the publication by any person of any journalistic, literary or artistic material which has not previously been published by the data controller,

he may make a determination in writing to that effect.

> **S.45(1)** - *See s.32(5). The Commissioner may determine that personal data are not being processed for special purposes or with a view to new publication of journalistic, literary or artistic material. If so, the court proceedings previously stayed pending this decision under s.32 will resume.*

(2) Notice of the determination shall be given to the data controller; and the notice must contain particulars of the right of appeal conferred by section 48.

(3) A determination under subsection (1) shall not take effect until the end of the period within which an appeal can be brought and, where an appeal is brought, shall not take effect pending the determination or withdrawal of the appeal.

46.– (1) The Commissioner may not at any time serve an enforcement notice on a data controller with respect to the processing of personal data for the special purposes unless-

(a) a determination under section 45(1) with respect to those data has taken effect, and

(b) the court has granted leave for the notice to be served.

> **S.46** - *The purpose of this section is to ensure that freedom of expression is not impeded lightly. Stringent rules must be followed.*

S.46(1) - *No enforcement notice can be served on a data controller unless a determination has taken effect under s.45(1) that the personal data are not being processed for the special purposes. The court must also grant leave for the notice to be served, which will only be granted in circumstances where suspected contravention of data protection principles is a matter of substantial public importance.*

(2) The court shall not grant leave for the purposes of subsection (1)(b) unless it is satisfied-

    (a) that the Commissioner has reason to suspect a contravention of the data protection principles which is of substantial public importance, and

    (b) except where the case is one of urgency, that the data controller has been given notice, in accordance with rules of court, of the application for leave.

(3) The Commissioner may not serve an information notice on a data controller with respect to the processing of personal data for the special purposes unless a determination under section 45(1) with respect to those data has taken effect.

S.46(3) - *Special information notices cannot be served unless a determination under s.45(1) has taken effect, but there is no requirement in this case to obtain leave from the court.*

47.– (1) A person who fails to comply with an enforcement notice, an information notice or a special information notice is guilty of an offence.

S.47(1) - *The offence could result in a maximum fine of £5,000 in the Magistrates' Court or an unlimited fine in the Crown Court.*

(2) A person who, in purported compliance with an information notice or a special information notice-

    (a) makes a statement which he knows to be false in a material respect, or

    (b) recklessly makes a statement which is false in a material respect,

is guilty of an offence.

(3) It is a defence for a person charged with an offence under subsection (1) to prove that he exercised all due diligence to comply with the notice in question.

48.– (1) A person on whom an enforcement notice, an information notice or a special information notice has been served may appeal to the Tribunal against the notice.

> **S.48(1)** - *There are numerous rights of appeal[62], not simply against the notices themselves, but against a refusal to vary or cancel a notice, the inclusion of a statement in the notices requiring urgent compliance, and a determination made under s.45.*
>
> ---
>
> 62   *See Sch 6 for more details.*

(2) A person on whom an enforcement notice has been served may appeal to the Tribunal against the refusal of an application under section 41(2) for cancellation or variation of the notice.

(3) Where an enforcement notice, an information notice or a special information notice contains a statement by the Commissioner in accordance with section 40(8), 43(5) or 44(6) then, whether or not the person appeals against the notice, he may appeal against-

(a) the Commissioner's decision to include the statement in the notice, or
(b) the effect of the inclusion of the statement as respects any part of the notice.

(4) A data controller in respect of whom a determination has been made under section 45 may appeal to the Tribunal against the determination.

(5) Schedule 6 has effect in relation to appeals under this section and the proceedings of the Tribunal in respect of any such appeal.

> **S.48** - *See commentary at Sch 6 relating to the appeals rules contained within The Data Protection Tribunal (Enforcement Appeals) Rules 2000 (SI 2000/189). They regulate the exercise of rights of appeal against decisions of the Commissioner and the practice and procedure of the Commissioner in such cases.*

49.– (1) If on an appeal under section 48(1) the Tribunal considers-

(a) that the notice against which the appeal is brought is not in accordance with the law, or
(b) to the extent that the notice involved an exercise of discretion by the Commissioner, that he ought to have exercised his discretion differently,

the Tribunal shall allow the appeal or substitute such other notice or decision as could have been served or made by the Commissioner; and in any other case the Tribunal shall dismiss the appeal.

(2) On such an appeal, the Tribunal may review any determination of fact on which the notice in question was based.

(3) If on an appeal under section 48(2) the Tribunal considers that the enforcement notice ought to be cancelled or varied by reason of a change in circumstances, the Tribunal shall cancel or vary the notice.

S.49(3) - *It is open to the Tribunal not simply to uphold or dismiss appeals, but also to substitute its own notice or decision in place of the Commissioner's. It can cancel or vary an enforcement notice and cancel a determination under s.45.*

(4) On an appeal under subsection (3) of section 48 the Tribunal may direct-

(a) that the notice in question shall have effect as if it did not contain any such statement as is mentioned in that subsection, or

(b) that the inclusion of the statement shall not have effect in relation to any part of the notice,

and may make such modifications in the notice as may be required for giving effect to the direction.

(5) On an appeal under section 48(4), the Tribunal may cancel the determination of the Commissioner.

(6) Any party to an appeal to the Tribunal under section 48 may appeal from the decision of the Tribunal on a point of law to the appropriate court; and that court shall be-

(a) the High Court of Justice in England if the address of the person who was the appellant before the Tribunal is in England or Wales,

(b) the Court of Session if that address is in Scotland, and

(c) the High Court of Justice in Northern Ireland if that address is in Northern Ireland.

S.49(6) - *Further appeals on points of law are available from a Tribunal decision to higher courts.*

(7) For the purposes of subsection (6)-

(a) the address of a registered company is that of its registered office, and

(b) the address of a person (other than a registered company) carrying on a business is that of his principal place of business in the United Kingdom.

50. Schedule 9 (powers of entry and inspection) has effect.

Part VI

Miscellaneous and General

Functions of Commissioner

51.– (1) It shall be the duty of the Commissioner to promote the following of good practice by data controllers and, in particular, so to perform his functions under this Act as to promote the observance of the requirements of this Act by data controllers.

> **S.51** - *The Commissioner has a number of new duties which reflect the increasing influence of European bodies and an emphasis on promoting best practice. This section provides examples of how she may achieve this, such as preparing codes of practice and guidance, encouraging trade associations to prepare their own codes, and disseminating EU decisions.*

(2) The Commissioner shall arrange for the dissemination in such form and manner as he considers appropriate of such information as it may appear to him expedient to give to the public about the operation of this Act, about good practice, and about other matters within the scope of his functions under this Act, and may give advice to any person as to any of those matters.

(3) Where-

    (a) the Secretary of State so directs by order, or
    (b) the Commissioner considers it appropriate to do so,

the Commissioner shall, after such consultation with trade associations, data subjects or persons representing data subjects as appears to him to be appropriate, prepare and disseminate to such persons as he considers appropriate codes of practice for guidance as to good practice.

> **S.51(3)** *An example of such a Code is the CCTV Draft Code of Practice which is available from the OIC. Compliance with this and other Codes is not a statutory requirement, although if CCTV users do comply with this Code it will ensure that they meet their legal obligations.*
>
> *The CCTV Draft Code of Practice covers such issues as:*
>
> •   *the siting of cameras (so that they monitor only those spaces to which the public have access);*

- *signs alerting the public to the fact that they are entering an area covered by surveillance equipment. It also stipulates the preferred wording on the signs and the size of the signs (at least A3 size) so as to cover the fair processing code (see Sch.1, Part II, paras 2 to 4);*

- *when it would be appropriate to dispense with such signs (ie for the prevention and detection of a specific criminal activity);*

- *quality of the images;*

- *retention of the images;*

- *access to and disclosure of images to third parties (usually restricted to law enforcement agencies, prosecution agencies and legal representatives);*

- *access by data subjects (and exemptions to the right of access - eg under s. 29);*

- *compliance with all the data protection principles.*

See also commentary in the Introduction on CCTV use.

At the time of writing, the Commissioner is in the process of finalising a Human Resources Code of Practice which will provide authoritative guidance to those responsible for human resources issues.[63] See the Introduction for further details and commentary.

---

63   *"The use of personal data in employer/employee relationships"*

---

(4) The Commissioner shall also-

    (a) where he considers it appropriate to do so, encourage trade associations to prepare, and to disseminate to their members, such codes of practice, and

    (b) where any trade association submits a code of practice to him for his consideration, consider the code and, after such consultation with data subjects or persons representing data subjects as appears to him to be appropriate, notify the trade association whether in his opinion the code promotes the following of good practice.

S.51(4)(b) - *The IOC does not have sufficient resources to prepare industry-specific codes of practice itself. However, the Commissioner has an obligation to consider a code submitted to her by a trade association (loosely defined as a body representing data controllers - see s.51(9)). After appropriate consultation, she must notify the trade association as to the suitability of the code. So that the Commissioner is not inundated with such requests, she is entitled to levy a charge for this service, pursuant to s.51(8).*

(5) An order under subsection (3) shall describe the personal data or processing to which the code of practice is to relate, and may also describe the persons or classes of persons to whom it is to relate.

(6) The Commissioner shall arrange for the dissemination in such form and manner as he considers appropriate of-

(a) any Community finding as defined by paragraph 15(2) of Part II of Schedule 1,

(b) any decision of the European Commission, under the procedure provided for in Article 31(2) of the Data Protection Directive, which is made for the purposes of Article 26(3) or (4) of the Directive, and

(c) such other information as it may appear to him to be expedient to give to data controllers in relation to any personal data about the protection of the rights and freedoms of data subjects in relation to the processing of personal data in countries and territories outside the European Economic Area.

S.51(6) -

(a) The Commissioner will disseminate Community findings regarding the adequacy of data protection in non-EEA countries.

(b) The Commissioner will also disseminate decisions made under the following procedures:

- *Article 31(2) procedure: The Commissioner and her counterparts in other EEA countries form a committee which is chaired by a representative of the European Commission. The chairman submits a draft of measures proposed by the Commission and the committee delivers its opinion about those measures. If the committee does not agree with the proposals of the Commission, the Commission will defer application of the measures for a period of three months and the European Council will be informed and may take a different decision within that three month time limit.*

- *Article 26(3) procedure: Member States may authorise transfers of data to a non-EEA country which does not ensure adequate level of data protection, so long as there are adequate safeguards with respect to the protection of the privacy and fundamental rights and freedoms of individuals. Member States must inform the Commission and other Member States of any such authorisations which are granted. If a Member State objects on justified grounds, the Commission shall take appropriate measures under the Article 31(2) procedure. The Member State would then have to take necessary measures to comply with the Commission's decision.*

- *Article 26(4): If, having followed the Article 31(2) procedure, the Commission decides that certain contractual clauses offer sufficient safeguards, Member States must take sufficient measures to comply with the Commission's decision.*

(c)   *The Commissioner will disseminate other information to protect rights and freedoms of data subjects in non-EEA countries.*

(7) The Commissioner may, with the consent of the data controller, assess any processing of personal data for the following of good practice and shall inform the data controller of the results of the assessment.

(8) The Commissioner may charge such sums as he may with the consent of the Secretary of State determine for any services provided by the Commissioner by virtue of this Part.

S.51(8) - *Where the Commissioner provides services (such as reviewing codes of practice for trade associations or assessing processing for the following of good practice under s.51(7)) she may make a charge for those services. The charge will be determined with the agreement of the Secretary of State. Under the 1984 Act, the costs of such services could not be recouped.*

(9) In this section-

"good practice" means such practice in the processing of personal data as appears to the Commissioner to be desirable having regard to the interests of data subjects and others, and includes (but is not limited to) compliance with the requirements of this Act;

"trade association" includes any body representing data controllers.

52.– (1) The Commissioner shall lay annually before each House of Parliament a general report on the exercise of his functions under this Act.

S.52(1) - *The annual report is a familiar feature of the 1984 Act and is published on the Commissioner's website.*

(2) The Commissioner may from time to time lay before each House of Parliament such other reports with respect to those functions as he thinks fit.

(3) The Commissioner shall lay before each House of Parliament any code of practice prepared under section 51(3) for complying with a direction of the Secretary of State, unless the code is included in any report laid under subsection (1) or (2).

53.– (1) An individual who is an actual or prospective party to any proceedings under section 7(9), 10(4), 12(8) or 14 or by virtue of section 13 which relate to personal data processed for the special purposes may apply to the Commissioner for assistance in relation to those proceedings.

S.53(1) - *Only in proceedings involving processing for the special purposes where there is "a matter of substantial public importance" can the Commissioner offer assistance to an individual. The intention is that important cases do not founder for lack of resources of the claimant. See s.32 for details.*

In proceedings involving special purposes processing and relating to:

- *subject access rights (s.7(9));*
- *the right to prevent processing (s.10(4));*
- *rights in relation to automated decision-taking (s.12(8));*
- *rights in relation to exempt manual data - see Sch 13 para 4 (until 24 October 2007 only);*
- *rights to rectification etc (s.14); and*
- *the right to compensation (s.13)*

an individual may apply for assistance from the Commissioner.

(2) The Commissioner shall, as soon as reasonably practicable after receiving an application under subsection (1), consider it and decide whether and to what extent to grant it, but he shall not grant the application unless, in his opinion, the case involves a matter of substantial public importance.

S.53(2) - *"substantial public importance": this term is not defined in the Act. The Commissioner will decide on the facts of each case. The Commissioner has discretion over whether to grant such assistance and there is no right of appeal against the Commissioner's decision.*

(3) If the Commissioner decides to provide assistance, he shall, as soon as reasonably practicable after making the decision, notify the applicant, stating the extent of the assistance to be provided.

> **S.53(3)** - *"the extent of the assistance": see Sch 10 for details. The assistance may include the cost of legal advice and/or representation in relation to the proceedings.*

(4) If the Commissioner decides not to provide assistance, he shall, as soon as reasonably practicable after making the decision, notify the applicant of his decision and, if he thinks fit, the reasons for it.

> **S.53(4)** - *There is no obligation on the part of the Commissioner to provide reasons for refusing to provide assistance.*

(5) In this section-

    (a) references to "proceedings" include references to prospective proceedings, and

    (b) "applicant", in relation to assistance under this section, means an individual who applies for assistance.

(6) Schedule 10 has effect for supplementing this section.

54.– (1) The Commissioner-

    (a) shall continue to be the designated authority in the United Kingdom for the purposes of Article 13 of the Convention, and

    (b) shall be the supervisory authority in the United Kingdom for the purposes of the Data Protection Directive.

> **S.54(1)** - *This section sets out a framework for new international arrangements.*
>
> *(1) "Convention": see definition in s.54(8).*

(2) The Secretary of State may by order make provision as to the functions to be discharged by the Commissioner as the designated authority in the United Kingdom for the purposes of Article 13 of the Convention.

> **S.54(2)** - *The Data Protection (Functions of Designated Authority) Order 2000 (SI 2000/186) specifies the functions to be discharged by the Commissioner in her capacity as the designated authority in the UK for the purposes of the Convention (defined at s.54(8)).*

> *The functions include:*
>
> - *furnishing particular information to (or a power to request information from) designated authorities in other Convention countries;*
>
> - *assisting persons resident outside the UK in exercising certain of their rights under Part II of the Act;*
>
> - *sending a request for assistance made by a UK resident, where the request relates to the exercise of rights of access to personal data in a Convention country, to the designated authority in that country.*

(3) The Secretary of State may by order make provision as to co-operation by the Commissioner with the European Commission and with supervisory authorities in other EEA States in connection with the performance of their respective duties and, in particular, as to-

    (a) the exchange of information with supervisory authorities in other EEA States or with the European Commission, and

    (b) the exercise within the United Kingdom at the request of a supervisory authority in another EEA State, in cases excluded by section 5 from the application of the other provisions of this Act, of functions of the Commissioner specified in the order.

> **S.54(3)** - *The Data Protection (International Co-operation) Order 2000 provides for co-operation between the Information Commissioner, the European Commission and other supervisory authorities in EEA States.*
>
> *Under this Order, the Commissioner has the following powers and obligations:*
>
> - *the Commissioner is obliged to inform the European Commission and supervisory authorities if she believes that a transfer or proposed transfer of personal data outside the EEA would involve a contravention of the eighth data protection principle (see Sch 1, para 8);*
>
> - *the Commissioner's enforcement powers are extended in relation to certain data controllers who are processing data in the UK but to whom the Act does not apply due to s.5 of the Act (relating to jurisdiction). However, such enforcement powers can only be exercised if the supervisory authority in the EEA state whose laws apply to the data controller makes a request to the Commissioner;*
>
> - *the Commissioner can supply other information to the European Commission or supervisory authorities to enable them to discharge their data protection functions.*

(4) The Commissioner shall also carry out any data protection functions which the Secretary of State may by order direct him to carry out for the purpose of enabling Her Majesty's Government in the United Kingdom to give effect to any international obligations of the United Kingdom.

(5) The Commissioner shall, if so directed by the Secretary of State, provide any authority exercising data protection functions under the law of a colony specified in the direction with such assistance in connection with the discharge of those functions as the Secretary of State may direct or approve, on such terms (including terms as to payment) as the Secretary of State may direct or approve.

(6) Where the European Commission makes a decision for the purposes of Article 26(3) or (4) of the Data Protection Directive under the procedure provided for in Article 31(2) of the Directive, the Commissioner shall comply with that decision in exercising his functions under paragraph 9 of Schedule 4 or, as the case may be, paragraph 8 of that Schedule.

S.54(6) - *Article 26(3) etc: see notes to s.51(6)(b) above.*

Schedule 4 - This schedule covers exemptions to the eighth data protection principle.

(7) The Commissioner shall inform the European Commission and the supervisory authorities in other EEA States-

(a) of any approvals granted for the purposes of paragraph 8 of Schedule 4, and
(b) of any authorisations granted for the purposes of paragraph 9 of that Schedule.

(8) In this section-

"the Convention" means the Convention for the Protection of Individuals with regard to Automatic Processing of Personal Data which was opened for signature on 28th January 1981;

"data protection functions" means functions relating to the protection of individuals with respect to the processing of personal information.

Unlawful obtaining etc. of personal data

55.- (1) A person must not knowingly or recklessly, without the consent of the data controller-

(a) obtain or disclose personal data or the information contained in personal data, or
(b) procure the disclosure to another person of the information contained in personal data.

> **S.55(1)** - *This section creates a criminal offence of unlawfully obtaining or disclosing personal data without the consent of the data controller. It has its origins in the Criminal Justice and Public Order Act 1994, which responded to concerns about the activities of private investigators who made a business out of obtaining personal data.*
>
> *This could be a useful tool for employers whose employees leave their service and take with them customer lists or other sensitive data. Even if they do not actually take such data with them, but disclose the information to another party, they will have fallen foul of s.55(1)(b) (subject to the provisions in s.55(2)). In such circumstances, the employer should inform the ex-employee that he or she has no right to obtain or disclose the data and that their actions constitute an offence under s.55(3).*

(2) Subsection (1) does not apply to a person who shows-

    (a) that the obtaining, disclosing or procuring-
        (i) was necessary for the purpose of preventing or detecting crime, or
        (ii) was required or authorised by or under any enactment, by any rule of law or by the order of a court,
    (b) that he acted in the reasonable belief that he had in law the right to obtain or disclose the data or information or, as the case may be, to procure the disclosure of the information to the other person,
    (c) that he acted in the reasonable belief that he would have had the consent of the data controller if the data controller had known of the obtaining, disclosing or procuring and the circumstances of it, or
    (d) that in the particular circumstances the obtaining, disclosing or procuring was justified as being in the public interest.

> **S.55(2)** - *The consent of the data subject is not specifically an excuse because the data controller may have a proprietary interest in the personal data of the data subject.*

(3) A person who contravenes subsection (1) is guilty of an offence.

(4) A person who sells personal data is guilty of an offence if he has obtained the data in contravention of subsection (1).

(5) A person who offers to sell personal data is guilty of an offence if-

    (a) he has obtained the data in contravention of subsection (1), or
    (b) he subsequently obtains the data in contravention of that subsection.

> **S.55(5)(b)** - *If a person offers to sell data before they have acquired it, they must ensure that the data controller is happy for the data to be obtained and disclosed by that person.*

(6) For the purposes of subsection (5), an advertisement indicating that personal data are or may be for sale is an offer to sell the data.

(7) Section 1(2) does not apply for the purposes of this section; and for the purposes of subsections (4) to (6), "personal data" includes information extracted from personal data.

> **S.55(7)** - *s.1(2) provides a definition of "obtaining", "recording", "using" and "disclosing".*

(8) References in this section to personal data do not include references to personal data which by virtue of section 28 are exempt from this section.

> **S.55(8)** - *s.28: exemptions relating to national security.*

Records obtained under data subject's right of access

56.– (1) A person must not, in connection with-

  (a) the recruitment of another person as an employee,
  (b) the continued employment of another person, or
  (c) any contract for the provision of services to him by another person,

require that other person or a third party to supply him with a relevant record or to produce a relevant record to him.

> **S.56(1)** - *Sections 112, 113 and 115 of the Police Act 1997 (now in force) deal with the three types of certificate which will become available from the new Criminal Records Bureau ("CRB"), which is due to be in operation in Autumn 2001:*

Police Act s.112 - criminal conviction certificate (referred to in the CRB's Code of Practice[64] as "Basic Disclosures")

This will record convictions held on central police records which are not "spent" under the Rehabilitation of Offenders Act 1974. Certificates will not be supplied directly to employers, but to applicants who may produce them to employers. Applications for Standard and Enhanced Disclosures (see s.115 below) must be countersigned by a person (including a company or other entity) registered with the CRB for this purpose.[65]

Such persons will undergo a check to assess their suitability to receive information for the CRB. If organisations (for reasons of practicality or cost) do not wish to register themselves, they may nevertheless be able to obtain Disclosure information via umbrella bodies which register on their behalf. Further details are available in the Code. It is expected that Basic Disclosures will be issued from 2002.

Police Act s.113 - criminal record certificate (referred to in the Code as "Standard Disclosures")

Standard Disclosures are available regarding portions within the terms of the Exceptions Order under the Rehabilitation of Offenders Act. This Disclosure will record both "spent" and "unspent" convictions and details of police cautions. Proposals for groups who can register include those involved in regular contact with vulnerable members of society such as children, the elderly and the sick; those checked in the interests of national security; professionals in the fields of health, pharmacy and the law; senior managers in banking and financial services. The Standard Disclosures will be available from Autumn 2001.

Police Act s.115 - enhanced criminal record certificate (referred to in the Code as "Enhanced Disclosures")

This will be available to prospective employees, trainees and volunteers with regular contact with children and youths under 18 or applicants for gaming, betting and lottery licences. The Disclosure will include all details on the Standard Disclosure together with information from a local police force record check and other "non-conviction information". The Enhanced Disclosures will be available from Autumn 2001.

---

64   *The Code of Practice for Registered Persons and other Recipients of Disclosure Information (available on the CRB's website, www.crb.gov.uk), ("the Code").*

65   *Police Act 1997 (Criminal Records) (Registration) (Amendment) Regulations 2001 (SI 2001/2498) in force August 2001, made under the Police Act s.120(3). These regulations require names and certain other details of individuals nominated by a registered body to act as countersignatories for applications for certificates to be entered into a register. The Secretary of State may refuse such nominations on specified grounds and may require a fee of £5 for each additional name to be entered in the register.*

Recent legislation relating to those who work with children or vulnerable people (such as the Criminal Justice and Courts Act 2000, the Care Standards Act 2000 and the Protection of Children Act 2000) requires employers to carry out checks on workers before they start work. The CRB will enable employers to make the appropriate checks.

Note that s.56 will not prevent an employer asking a prospective employee if they have a criminal record, but they cannot require the prospective employee or a third party to supply them with a copy of their criminal record or prison record. Nor can the employer require an employee to ask the Department of Social Security to provide a copy of the individual's contributions record. Some employers currently insist on receiving a copy of this record as a pre-requisite for recruitment in the belief that gaps indicate a period of time in custody.

It is suggested that an employer who does not wish to employ people with unspent convictions should make it clear that it is a condition of the employment contract that employees have no unspent convictions at the time of their appointment. The employer may ask employees if they would mind obtaining a copy of their criminal record (or appropriate level of certificate) but should make it clear that in doing so, the employer is not insisting upon the employee exercising his or her subject access rights under the Act.

The Code sets out proposals to closely regulate the handling of Disclosure information received from the CRB. Mishandling of the disclosure information could amount to a criminal offence. Any organisation wishing to register with the CRB to obtain access to criminal records for current or prospective employees will have to comply with the Code. Such organisations will have to follow a range of obligations, including:

- *implementing a written policy on the recruitment of ex-offenders, and giving a copy to applicants for positions where a Disclosure is requested;*

- *ensuring that application forms for positions where Disclosures are requested inform applicants of this fact;*

- *discussing any matters revealed in Disclosure information with the person seeking the position before withdrawing the offer of employment;*

- *putting in application forms a statement to the effect that a criminal record will not necessarily debar someone from a job simply because they have a conviction;*

- *not passing on Disclosure information to persons not authorised to receive it under section 124 of the Police Act 1997;*

- *securely storing Disclosures and the information they contain;*

- *implementing a written security policy covering the correct handling and safekeeping of Disclosure information;*

> • reporting to the CRB any suspected malpractice under the Code or offences in relation to the misuse of Disclosures.
>
> **S.56(1)** - *"relevant record"- see s.56(6) below.*

(2) A person concerned with the provision (for payment or not) of goods, facilities or services to the public or a section of the public must not, as a condition of providing or offering to provide any goods, facilities or services to another person, require that other person or a third party to supply him with a relevant record or to produce a relevant record to him.

> **S.56(2)** - *The prohibition extends beyond the employment context. So if an individual takes out an insurance policy, they cannot be required to provide the insurance company with a record of their criminal conviction.*

(3) Subsections (1) and (2) do not apply to a person who shows-

(a) that the imposition of the requirement was required or authorised by or under any enactment, by any rule of law or by the order of a court, or

(b) that in the particular circumstances the imposition of the requirement was justified as being in the public interest.

> **S.56(3)** - *Enforced subject access is lawful where it is allowed under this section.*

(4) Having regard to the provisions of Part V of the Police Act 1997 (certificates of criminal records etc.), the imposition of the requirement referred to in subsection (1) or (2) is not to be regarded as being justified as being in the public interest on the ground that it would assist in the prevention or detection of crime.

> **S.56(4)** - *see s.56(1) above.*

(5) A person who contravenes subsection (1) or (2) is guilty of an offence.

S.56(5) - *The mere imposition of a requirement to provide a "relevant record" will be an offence, so policies should be updated now in readiness for this section coming into force.*

(6) In this section "a relevant record" means any record which-

    (a) has been or is to be obtained by a data subject from any data controller specified in the first column of the Table below in the exercise of the right conferred by section 7, and

    (b) contains information relating to any matter specified in relation to that data controller in the second column,

and includes a copy of such a record or a part of such a record.

TABLE

Data controller	Subject-matter
1. Any of the following persons- (a) a chief officer of police of a police force in England and Wales. (b) a chief constable of a police force in Scotland. (c) the Chief Constable of the Royal Ulster Constabulary. (d) the Director General of the National Criminal Intelligence Service. (e) the Director General of the National Crime Squad.	(a) Convictions. (b) Cautions.
2. The Secretary of State.	(a) Convictions (b) Cautions (c) His functions under section 53 of the Children and Young Persons Act 1933, section 205(2) or 208 of the Criminal Procedure (Scotland) Act 1995 or section 73 of the Children and Young Persons Act (Northern Ireland) 1968 in relation to any person sentenced to detention. (d) His functions under the Prison Act 1952, the Prisons (Scotland) Act 1989 or the Prison Act (Northern Ireland) 1953 in relation to any person imprisoned or detained. (e) His functions under the Social Security Contributions and Benefits Act 1992, the Social Security Administration Act 1992 or the Jobseekers Act 1995. (f) His functions under Part V of the Police Act 1997.
3. The Department of Health and Social Services for Northern Ireland.	Its functions under the Social Security Contributions and Benefits (Northern Ireland) Act 1992, the Social Security Administration (Northern Ireland) Act 1992 or the Jobseekers (Northern Ireland) Order 1995.

> **S.56(6)** - *"Relevant record": the record has to be obtained via s.7 (i.e. the data subject has to be required to obtain access to the record him/herself). As to the sort of record which is covered, refer to the table, which can be amended by order. Essentially, this covers criminal records, prison records and Social Security contributions records.*

(7) In the Table in subsection (6)-

"caution" means a caution given to any person in England and Wales or Northern Ireland in respect of an offence which, at the time when the caution is given, is admitted;

"conviction" has the same meaning as in the Rehabilitation of Offenders Act 1974 or the Rehabilitation of Offenders (Northern Ireland) Order 1978.

(8) The Secretary of State may by order amend-

(a) the Table in subsection (6), and
(b) subsection (7).

> **S.56(8)** - *Concerns have been expressed in Parliamentary debates[66] that data controllers will find a new method of obtaining the information they require by abusing subject access rights in a different way, thus contravening the provisions of the Police Act 1997. If this occurs, the Secretary of State will be able to amend the table accordingly.*
>
> ---
> 66 *House of Commons, Standing Committee D, 2 June 1998*

(9) For the purposes of this section a record which states that a data controller is not processing any personal data relating to a particular matter shall be taken to be a record containing information relating to that matter.

(10) In this section "employee" means an individual who-

(a) works under a contract of employment, as defined by section 230(2) of the Employment Rights Act 1996, or
(b) holds any office,

whether or not he is entitled to remuneration; and "employment" shall be construed accordingly.

S.56(10) - *This stipulates a wider definition of "employee" than just those under a contract of employment, which may include contractors or consultants if they hold positions of trust or responsibility.*

57.– (1) Any term or condition of a contract is void in so far as it purports to require an individual-

(a) to supply any other person with a record to which this section applies, or with a copy of such a record or a part of such a record, or

(b) to produce to any other person such a record, copy or part.

S.57(1) - *Some contracts of employment have a standard term which requires employees, upon request in appropriate circumstances, to supply a copy of their medical record to the occupational health adviser in strictest confidence. Such a term will be void under this section. This will not prevent employers from requiring employees to undergo medicals so long as those medicals are carried out for employment or insurance purposes and not in connection with "the care of that individual" (see s.68(2)(b)). See also s.69 which sets out a long list of those who are considered to be "health professionals"; it includes doctors, dentists, opticians and nurses.*

Employers may be concerned about how to deal with a request to disclose medical records, for example, to enable the company to obtain key man insurance. Section 3 of the Access to Medical Reports Act 1988 still applies, so consent of the individual must be obtained (and requisite information about the right to withhold consent) before a medical report can be obtained. The Access to Medical Records Act 1990 governs the disclosure of medical notes. The idea behind s.57 is to avoid the reliance on "blanket consent" - fresh consent should be obtained each time medical records are sought.

Under Section 60 of the Health and Social Care Act 2001, the Secretary of State for Health is able to allow access to medical records to such "prescribed person" as he considers "necessary or expedient in the interest of improving patient care or in the public interest".[67] Such disclosures can be made without the consent of the patient and will be permitted as laid down by forthcoming regulations. This provision may benefit organisations such as the Institute of Cancer Research which relies on access to health data for research purposes. Professor Peto, head of epidemiology at the Institute of Cancer Research is reported to have claimed that "it's no understatement to say that the Data Protection Act is killing people".[68] He made this statement after a £600,000 investigation into the cancer dangers of asbestos had been delayed for 18 months by health authorities and companies concerned about breaching the Act. The Department of Health refused to release names of doctors with eligible patients because such records had not been gathered for that purpose. Obtaining consents will not necessarily resolve the issue either. Dr Peter Sasieni, head of mathematics and statistics at Imperial Cancer Research Fund has commented that "a reliable overview of the [cervical] screening programme must be representative of the whole population. By only looking at the experience of consenting women we are likely to get a biased and misleading picture".[69] It remains to be seen how the Health and Social Care Act and secondary legislation can ameliorate the problem.

67   *Section 60(1) Health and Social Care Act 2001*
68   *Quoted in The Times 15 May 2001*
69   *Quoted in The Times 15 May 2001*

(2) This section applies to any record which-

    (a) has been or is to be obtained by a data subject in the exercise of the right conferred by section 7, and

    (b) consists of the information contained in any health record as defined by section 68(2).

Information provided to Commissioner or Tribunal

58. No enactment or rule of law prohibiting or restricting the disclosure of information shall preclude a person from furnishing the Commissioner or the Tribunal with any information necessary for the discharge of their functions under this Act.

S.58 - *Organisations should ensure that all confidentiality agreements or clauses relating to information containing personal data will permit the disclosure of that information should the Act require such disclosure (e.g. to comply with a subject access request). Otherwise a position may arise where an organisation has to decide between breaching the requirements of the Act or breaching an obligation of confidentiality.*

59.– (1) No person who is or has been the Commissioner, a member of the Commissioner's staff or an agent of the Commissioner shall disclose any information which-

    (a) has been obtained by, or furnished to, the Commissioner under or for the purposes of this Act,

    (b) relates to an identified or identifiable individual or business, and

    (c) is not at the time of the disclosure, and has not previously been, available to the public from other sources,

unless the disclosure is made with lawful authority.

> **S.59(1)** - *This section imposes a restriction upon the Commissioner, her staff and agents regarding information identifying a person or organisation disclosed pursuant to the Act. It will be interesting to see whether this impacts upon the Commissioner's ability to name and shame organisations or report on her activities. The Commissioner may find herself having to justify the disclosure of an organisation's data protection practices on grounds of public interest (s.59(2)(e)) if such disclosure has not been consented to, or has not previously been made publicly available by another source (s.59(1)(c)).*

(2) For the purposes of subsection (1) a disclosure of information is made with lawful authority only if, and to the extent that-

    (a) the disclosure is made with the consent of the individual or of the person for the time being carrying on the business,

    (b) the information was provided for the purpose of its being made available to the public (in whatever manner) under any provision of this Act,

    (c) the disclosure is made for the purposes of, and is necessary for, the discharge of-

        (i) any functions under this Act, or

        (ii) any Community obligation,

    (d) the disclosure is made for the purposes of any proceedings, whether criminal or civil and whether arising under, or by virtue of, this Act or otherwise, or

    (e) having regard to the rights and freedoms or legitimate interests of any person, the disclosure is necessary in the public interest.

(3) Any person who knowingly or recklessly discloses information in contravention of subsection (1) is guilty of an offence.

General provisions relating to offences

60.– (1) No proceedings for an offence under this Act shall be instituted-

    (a) in England or Wales, except by the Commissioner or by or with the consent of the Director of Public Prosecutions;

    (b) in Northern Ireland, except by the Commissioner or by or with the consent of the Director of Public Prosecutions for Northern Ireland.

> **S.60(1)** - *In Scotland criminal proceedings will normally be bought by the Procurator Fiscal.*

(2) A person guilty of an offence under any provision of this Act other than paragraph 12 of Schedule 9 is liable-

(a) on summary conviction, to a fine not exceeding the statutory maximum, or

(b) on conviction on indictment, to a fine.

> **S.60(2)** - *The "offence...under Sch 9, para 12" is intentional obstruction of or failure to give reasonable assistance in the execution of a warrant authorising the Commissioner to enter and inspect a set of premises. This offence is only triable in a Magistrates Court and carries a maximum fine on conviction of £5,000 (see s.60(3)). All other offences are triable in either a Magistrates Court (which carries a maximum fine of £5,000) or a Crown Court, where an unlimited fine may be imposed.*
>
> *Company directors, managers, secretaries, or (in the case of a shareholder managed business) shareholders may be made personally liable for breaches by their companies of the Act if they are shown to have consented to the breach, or it is made with their connivance or negligence (see s.61(1)). For identical reasons, an individual partner in a Scottish partnership may also be made personally liable for breaches of the Act by his or her firm (see s.61(3)).*

(3) A person guilty of an offence under paragraph 12 of Schedule 9 is liable on summary conviction to a fine not exceeding level 5 on the standard scale.

> **S.60(3)** - *see s.60(2) for details of potential penalties.*

(4) Subject to subsection (5), the court by or before which a person is convicted of-

    (a) an offence under section 21(1), 22(6), 55 or 56,

> **S.60(4)(a)** - *i.e.:*
>
> - *processing personal data without having notified the Commisioner, if required to do so (s.21(1));*
>
> - *processing in breach of an assessable processing order (see s.22);*
>
> - *unlawful obtaining or disclosure of personal data without the consent of the data controller (s.55 (1)); and*
>
> - *breach of the prohibition on not disclosing a "relevant record" (see s.56(6)).*

(b) an offence under section 21(2) relating to processing which is assessable processing for the purposes of section 22, or

(c) an offence under section 47(1) relating to an enforcement notice,

may order any document or other material used in connection with the processing of personal data and appearing to the court to be connected with the commission of the offence to be forfeited, destroyed or erased.

(5) The court shall not make an order under subsection (4) in relation to any material where a person (other than the offender) claiming to be the owner of or otherwise interested in the material applies to be heard by the court, unless an opportunity is given to him to show cause why the order should not be made.

61.– (1) Where an offence under this Act has been committed by a body corporate and is proved to have been committed with the consent or connivance of or to be attributable to any neglect on the part of any director, manager, secretary or similar officer of the body corporate or any person who was purporting to act in any such capacity, he as well as the body corporate shall be guilty of that offence and be liable to be proceeded against and punished accordingly.

(2) Where the affairs of a body corporate are managed by its members subsection (1) shall apply in relation to the acts and defaults of a member in connection with his functions of management as if he were a director of the body corporate.

(3) Where an offence under this Act has been committed by a Scottish partnership and the contravention in question is proved to have occurred with the consent or connivance of, or to be attributable to any neglect on the part of, a partner, he as well as the partnership shall be guilty of that offence and shall be liable to be proceeded against and punished accordingly.

Amendments of Consumer Credit Act 1974

62.– (1) In section 158 of the Consumer Credit Act 1974 (duty of agency to disclose filed information)-

(a) in subsection (1)-
   (i) in paragraph (a) for "individual" there is substituted "partnership or other unincorporated body of persons not consisting entirely of bodies corporate", and
   (ii) for "him" there is substituted "it",
(b) in subsection (2), for "his" there is substituted "the consumer's", and
(c) in subsection (3), for "him" there is substituted "the consumer".

(2) In section 159 of that Act (correction of wrong information) for subsection (1) there is substituted-

"(1) Any individual (the "objector") given-

(a) information under section 7 of the Data Protection Act 1998 by a credit reference agency, or

(b) information under section 158,

who considers that an entry in his file is incorrect, and that if it is not corrected he is likely to be prejudiced, may give notice to the agency requiring it either to remove the entry from the file or amend it.

"(3) In subsections (2) to (6) of that section-

(a) for "consumer", wherever occurring, there is substituted "objector", and
(b) for "Director", wherever occurring, there is substituted "the relevant authority".

(4) After subsection (6) of that section there is inserted-

"(7) The Information Commissioner may vary or revoke any order made by him under this section.

(8) In this section "the relevant authority" means-

(a) where the objector is a partnership or other unincorporated body of persons, the Director, and
(b) in any other case, the Information Commissioner."

(5) In section 160 of that Act (alternative procedure for business consumers)-

(a) in subsection (4)-
    (i) for "him" there is substituted "to the consumer", and
    (ii) in paragraphs (a) and (b) for "he" there is substituted "the consumer" and for "his" there is substituted "the consumer's", and
(b) after subsection (6) there is inserted-
    "(7) In this section "consumer" has the same meaning as in section 158.""

General

63.– (1) This Act binds the Crown.

> **S.63** - *The Government, which is responsible for processing vast quantities of personal data, including tax and social security records, must comply with the Act. Government departments cannot however be prosecuted for offences, although s.55 and para 12 of Sch 9 apply to them (see s.63(5) below).*

(2) For the purposes of this Act each government department shall be treated as a person separate from any other government department.

(3) Where the purposes for which and the manner in which any personal data are, or are to be, processed are determined by any person acting on behalf of the Royal Household, the Duchy of Lancaster or the Duchy of Cornwall, the data controller in respect of those data for the purposes of this Act shall be-

(a) in relation to the Royal Household, the Keeper of the Privy Purse,

(b) in relation to the Duchy of Lancaster, such person as the Chancellor of the Duchy appoints, and

(c) in relation to the Duchy of Cornwall, such person as the Duke of Cornwall, or the possessor for the time being of the Duchy of Cornwall, appoints.

(4) Different persons may be appointed under subsection (3)(b) or (c) for different purposes.

(5) Neither a government department nor a person who is a data controller by virtue of subsection (3) shall be liable to prosecution under this Act, but section 55 and paragraph 12 of Schedule 9 shall apply to a person in the service of the Crown as they apply to any other person.

> **S.63(5)** - *S.55 refers to unlawful obtaining of personal data.*
>
> *Under para 12 of Sch 9 anybody who intentionally obstructs or fails to provide appropriate assistance to an official with a warrant to enter and inspect the premises, shall be guilty of an offence.*

64.– (1) This section applies to-

(a) a notice or request under any provision of Part II,

> **S.64(1)(a)** - *Notice or request under Part II - Request for information about personal data (s.7), notice to prevent processing and counter-notice from data controller (s.10), notice to prevent processing for direct marketing (s.11) and notice in relation to automated decision-taking (s.12).*

(b) a notice under subsection (1) of section 24 or particulars made available under that subsection, or

> **S.64(1)(b)** - *s.24(1) - Request for relevant particulars: in certain circumstances, set out in ss.17(2) and (3), processing can take place without the need for notification. If such circumstances apply and the data controller has not provided relevant particulars to the Commissioner, the data controller must nevertheless provide the data subject with relevant particulars within 21 days of receiving a written request.*

(c) an application under section 41(2),

S.64(1)(c) - *s.41(2) - An application to vary or cancel an enforcement notice due to a change in circumstances.*

but does not apply to anything which is required to be served in accordance with rules of court.

(2) The requirement that any notice, request, particulars or application to which this section applies should be in writing is satisfied where the text of the notice, request, particulars or application-

(a) is transmitted by electronic means,
(b) is received in legible form, and
(c) is capable of being used for subsequent reference.

S.64(2) - *It would appear that e-mail and fax are suitable means by which to transmit such notices (etc). However, official notices issued for the purposes of litigation or by the Commissioner in connection with enforcement arrangements must not be served in such a manner.*

(3) The Secretary of State may by regulations provide that any requirement that any notice, request, particulars or application to which this section applies should be in writing is not to apply in such circumstances as may be prescribed by the regulations.

65.– (1) Any notice authorised or required by this Act to be served on or given to any person by the Commissioner may-

(a) if that person is an individual, be served on him-
　　(i) by delivering it to him, or
　　(ii) by sending it to him by post addressed to him at his usual or last-known place of residence or business, or
　　(iii) by leaving it for him at that place;
(b) if that person is a body corporate or unincorporate, be served on that body-
　　(i) by sending it by post to the proper officer of the body at its principal office, or
　　(ii) by addressing it to the proper officer of the body and leaving it at that office;
(c) if that person is a partnership in Scotland, be served on that partnership-
　　(i) by sending it by post to the principal office of the partnership, or
　　(ii) by addressing it to that partnership and leaving it at that office.

(2) In subsection (1)(b) "principal office", in relation to a registered company, means its registered office and "proper officer", in relation to any body, means the secretary or other executive officer charged with the conduct of its general affairs.

(3) This section is without prejudice to any other lawful method of serving or giving a notice.

66.– (1) Where a question falls to be determined in Scotland as to the legal capacity of a person under the age of sixteen years to exercise any right conferred by any provision of this Act, that person shall be taken to have that capacity where he has a general understanding of what it means to exercise that right.

(2) Without prejudice to the generality of subsection (1), a person of twelve years of age or more shall be presumed to be of sufficient age and maturity to have such understanding as is mentioned in that subsection.

67.– (1) Any power conferred by this Act on the Secretary of State to make an order, regulations or rules shall be exercisable by statutory instrument.

(2) Any order, regulations or rules made by the Secretary of State under this Act may-

(a) make different provision for different cases, and
(b) make such supplemental, incidental, consequential or transitional provision or savings as the Secretary of State considers appropriate;

and nothing in section 7(11), 19(5), 26(1) or 30(4) limits the generality of paragraph (a).

> **S.67(2)** - *s.7(11), 19(5), 26(1) and 30(4) relate to orders and regulations which may stipulate different provisions for different cases (e.g. different fees or different periods of time).*

(3) Before making-

(a) an order under any provision of this Act other than section 75(3),
(b) any regulations under this Act other than notification regulations (as defined by section 16(2)),

the Secretary of State shall consult the Commissioner.

> **S.67(3)** - *s.75(3) - orders relating to the commencement of different provisions of the Act.*

(4) A statutory instrument containing (whether alone or with other provisions) an order under-

> section 10(2)(b),
>
> section 12(5)(b),
>
> section 22(1),
>
> section 30,
>
> section 32(3),
>
> section 38,
>
> section 56(8),
>
> paragraph 10 of Schedule 3, or
>
> paragraph 4 of Schedule 7,

shall not be made unless a draft of the instrument has been laid before and approved by a resolution of each House of Parliament.

S.67(4) - *The following orders must be approved by Parliament before they can be implemented:*

- *S.10(2)(b) - an order setting out situations where individuals will not be entitled to require processing likely to cause damage or distress to cease or not begin.*

- *S.12(5)(b) - an order setting out situations where individuals will not be entitled to require that no significant decision is taken solely as a result of processing of personal data by automated means.*

- *S.22(1) - an order describing processing which is "assessable processing"; i.e. of a type which is particularly likely to cause substantial damage or distress or prejudice rights and freedoms of data subjects.*

- *S.30 - an order providing an exemption from (or modification of rules regarding) subject information provisions in relation to information about the physical or mental health or condition of a data subject [now in force].*

- *S.32(3) - an order designating codes of practice in the spheres of journalism, literature and art. Certain exemptions relate to processing of data for the "special purposes" provided that publication is reasonably believed to be in the public interest. Codes of practice may be designated to ascertain the reasonableness of this belief [now in force].*

- *S.38 - an order providing further exemptions to subject information and non-disclosure provisions [now in force].*

- *S.56(8) - an order amending the table setting out details relating to "relevant records".*

- *Sch 3 para 10 - an order providing further conditions for processing sensitive personal data [now in force].*

- *Sch 7 para 4 - an order providing further exemptions from subject information provisions for those being assessed for suitability for Crown employment or similar appointments [now in force].*

(5) A statutory instrument which contains (whether alone or with other provisions)-

    (a) an order under-

        section 22(7),

        section 23,

        section 51(3),

        section 54(2), (3) or (4),

        paragraph 3, 4 or 14 of Part II of Schedule 1,

        paragraph 6 of Schedule 2,

        paragraph 2, 7 or 9 of Schedule 3,

        paragraph 4 of Schedule 4,

        paragraph 6 of Schedule 7,

S.67(5)(a) - *Parliament can annul any of the following which have not otherwise been approved by Parliament under s.67(4):*

Orders under:

- *S.22(7) - changes of time periods in relation to "assessable processing".*

- *S.23 - appointment of data protection supervisors.*

- *S.51(3) - codes of practice for guidance as to good practice regarding data protection.*

- *S.54(2), (3) or (4) - functions of the Commissioner on the international stage.*

- *Sch 1 Part II para 3 - circumstances in which fair processing will have taken place even though specified information (under Sch 1 Part II para 2(3)) has not been provided to the data subject.*

- *Sch 1 Part II para 4 - conditions relating to the processing of personal data containing general identifiers.*

- *Sch 1 Part II para 14 - circumstances in which the 8th principle will apply, regardless of the provisions of Schedule 4 (exemptions from the 8th principle).*

- *Sch 2 para 6 - circumstances in which the "legitimate interests" condition is satisfied.*

- *Sch 3 para 2 and 7 - circumstances in which the conditions relating to "legal right or obligation" and "administration of justice (etc)" are not applicable or where further conditions must be satisfied.*

- *Sch 3 para 9 - circumstances in which the ethnic monitoring condition is or is not properly satisfied.*

- *Sch 4 para 4 - circumstances in which a transfer is necessary for public interest reasons.*

- *Sch 7 para 6 - whether the subject information exemption applies for corporate finance services.*

(b) regulations under section 7 which-
    (i) prescribe cases for the purposes of subsection (2)(b),
    (ii) are made by virtue of subsection (7), or
    (iii) relate to the definition of "the prescribed period",

S.67(5)(b) - *Parliament can annul any of the following regulations which have not otherwise been approved under s.67(4):*

(i) those cases where no fee is payable when the data subject requests information;

(ii) definitions of "prescribed cases" and personal data of a "prescribed description" by which an individual can limit his/her request for information;

(iii) in SI 2000/191, the prescribed period is between 7 and 40 days, depending on the nature of the data being accessed.

(c) regulations under section 8(1) or 9(3),

S.67(5)(c) *s.8(1) - in prescribed cases, a request for information under one subsection of s.7(1) is extended to include a request for information under the other subsections of s.7(1) (SI 2000/191);*

> *s.9(3) - credit reference agencies may be required to provide data subjects making information requests with a statement of their rights under the Act and the Consumer Credit Act 1974.*

(d) regulations under section 64,

(e) notification regulations (as defined by section 16(2)), or

(f) rules under paragraph 7 of Schedule 6,

and which is not subject to the requirement in subsection (4) that a draft of the instrument be laid before and approved by a resolution of each House of Parliament, shall be subject to annulment in pursuance of a resolution of either House of Parliament.

(6) A statutory instrument which contains only-

(a) regulations prescribing fees for the purposes of any provision of this Act, or

(b) regulations under section 7 prescribing fees for the purposes of any other enactment,

shall be laid before Parliament after being made.

> **·S.67(6)(b)** *s.7 - right of access to personal data.*

68.– (1) In this Act "accessible record" means-

(a) a health record as defined by subsection (2),

(b) an educational record as defined by Schedule 11, or

> **S.68.(1)(b)** *- generally, this involves information relating to former or current school pupils.*

(c) an accessible public record as defined by Schedule 12.

> **S.68(1)(c)** *- generally, this involves information relating to local authority tenancies and social services.*

(2) In subsection (1)(a) "health record" means any record which-

(a) consists of information relating to the physical or mental health or condition of an individual, and

(b) has been made by or on behalf of a health professional in connection with the care of that individual.

S.68(2)(b) - *"care of that individual"* - *see commentary to s.57.*

69.– (1) In this Act "health professional" means any of the following-

(a) a registered medical practitioner,

(b) a registered dentist as defined by section 53(1) of the Dentists Act 1984,

(c) a registered optician as defined by section 36(1) of the Opticians Act 1989,

(d) a registered pharmaceutical chemist as defined by section 24(1) of the Pharmacy Act 1954 or a registered person as defined by Article 2(2) of the Pharmacy (Northern Ireland) Order 1976,

(e) a registered nurse, midwife or health visitor,

(f) a registered osteopath as defined by section 41 of the Osteopaths Act 1993,

(g) a registered chiropractor as defined by section 43 of the Chiropractors Act 1994,

(h) any person who is registered as a member of a profession to which the Professions Supplementary to Medicine Act 1960 for the time being extends,

(i) a clinical psychologist, child psychotherapist or speech therapist,

(j) a music therapist employed by a health service body, and

(k) a scientist employed by such a body as head of a department.

(2) In subsection (1)(a) "registered medical practitioner" includes any person who is provisionally registered under section 15 or 21 of the Medical Act 1983 and is engaged in such employment as is mentioned in subsection (3) of that section.

(3) In subsection (1) "health service body" means-

(a) a Health Authority established under section 8 of the National Health Service Act 1977,

(b) a Special Health Authority established under section 11 of that Act,

(c) a Health Board within the meaning of the National Health Service (Scotland) Act 1978,

(d) a Special Health Board within the meaning of that Act,

(e) the managers of a State Hospital provided under section 102 of that Act,

(f) a National Health Service trust first established under section 5 of the National Health Service and Community Care Act 1990 or section 12A of the National Health Service (Scotland) Act 1978,

(g) a Health and Social Services Board established under Article 16 of the Health and Personal Social Services (Northern Ireland) Order 1972,

(h) a special health and social services agency established under the Health and Personal Social Services (Special Agencies) (Northern Ireland) Order 1990, or

(i) a Health and Social Services trust established under Article 10 of the Health and Personal Social Services (Northern Ireland) Order 1991.

S.70 - *Supplementary definitions - if a definition does not appear in this section or in s.71, it is worth looking in another part of the section in which the term first appears.*

70.– (1) In this Act, unless the context otherwise requires-

"business" includes any trade or profession;

"the Commissioner" means the Information Commissioner;

"credit reference agency" has the same meaning as in the Consumer Credit Act 1974;

"the Data Protection Directive" means Directive 95/46/EC on the protection of individuals with regard to the processing of personal data and on the free movement of such data;

"EEA State" means a State which is a contracting party to the Agreement on the European Economic Area signed at Oporto on 2nd May 1992 as adjusted by the Protocol signed at Brussels on 17th March 1993;

"enactment" includes an enactment passed after this Act;

"government department" includes a Northern Ireland department and any body or authority exercising statutory functions on behalf of the Crown;

"Minister of the Crown" has the same meaning as in the Ministers of the Crown Act 1975;

"public register" means any register which pursuant to a requirement imposed-

(a) by or under any enactment, or
(b) in pursuance of any international agreement,

is open to public inspection or open to inspection by any person having a legitimate interest;

"pupil"-

(a) in relation to a school in England and Wales, means a registered pupil within the meaning of the Education Act 1996,
(b) in relation to a school in Scotland, means a pupil within the meaning of the Education (Scotland) Act 1980, and
(c) in relation to a school in Northern Ireland, means a registered pupil within the meaning of the Education and Libraries (Northern Ireland) Order 1986;

"recipient", in relation to any personal data, means any person to whom the data are disclosed, including any person (such as an employee or agent of the data controller, a data processor or an employee or agent of a data processor) to whom they are disclosed in the course of processing the data for the data controller, but does not include any person to whom disclosure is or may be made as a result of, or with a view to, a particular inquiry by or on behalf of that person made in the exercise of any power conferred by law;

"registered company" means a company registered under the enactments relating to companies for the time being in force in the United Kingdom;

"school"-

(a) in relation to England and Wales, has the same meaning as in the Education Act 1996,

(b) in relation to Scotland, has the same meaning as in the Education (Scotland) Act 1980, and

(c) in relation to Northern Ireland, has the same meaning as in the Education and Libraries (Northern Ireland) Order 1986;

"teacher" includes-

(a) in Great Britain, head teacher, and

(b) in Northern Ireland, the principal of a school;

"third party", in relation to personal data, means any person other than-

(a) the data subject,

(b) the data controller, or

(c) any data processor or other person authorised to process data for the data controller or processor;

"the Tribunal" means the Data Protection Tribunal.

(2) For the purposes of this Act data are inaccurate if they are incorrect or misleading as to any matter of fact.

71. The following Table shows provisions defining or otherwise explaining expressions used in this Act (other than provisions defining or explaining an expression only used in the same section or Schedule)-

accessible record	section 68
address (in Part III)	section 16(3)
business	section 70(1)
the Commissioner	section 70(1)
credit reference agency	section 70(1)
data	section 1(1)
data controller	sections 1(1) and (4) and 63(3)
data processor	section 1(1)
the Data Protection Directive	section 70(1)
data protection principles	section 4 and Schedule 1

data subject	section 1(1)
disclosing (of personal data)	section 1(2)(b)
EEA State	section 70(1)
enactment	section 70(1)
enforcement notice	section 40(1)
fees regulations (in Part III)	section 16(2)
government department	section 70(1)
health professional	section 69
inaccurate (in relation to data)	section 70(2)
information notice	section 43(1)
Minister of the Crown	section 70(1)
the non-disclosure provisions (in Part IV)	section 27(3)
notification regulations (in Part III)	section 16(2)
obtaining (of personal data)	section 1(2)(a)
personal data	section 1(1)
prescribed (in Part III)	section 16(2)
processing (of information or data)	section 1(1) and paragraph 5 of Schedule 8
public register	section 70(1)
publish (in relation to journalistic, literary or artistic material)	section 32(6)
pupil (in relation to a school)	section 70(1)
recipient (in relation to personal data)	section 70(1)
recording (of personal data)	section 1(2)(a)
registered company	section 70(1)
registrable particulars (in Part III)	section 16(1)
relevant filing system	section 1(1)
school	section 70(1)
sensitive personal data	section 2
special information notice	section 44(1)
the special purposes	section 3
the subject information provisions (in Part IV)	section 27(2)
teacher	section 70(1)
third party (in relation to processing of personal data)	section 70(1)
the Tribunal	section 70(1)
using (of personal data)	section 1(2)(b).

72. During the period beginning with the commencement of this section and ending with 23rd October 2007, the provisions of this Act shall have effect subject to the modifications set out in Schedule 13.

S.72 - *Sch 13 provides for a s.12A which applies only until 23 October 2007 and gives rights to data subjects in relation to exempt manual data.*

73. Schedule 14 (which contains transitional provisions and savings) has effect.

S.73 - *Sch 14 sets out the procedure in cases where part but not all of the Act is in force and the effect of repealing other legislation.*

74.– (1) Schedule 15 (which contains minor and consequential amendments) has effect.

(2) The enactments and instruments specified in Schedule 16 are repealed or revoked to the extent specified.

75.– (1) This Act may be cited as the Data Protection Act 1998.

(2) The following provisions of this Act-

   (a) sections 1 to 3,
   (b) section 25(1) and (4),
   (c) section 26,
   (d) sections 67 to 71,
   (e) this section,
   (f) paragraph 17 of Schedule 5,
   (g) Schedule 11,
   (h) Schedule 12, and
   (i) so much of any other provision of this Act as confers any power to make subordinate legislation,

shall come into force on the day on which this Act is passed.

(3) The remaining provisions of this Act shall come into force on such day as the Secretary of State may by order appoint; and different days may be appointed for different purposes.

S.75(3) - *As at the date of writing, only s56 is yet to come into force (see s.75(4)).*

(4) The day appointed under subsection (3) for the coming into force of section 56 must not be earlier than the first day on which sections 112, 113 and 115 of the Police Act 1997 (which provide for the issue by the Secretary of State of criminal conviction certificates, criminal record certificates and enhanced criminal record certificates) are all in force.

S.75(4) - *s.56: it will be an offence in certain circumstances for a person to require a data subject or third party to supply that person with a copy of the data subject's criminal, prison or social security contributions record. (see s.56).*

(5) Subject to subsection (6), this Act extends to Northern Ireland.

(6) Any amendment, repeal or revocation made by Schedule 15 or 16 has the same extent as that of the enactment or instrument to which it relates.

SCHEDULES

SCHEDULE 1

THE DATA PROTECTION PRINCIPLES

PART I

The data protection principles form the fundamental core of the Act, setting out the ground rules for obtaining, holding, disclosing, securing, transferring and destroying personal data. On the face of it, they seem very similar to the principles contained in the 1984 Act although the wider significance of the terminology means that their application has been broadened. The eighth principle (transfer of data outside the EEA) is the only entirely new principle.

Not all personal data are subject to the principles - see Part IV Exemptions.

THE PRINCIPLES

1. Personal data shall be processed fairly and lawfully and, in particular, shall not be processed unless-

   (a) at least one of the conditions in Schedule 2 is met, and
   (b) in the case of sensitive personal data, at least one of the conditions in Schedule 3 is also met.

Fair processing code

1.   The fair processing code is divided into two stages: (a) fair obtaining of personal data - Schedule 1, Part II, para 1; (b) information provided or made readily available to data subjects - Schedule 1, Part II, paras 2-4. In addition, there must be compliance with the conditions of Schedule 2 and 3.

Data controllers must consider each of these elements when they first collect personal data.

2. Personal data shall be obtained only for one or more specified and lawful purposes, and shall not be further processed in any manner incompatible with that purpose or those purposes.

2.   See Sch 1 Part II paras 5-6.

3. Personal data shall be adequate, relevant and not excessive in relation to the purpose or purposes for which they are processed.

> *3.   No further interpretation is given. This is similar to the fourth data protection principle under the 1984 Act, although the definition of "processing" is now much wider. Data controllers should ensure they do not obtain more data than they need and discard any irrelevant data. It may be that certain information is required in relation to some data subjects, but not others. Care should be exercised in such circumstances to ensure that the same level of information is not obtained from all data subjects. An example is in the request for information in job application forms, in which all potential employees, regardless of the position they are applying for, are asked the same in-depth questions. Under the 1984 Act, the Registrar published a list of factors which she would consider where an item of data is held for all data subjects, although is not required for all of them. Such factors included the length of time for which the item is held, the purpose for holding it and possible consequences of holding or destroying it.*

4. Personal data shall be accurate and, where necessary, kept up to date.

> *4.   See Sch 1 Part II para 7.*

5. Personal data processed for any purpose or purposes shall not be kept for longer than is necessary for that purpose or those purposes.

> *5.   The Commissioner has indicated that the first principle should be considered in relation to this obligation as that principle requires processors to detail for what purposes they intend to use personal data. No further interpretation is given, although this is similar to the sixth data protection principle under the 1984 Act. Data should be reviewed regularly and what is no longer required should be discarded although care should be taken to consider all potential legitimate uses to which the data could be put before valuable information is destroyed. An example is disciplinary records; over-zealous deletion could backfire on a well-meaning employer who subsequently may not be able to refute allegations of harassment carried out during disciplinary hearings if records of those hearings have been prematurely destroyed. In the past, the Registrar has recommended a systematic*

policy of data deletion. In some circumstances, data may be legitimately retained for many years, and the Institute of Chartered Secretaries and Administrators provides useful guidance on the retention of different types of records.[70] Also, the Commissioner has included a schedule of retention times for employment related documentation in her Code of Practice ("The use of personal data in employer/employee relationships"). It is suggested that data which could relate to a potential legal claim should be retained until the time limit for bringing an action has expired. In the case of contractual disputes, that is 6 years. In the case of personal injury, that is three years from the date on which the injury is discovered. That could, potentially, be many years later. A sensible approach should be taken, and only those documents which could assist the data controller in defending such a claim should be retained.

70　*A Short Guide to the Retention of Documents, by Andrew C Hamer (the Institute of Chartered Secretaries & Administrators, 1996)*

6.　Personal data shall be processed in accordance with the rights of data subjects under this Act.

6.　*See Sch 1 Part II para 8.*

7.　Appropriate technical and organisational measures shall be taken against unauthorised or unlawful processing of personal data and against accidental loss or destruction of, or damage to, personal data.

7.　*See Sch 1 Part II paras 9-12.*

8.　Personal data shall not be transferred to a country or territory outside the European Economic Area unless that country or territory ensures an adequate level of protection for the rights and freedoms of data subjects in relation to the processing of personal data.

8.　*See Sch 1 Part II paras 13-15.*

PART II

INTERPRETATION OF THE PRINCIPLES IN PART I

The first principle

> **1st Principle: para 1: fair and lawful processing**
>
> *is set out in paragraph 1 of Part I of Schedule 1. See also Schedules 2 and 3.*

1.– (1) In determining for the purposes of the first principle whether personal data are processed fairly, regard is to be had to the method by which they are obtained, including in particular whether any person from whom they are obtained is deceived or misled as to the purpose or purposes for which they are to be processed.

> *1.   Fairly obtained: Data controllers must ensure that data subjects are not misled or deceived as to the purpose or purposes for the processing. Personal data will be treated as having been fairly obtained if they have been obtained from a person who is either authorised or required under any enactment or international obligation to supply such data.*
>
> *Data controllers who purchase marketing lists from reputable companies should ensure that the lists are "clean" (ie have been tested against the Mailing, Fax and Telephone Preference Services) and have been fairly and lawfully obtained. It is wise to seek warranties from list brokers as to the quality of the data obtained and as to the fair and lawful collection of such data.*

(2) Subject to paragraph 2, for the purposes of the first principle data are to be treated as obtained fairly if they consist of information obtained from a person who-

(a) is authorised by or under any enactment to supply it, or

(b) is required to supply it by or under any enactment or by any convention or other instrument imposing an international obligation on the United Kingdom.

2.– (1) Subject to paragraph 3, for the purposes of the first principle personal data are not to be treated as processed fairly unless-

(a) in the case of data obtained from the data subject, the data controller ensures so far as practicable that the data subject has, is provided with, or has made readily available to him, the information specified in sub-paragraph (3), and

(b) in any other case, the data controller ensures so far as practicable that, before the relevant time or as soon as practicable after that time, the data subject has, is provided with, or has made readily available to him, the information specified in sub-paragraph (3).

2(1) Although there is no stipulation about how data controllers should go about notifying their data subjects (ie regarding the type size of notifications and their prominence), it is suggested that the more vulnerable the group of data subjects (eg children and the elderly), the simpler and clearer the notification. Any non-obvious intended uses must be pointed out. Where a data controller undergoes a change of business or a shift in emphasis from one area to another, the data controller must ensure that such developments are within the customer's expectations. If not, the data controller should obtain the consent of the customers before marketing the new product or service to them.

When obtaining customer details from list brokers or other third parties, data controllers should ensure they receive adequate warranties regarding the collection of details on the list and the purposes for which the data may be used.

(2) In sub-paragraph (1)(b) "the relevant time" means-
  (a) the time when the data controller first processes the data, or
  (b) in a case where at that time disclosure to a third party within a reasonable period is envisaged-
     (i) if the data are in fact disclosed to such a person within that period, the time when the data are first disclosed,
     (ii) if within that period the data controller becomes, or ought to become, aware that the data are unlikely to be disclosed to such a person within that period, the time when the data controller does become, or ought to become, so aware, or
     (iii) in any other case, the end of that period.

2. Providing information: "so far as practicable": there is no further guidance about the meaning of this phrase which, if taken to extremes, could be used to excuse fair processing. Under the 1984 Act, Innovations (Mail Order) Ltd[71] was served with an enforcement notice by the Registrar for failing to notify potential customers in its advertisements of its list rental practices (ie the practice of selling lists of customer names and addresses). It was deemed to be reasonably practicable for Innovations to "contain within any form of advertising currently available a statement informing of the purpose to trade in names and addresses." Unless para 3 applies, data controllers must provide information set out in sub-paragraph (3), or

---

71   *Innovations (Mail Order) Ltd v Data Protection Registrar 1993*

make it readily available. The distinction is important: although "readily available" is not defined in the Act, the Commissioner's office has indicated that communicating

a telephone number would constitute making the information "readily available". In practical terms, the person who is likely to answer the telephone call should have that information at his or her fingertips.

It is the authors' view that only the information set out in sub-paragraph (3)(a) to (c) can be made "readily available" in this way; data controllers who propose to use personal data in a way which a data subject would not reasonably expect (eg direct marketing or disclosure to a third party not directly linked to the purposes for obtaining the data) must actively inform the data subject. Therefore any further information which should be supplied in accordance with sub-paragraph (3)(d) should be actively presented to the data subject to ensure that its processing is fair.

Privacy Statements

With many organisations now collecting personal data through their websites, an excellent opportunity exists for providing the requisite information to data subjects. "Privacy statements" are becoming more commonplace and the Commissioner welcomes their introduction. Such statements can either be accessed via an icon (which could be the "information padlock" signpost) or, better still, must be viewed before personal data can be left on a website. That way, there would be no question that the fair processing code had been followed, and would also show that consent to the processing had been given, thereby fulfilling a Schedule 2 condition (see below).

*(2)   **Timing:** when should the data controller provide/make readily available the necessary information? It will depend upon whether the data were obtained from the data subject or not. If they were, there are no specific provisions as to timing, although the Guidelines state that the data subject should be provided with the information at the time the data are obtained[72]. If the data were not obtained from the data subject, the information must be provided either before the "relevant time" or as soon as practicable afterwards. In many cases, the "relevant time" will be the time when the data are first obtained. Only if the data controller plans to disclose the data to a third party within a reasonable time period do different rules apply (see sub-paragraph 2 (2)(b)).*

Data controllers may find it considerably easier simply to provide the requisite information by way of a notice to all those customers or other data subjects at the point when their personal data are sought. The notice should state the name of the data controller, explaining briefly why the data are required and giving a general description of any other organisations which will use the information. Such a notice will also satisfy the requirements of the second principle.

---

72   *Guidelines, Chapter 3, para 1.12.3*

(3) The information referred to in sub-paragraph (1) is as follows, namely-

    (a) the identity of the data controller,

    (b) if he has nominated a representative for the purposes of this Act, the identity of that representative,

    (c) the purpose or purposes for which the data are intended to be processed, and

    (d) any further information which is necessary, having regard to the specific circumstances in which the data are or are to be processed, to enable processing in respect of the data subject to be fair.

---

2.   (3) Content of information: (d) "any further information which is necessary": the Guidelines provide further assistance on this matter: "the more unforeseen the consequences of processing, the more likely it is that the data controller will be expected to provide further information[73]. For consent to be informed, the data subject should know the purposes for which their data are to be processed, the likely consequences of such processing and whether particular disclosures can be reasonably envisaged.

---

[73]   *Guidelines, Chapter 3, para 1.11.1*

3.– (1) Paragraph 2(1)(b) does not apply where either of the primary conditions in sub-paragraph (2), together with such further conditions as may be prescribed by the Secretary of State by order, are met.

(2) The primary conditions referred to in sub-paragraph (1) are-

    (a) that the provision of that information would involve a disproportionate effort, or

    (b) that the recording of the information to be contained in the data by, or the disclosure of the data by, the data controller is necessary for compliance with any legal obligation to which the data controller is subject, other than an obligation imposed by contract.

---

3.   In most cases, data controllers must ensure that they comply with the fair processing code by providing, (or making readily available to) their data subjects, the information contained in para 2(3) above. However, there are some circumstances in which data controllers can disregard that requirement.

Those circumstances are where:

•   the data are obtained from someone other than the data subject (para 2(1)(b)); and

•   either of the primary conditions apply (paras 3(2)(a) or (b)).

> *If the above conditions are fulfilled, this Order places certain additional obligations on data controllers who wish to benefit from the disapplication of the information requirements:*
>
> - *the data controller must provide the relevant information to any data subject who requests it;*
>
> - *if the data controller cannot readily determine whether he is processing information about the individual concerned because of a lack of identifying information, he must write to the individual explaining the position;*
>
> - *in the case of the "disproportionate effort" condition (para 3(2)(a)), the data controller must keep a record of the reasons why he believes the disapplication of the information requirements is necessary.*
>
> *See also commentary at s.34 relating to the electoral register (in relation to which, where the data are collected from third parties, sub-paragraph (2)(b) will apply).*
>
> *"Disproportionate effort": the Guidelines set out a number of factors which the Commissioner will take into account[74]. Such factors include: cost, length of time and ease of providing the information as against the benefit to the data subject. The factors are then balanced against the adverse effect on the data subject of not providing the information.*
>
> *In the Guidelines, emphasis is placed on the "overriding duty to process data fairly", regardless of the availability of the exceptions[75].*
>
> ---
>
> 74   *Guidelines, Chapter 3, para 1.12.2*
>
> 75   *Guidelines, Chapter 3, para 1.12.1*

4.– (1) Personal data which contain a general identifier falling within a description prescribed by the Secretary of State by order are not to be treated as processed fairly and lawfully unless they are processed in compliance with any conditions so prescribed in relation to general identifiers of that description.

(2) In sub-paragraph (1) "a general identifier" means any identifier (such as, for example, a number or code used for identification purposes) which-

(a) relates to an individual, and
(b) forms part of a set of similar identifiers which is of general application.

4 General identifiers: these may be, for instance, numbers or codes used for identification purposes. The Secretary of State may prescribe regulations which set out conditions which must be complied with to ensure that personal data containing such identifiers are processed fairly and lawfully, although at the time of writing no such regulations have been prescribed.

The second principle

2nd Principle: para 5: lawful purposes

is set out in para 2 of Part I of Schedule 1.

5. The purpose or purposes for which personal data are obtained may in particular be specified-

    (a) in a notice given for the purposes of paragraph 2 by the data controller to the data subject, or

    (b) in a notification given to the Commissioner under Part III of this Act.

5.   A notice to a data subject should state why the personal data are being processed and provide an indication of the likely recipients of the data, e.g. companies which market similar products to those of the data controller who is providing the notice.

5(b) See s.18.

Change of Purpose

Where a data controller, having collected personal data, subsequently wishes to change the use to which the data are put (eg a local authority which originally collected data for council tax purposes, subsequently wants to market its new arts programme to the same people) it cannot simply rely on the purposes notified to the Commissioner to enable it to fairly change the purposes for which it originally collected the data. It must effectively start the process again, following the fair processing code set out in the first principle. It must then consider a Schedule 2 (and, if applicable, Schedule 3) condition which will apply; in most cases, the data subject's consent will have to be obtained.

6. In determining whether any disclosure of personal data is compatible with the purpose or purposes for which the data were obtained, regard is to be had to the purpose or purposes for which the personal data are intended to be processed by any person to whom they are disclosed.

> 6.   *Disclosure: companies which intend to sell on customer lists to other companies should notify data subjects of this fact and explain the intentions of the purchasers of the lists, who will usually wish to market to some or all of the customers on the lists. Data subjects should be given the opportunity to "opt out" of this purpose, and their details should not be sold on until either their explicit consent to the rate of their details has been obtained or their failure to object to such processing has been notified to the data controller. See commentary at Sch 2 para 1. As to the timing of this, see Schedules 1 Part II, para 2. See also s.11, which allows data subjects the right to prevent processing for the purposes of direct marketing.*

The fourth principle

> **4th Principle: para 7: Accurate and (where necessary) up to date**
>
> *is set out in para 4 of Part I of Schedule 1.*

7. The fourth principle is not to be regarded as being contravened by reason of any inaccuracy in personal data which accurately record information obtained by the data controller from the data subject or a third party in a case where-

   (a) having regard to the purpose or purposes for which the data were obtained and further processed, the data controller has taken reasonable steps to ensure the accuracy of the data, and
   (b) if the data subject has notified the data controller of the data subject's view that the data are inaccurate, the data indicate that fact.

> 7.   *It is not enough for data controllers to rely on the fact that the personal data were provided by the data subject or third party as evidence of their accuracy. Data controllers should take reasonable steps to ensure the accuracy of data which they process and, if the data subject believes the data are inaccurate, the data should indicate that fact.*

The Commissioner is likely to take into account those factors which were relevant under the 1984 Act when deciding what action to take regarding the inaccuracy of data. Data controllers confronting this problem should consider the following questions:

- *How significant was the inaccuracy and did it or is it likely to cause the data subject damage or distress?*

- *From where was the inaccurate information obtained and was it reasonable to rely on that source?*

- *Were any steps taken to verify the information?*

- *How reliable is the data controller's procedure for data entry?*

- *What procedures were followed when the inaccuracy was discovered?*

Significantly, data controllers need only keep data up to date "where necessary". If the purpose for which the data are processed is to establish a historical record, it will clearly defeat the purpose if the data are updated. In most cases, it will be in the interests of the data controller to ensure that the data are up to date, otherwise valuable custom may be lost. In some cases, the repercussions of a failure to keep up to date records of a person's next of kin details could be catastrophic. Regular reviews should take place and a record kept of the date of the last review. Particular care should be taken if the fact that data are out of date may cause damage or distress to the data subject.

See also s.40(4) - enforcement notice in respect of a contravention of this principle.

The sixth principle

6th Principle: para 8: Processing in accordance with data subject rights

is set out in para 6 of Part I of Schedule 1. See also Part II of the Act.

8. A person is to be regarded as contravening the sixth principle if, but only if-

   (a) he contravenes section 7 by failing to supply information in accordance with that section,
   (b) he contravenes section 10 by failing to comply with a notice given under subsection (1) of that section to the extent that the notice is justified or by failing to give a notice under subsection (3) of that section,
   (c) he contravenes section 11 by failing to comply with a notice given under subsection (1) of that section, or

(d) he contravenes section 12 by failing to comply with a notice given under subsection (1) or (2)(b) of that section or by failing to give a notification under subsection (2)(a) of that section or a notice under subsection (3) of that section.

> 8.   *Only in the circumstances set out in this paragraph will a contravention of this principle have occurred.*
>
> *8(a)   A contravention will have occurred if the data controller fails to supply information in accordance with a s.7 subject access request.*
>
> *8(b) (c) (d)   A contravention will have occurred if the data controller fails to comply with notices under ss.10 to 12 and 12A.*
>
> *(e)   Schedule 13 para 5 inserts sub-paragraph (e). It is applicable only up to 24 October 2007, and provides rights to data subjects in relation to exempt manual data. Contravention of a s.12A notice will amount to a breach of this principle.*

The seventh principle

> **7th Principle: paras 9 to 12: Security measures**
>
> *is set out in para 7 of Part I of Schedule 1.*
>
> *Data controllers need to focus on two distinct, but related, areas of security (technical and organisational), to ensure that personal data are not subjected to unauthorised or unlawful processing or accidental loss, destruction or damage.*

9.   Having regard to the state of technological development and the cost of implementing any measures, the measures must ensure a level of security appropriate to-

    (a) the harm that might result from such unauthorised or unlawful processing or accidental loss, destruction or damage as are mentioned in the seventh principle, and

    (b) the nature of the data to be protected.

> 9.   **Technical:**
>
> *Suggestions include:*
>
> • *putting in place comprehensive back up procedures;*

- *introducing measures to prevent computer hacking;*

- *implementing virus detection software;*

- *insisting on the use and regular changing of passwords;*

- *placing restrictions on access so that individuals only have access to those parts of the computer system to which they have a legitimate interest.*

The extent to which the above (or similar) measures should be implemented will depend on a number of factors, including the cost of the measures, the state of technological development, the harm which might ensue from a failure to apply such measures and the sensitivity of the data being protected.

One of the requirements of the new notification procedure is for data controllers to provide "a general description of measures to be taken for the purpose of complying with the seventh data protection principle" (s.18(2)(b)).

One question which is asked in the notification procedure is whether the data controller has sought to comply with BS7799 (British Standard Code of Practice for information security management). See commentary below para 10 for further information.

10. The data controller must take reasonable steps to ensure the reliability of any employees of his who have access to the personal data.

10. **Organisational:**

Employees with access to personal data must be reliable and trustworthy. Appropriate checks should be made on those who are to be recruited for data entry work or who are to undertake such work for the first time (subject to the constraints in s.56). Such employees should be given proper training and provided with regular updates on the requirements of the Act. Any deliberate or negligent contravention of the Act should be made a specific disciplinary offence and access to personal data should be immediately withdrawn pending the outcome of a disciplinary hearing.

Companies may consider appointing a data protection officer to oversee the implementation of the data protection principles in the workplace. The officer should:

- *be the point of contact for the Commissioner and for members of staff with data protection queries;*

- *organise training sessions for staff;*

- *draft a data protection policy;*

> • *assist in the disciplinary process and assess the likely harm that any transgression may cause.*
>
> *Organisational measures are not restricted to the employment of reliable staff. Data controllers also need to consider other arrangements for the protection of personal data. A risk assessment should be carried out to establish whether precautions taken against burglary, fire or natural disasters are adequate. Similarly, the storage and disposal of items containing personal data (such as computer disks and print-outs) should be reviewed. It is advisable for waste paper containing personal data to be placed in a separate "confidential" waste bin and shredded by a reputable contractor.*
>
> *BSI Standard 7799: Businesses might like to consider the advantages of adopting this British Standards Institute Standard in relation to the seventh principle. The standard relates (amongst other things) to the way in which a business protects and regulates access to information held by it. For instance, it requires businesses to categorise data according to their sensitivity and to decide, given that categorisation, whether internal access to such data should be restricted accordingly. It also requires policies to be introduced ensuring that data are securely handled when transferred or used off-site by a business (a policy governing use of personal data on laptop computers, for example, could be adopted to assist in this regard). Adoption of BS:7799 has the advantage not only of providing a strong argument that a business complies with the seventh principle, but also may entitle that business to pay lower insurance premiums.*

11. Where processing of personal data is carried out by a data processor on behalf of a data controller, the data controller must in order to comply with the seventh principle-

    (a) choose a data processor providing sufficient guarantees in respect of the technical and organisational security measures governing the processing to be carried out, and

    (b) take reasonable steps to ensure compliance with those measures.

12. Where processing of personal data is carried out by a data processor on behalf of a data controller, the data controller is not to be regarded as complying with the seventh principle unless-

    (a) the processing is carried out under a contract-

        (i) which is made or evidenced in writing, and

        (ii) under which the data processor is to act only on instructions from the data controller, and

    (b) the contract requires the data processor to comply with obligations equivalent to those imposed on a data controller by the seventh principle.

11 and 12. **Data processors:** *see s.1(1) definition. Data controllers who use the services of data processors cannot absolve themselves of responsibility easily. An example is Company A which outsources its payroll functions to Company B. Company A must obtain guarantees regarding security measures and must take reasonable steps to ensure compliance with those measures. In addition, there must be a written contract between Company A and Company B, which must contain the details set out in para 12. Existing contracts between data controllers and processors should be reviewed to ensure compliance with para 12.*

The eighth principle

8th Principle: para 13: transfers outside the EEA

is set out in para 8 of Part I of Schedule 1.

13. An adequate level of protection is one which is adequate in all the circumstances of the case, having regard in particular to-

(a) the nature of the personal data,
(b) the country or territory of origin of the information contained in the data,
(c) the country or territory of final destination of that information,
(d) the purposes for which and period during which the data are intended to be processed,
(e) the law in force in the country or territory in question,
(f) the international obligations of that country or territory,
(g) any relevant codes of conduct or other rules which are enforceable in that country or territory (whether generally or by arrangement in particular cases), and
(h) any security measures taken in respect of the data in that country or territory.

13. Personal data are transferred to a country or territory outside the EEA whenever the data are disclosed, held or made readily available in such a place. This means that if a company places personal data on its website, because that information can be accessed from anywhere in the world, the company may be in breach of this principle. This principle will also concern those companies with overseas customers or subsidiaries.

However, the Commissioner has stated (as a preliminary opinion) that a transfer of data does not occur where information merely passes through a non-EEA country on its way to an EEA country. So if sending an e-mail from London to Llandudno in fact involves the e-mail being carried via servers in the USA this will not constitute a data transfer outside the EEA. If some substantial processing takes place in the USA (eg the data can be accessed, changed or added to) then a transfer outside the EEA is likely to be deemed to have occurred.[76]

If the level of data protection in the country or territory of destination is "adequate", there is no breach of this principle. Factors which should be considered are set out in this paragraph but they are not definitive. According to the Commissioner's guidance[77] a data controller can come to its own conclusion that a country has an adequate level of security given individual circumstances relevant to its situation.

---

76   *See the Commissioner's guidance note "International Transfers of Personal Data, Advice on Compliance with the 8th Data Protection Principle", para 4.1.*

77   *Ditto, para 7.*

14. The eighth principle does not apply to a transfer falling within any paragraph of Schedule 4, except in such circumstances and to such extent as the Secretary of State may by order provide.

14.   See also Schedule 4 for exemptions to this principle, although this is subject to any further order to be made by the Secretary of State.

15.– (1) Where-

(a) in any proceedings under this Act any question arises as to whether the requirement of the eighth principle as to an adequate level of protection is met in relation to the transfer of any personal data to a country or territory outside the European Economic Area, and

(b) a Community finding has been made in relation to transfers of the kind in question,

that question is to be determined in accordance with that finding.

(2) In sub-paragraph (1) "Community finding" means a finding of the European Commission, under the procedure provided for in Article 31(2) of the Data Protection Directive, that a country or territory outside the European Economic Area does, or does not, ensure an adequate level of protection within the meaning of Article 25(2) of the Directive.

15. *If the European Commission makes a finding that a country or territory outside the EEA does or does not provide adequate level of protection, such a finding will be conclusive. As mentioned in the Introduction, the European Commission at the time of writing has found that Switzerland and Hungary provide adequate levels of protection. However, the Commissioner has named thirteen additional countries which she considers very likely to have a suitably adequate level of protection given that they have all adopted data protection laws[78]. The countries are Australia, Canada, Guernsey, Hong Kong, Isle of Man, Israel, Japan, Jersey, New Zealand, Poland, Slovak Republic, Slovenia and Taiwan.*

The "Safe Harbour" provisions:

After long negotiations the European Commission and the US Department of Commerce concluded negotiations on the implementation of a system which, to their mutual satisfaction, ensures that in certain circumstances transfers of personal data to the US involve an adequate level of protection. The provisions apply where the US recipient of the data agrees to adhere to certain Safe Harbour Principles (the "Principles") (detailed below). At the time of writing several major US corporations have signed up to the Principles, including Microsoft, Hewlett Packard and Intel.

The provisions will apply where US organisations voluntarily agree to the Principles by either (i) agreeing to comply with a private sector privacy programme which incorporates the Principles into its rules, (ii) complying with a statutory, regulatory or administrative authority which has dispute resolution and complaints procedure powers, (iii) agreeing to adhere to any data protection authorities located in Europe (so long as the authority in question agrees to accept the US organisation), or (iv) agreeing to comply with any other private sector self-regulatory scheme provided that the scheme complies with the enforcement Principle (detailed below) and provided that any failure of the scheme to self-regulate is actionable under Section 5 of the US Federal Trade Commission Act.

If the Principles are met by any of the above routes the Safe Harbour provisions apply as soon as an organisation self-certifies to the US Department of Commerce (or its designee) that it adheres to the Principles. Exceptions apply to the need to meet the Principles (for example where US national security, public interest or law enforcement requirements must be met, where local case law is conflicted with, or where EU law provides a comparable exemption). It should also be noted that as initially proposed US organisations are not obliged to apply the Principles to manually processed filing systems. Further, as the Federal Trade Commission has no jurisdiction over certain industry sectors (most notably the banking and insurance sectors) not all businesses have been able to take advantage of the Principles.

---

78   *See the Commissioner's guidance note "International Transfers of Personal Data, Advice on Compliance with the 8th Data Protection Principle", para 6.2.*

The Safe Harbour provisions' Principles can be summarised as follows[79]:

1.   Notice

Individuals must be informed by an organisation of (i) the purposes for which it will use information about them, (ii) how to make enquiries or complaints to the organisation, (iii) the types of third party to whom it will disclose information, and (iv) the choices and means offered to limit disclosures and use of information about an individual. Notices detailing this information must be clear and conspicuous and provided when information is first obtained by an organisation (or at least before it is first used).

2.   Choice

Individuals must be offered an opportunity to opt out of having their information (a) disclosed or (b) used for purposes unrelated to those for which it was collected. In relation to sensitive personal data (as defined under Section 2 of the 1998 Act, except that information as to convictions and/or offences are not included) such opt-in consent must be explicit.

3.   Onward Transfer

If Principles (1) and (2) have not been met, personal information may only be disclosed to another organisation which subscribes to the Principles, or to an organisation which is subject to the EU's Data Protection Directive, or where a contract is made with the recipient requiring it to obey a level of security equivalent to that contained in the Principles.

4.   Security

Organisations must adopt reasonable precautions to protect personal information created, maintained, used or disseminated by them from loss, misuse and unauthorised access, disclosure, alteration and destruction.

5.   Data Integrity

Organisations must not use personal information for purposes for which it was not collected or authorised, and steps should be taken to ensure data are reliable, accurate, complete and current, given the intended uses.

6.   Access

Organisations must give individuals access to personal information which they hold about them. Organisations should also be able to correct, amend or delete inaccurate information unless the burden or expense of providing access is disproportionate to the risks to an individual's privacy or where a third party's rights would be violated.

---

[79]   *As detailed in the US Department of Commerce's draft "International Safe Harbour Privacy Principles" - 14 March 2000.*

7. Enforcement

Mechanisms for correcting non-compliance with any of the Principles must exist and must include (a) readily available, affordable and independent resource mechanisms for individuals' complaints and disputes allowing for the award of damages, (b) follow up procedures to verify that the attestations and assertions made by businesses regarding their privacy policies are true and that privacy practices have been implemented as presented and (c) obligations to remedy non-compliance with the Principles and "sufficiently rigorous" sanctions to ensure compliance.

SCHEDULE 2

CONDITIONS RELEVANT FOR PURPOSES OF THE FIRST PRINCIPLE:
PROCESSING OF ANY PERSONAL DATA

See definition of "personal data" and "sensitive personal data" in s.1(1).

Schedules 2 and 3 form part of the first principle, which stipulates that personal data must be processed fairly and lawfully. This is achieved by, firstly, following the fair processing code (Sch 1, Part I, paras 1 to 4) and, secondly, by complying with at least one condition from Schedule 2 (in the case of personal data) or at least one condition from each of Schedules 2 and 3 (in the case of sensitive personal data).

1. The data subject has given his consent to the processing.

1. **Consent:** *compare "explicit consent" in para 1 of Schedule 3. Here, simple "consent" suffices. Article 2 of the Directive defines the data subject's consent as "...any freely given specific and informed indication of his wishes by which the data subject signifies his agreement to personal data relating to him being processed". The Guidelines state that "data controllers cannot infer consent from non-response to a communication, for example from a customer's failure to return or respond to a leaflet".*[80]

The issue of consent was dealt with in some detail in the case of British Gas Trading Limited -v- The Data Protection Registrar (1998). The Registrar had issued an enforcement notice against British Gas Trading Limited ("BGTL") in respect of

---

[80] *Guidelines, Chapter 3, para 1.6*

contraventions of the first three data protection principles. BGTL had intended to promote the sale of electricity by using its existing database which was set up for billing its 19 million customers. In a leaflet enclosed with quarterly bills, customers were informed of their right to object to the processing of their data for the promotion of other products and services. If they had such an objection, the leaflet said they should tear off the coupon attached to the leaflet and return it to a freepost address. In the decision of the Data Protection Tribunal, hearing the appeal by BGTL against the enforcement notice, the Chairman, JAC Spokes QC, indicated that data controllers cannot infer consent from a failure to return a notice of objection. This would require data subjects having to take an active step in order to register their objection. However, the Tribunal could see nothing wrong with data controllers relying on passive consent, such as where a data subject does not tick an "opt-out box" (inviting the customer to tick if he or she objects to receiving future mailings of a specified type) on a form which is returned to the data controller. This was considered sufficient indication of the customer's consent to that type of processing. Examples of returned documents included a direct debit mandate, part of a bill or a purpose designed leaflet.

2. The processing is necessary-

   (a) for the performance of a contract to which the data subject is a party, or
   (b) for the taking of steps at the request of the data subject with a view to entering into a contract.

2.   Contract: e.g. employment contract. The personnel department of an organisation which processes monthly salary details should be able to do so without consent. Other contracts might include contracts to supply goods or services where the processing of personal data is essential for the supply to be carried out.

3. The processing is necessary for compliance with any legal obligation to which the data controller is subject, other than an obligation imposed by contract.

3.   Legal obligations: e.g. an employer is required to process personal data in relation to PAYE and National Insurance obligations.

4. The processing is necessary in order to protect the vital interests of the data subject.

> 4.   *Vital interests of the data subject: the Commissioner has advised that reliance on this condition "may only be claimed where the processing is necessary for matters of life and death, for example, the disclosure of a data subject's medical history to a hospital casualty department treating the data subject after a serious road accident"*[81].
>
> ---
>
> 81   *Guidelines, Chapter 3, para 1.2*

5.   The processing is necessary-

   (a) for the administration of justice,

   (b) for the exercise of any functions conferred on any person by or under any enactment,

   (c) for the exercise of any functions of the Crown, a Minister of the Crown or a government department, or

   (d) for the exercise of any other functions of a public nature exercised in the public interest by any person.

6.– (1) The processing is necessary for the purposes of legitimate interests pursued by the data controller or by the third party or parties to whom the data are disclosed, except where the processing is unwarranted in any particular case by reason of prejudice to the rights and freedoms or legitimate interests of the data subject.

(2) The Secretary of State may by order specify particular circumstances in which this condition is, or is not, to be taken to be satisfied.

> 6.   *Legitimate interests of the data controller: this appears to be something of a catch-all category, although when contemplating disclosure to third parties, data controllers should satisfy themselves that future processing will not have an adverse effect on the legitimate interests of the data subject. Further guidance may be given if the Secretary of State makes an order specifying the circumstances when this condition is satisfied, although no such guidance has been given at the date of writing.*
>
> *See definition of "sensitive personal data" in s.2.*

SCHEDULE 3

CONDITIONS RELEVANT FOR PURPOSES OF THE FIRST PRINCIPLE:
PROCESSING OF SENSITIVE PERSONAL DATA

This Schedule forms part of the first principle, relating to the fair and lawful processing of personal data. In order to process sensitive personal data lawfully and fairly, at least one condition from each of Schedules 2 and 3 must be satisfied. See s.1 for a definition of "sensitive personal data"

1. The data subject has given his explicit consent to the processing of the personal data.

1. Explicit consent: compare "consent" in para 1 of Schedule 2. The Guidelines provide that "the use of the word 'explicit' suggests that the consent of the data subject should be absolutely clear".[82] So long as data controllers adhere to the principles contained in the fair processing code, they should not go far wrong. (See notes to Sch I Part II, paras 1 to 4 above.) This may involve obtaining consent to a specific type of data to be processed, to particular purposes and particular disclosures. The Commissioner has indicated that "explicit consent" need not necessarily be written consent, so long as it is unequivocal; she has advised data controllers to "consider the extent to which the use of personal data by them is or is not reasonably foreseeable by data subjects"[83].

82 *Guidelines, Chapter 3, para 1.6*

83 *Guidelines, Chapter 3, para 1.6*

2.– (1) The processing is necessary for the purposes of exercising or performing any right or obligation which is conferred or imposed by law on the data controller in connection with employment.

2. (1) Such an obligation might include the processing of sickness absence information in order to comply with obligations relating to statutory sick pay.

(2) The Secretary of State may by order-

    (a) exclude the application of sub-paragraph (1) in such cases as may be specified, or

(b) provide that, in such cases as may be specified, the condition in sub-paragraph (1) is not to be regarded as satisfied unless such further conditions as may be specified in the order are also satisfied.

> 2.   *(2) The Secretary of State may set out circumstances in which this condition will not apply, or will only apply if further conditions are also satisfied.*

3. The processing is necessary-

(a) in order to protect the vital interests of the data subject or another person, in a case where-
  (i) consent cannot be given by or on behalf of the data subject, or
  (ii) the data controller cannot reasonably be expected to obtain the consent of the data subject, or
(b) in order to protect the vital interests of another person, in a case where consent by or on behalf of the data subject has been unreasonably withheld.

> 3.   *Vital interests: see Sch 2, para 4 above. This condition may be applied not merely to the vital interests of the data subject (as in Schedule 2) but also to another person. It is difficult to envisage circumstances in which this condition would apply. There could be a situation in which the survival of an individual depends upon the disclosure of the mental health or criminal record of another individual. Even if the data subject refuses to consent to such a disclosure, such a disclosure will nevertheless be allowable in rare circumstances. See also para 8 - processing for medical purposes.*

4. The processing-

(a) is carried out in the course of its legitimate activities by any body or association which-
  (i) is not established or conducted for profit, and
  (ii) exists for political, philosophical, religious or trade-union purposes,
(b) is carried out with appropriate safeguards for the rights and freedoms of data subjects,
(c) relates only to individuals who either are members of the body or association or have regular contact with it in connection with its purposes, and
(d) does not involve disclosure of the personal data to a third party without the consent of the data subject.

> *4. Trade unions, political and religious (or similar) groups logically have to be provided with special rights as far as the processing of sensitive personal data is concerned because the very fact that their members share their beliefs is a matter of sensitive personal data. Such groups should be careful that, in relying on this condition, they do not process sensitive personal data relating to anyone other than their members or quasi-members. Groups which are established in order to make profit cannot benefit from this condition. Each of the sub-paragraphs (a) to (d) must apply for this condition to be satisfied.*

5. The information contained in the personal data has been made public as a result of steps deliberately taken by the data subject.

> *5. If no other condition applies, data controllers can check to see whether the data subject has deliberately made public that aspect of their sensitive personal data which the data controller intends to process or is processing.*

6. The processing-

   (a) is necessary for the purpose of, or in connection with, any legal proceedings (including prospective legal proceedings),
   (b) is necessary for the purpose of obtaining legal advice, or
   (c) is otherwise necessary for the purposes of establishing, exercising or defending legal rights.

> *6. This would enable employers to disclose sensitive personal data to appropriate persons, say, in relation to whether an employee is suffering from a disability within the meaning of section 1 of the Disability Discrimination Act 1995. It would also enable them to disclose details contained in an employee's personnel file in order to defend an employment tribunal claim. The scope of this condition may however be narrowed by order of the Secretary of State.*

7.– (1) The processing is necessary-

   (a) for the administration of justice,
   (b) for the exercise of any functions conferred on any person by or under an enactment, or
   (c) for the exercise of any functions of the Crown, a Minister of the Crown or a government department.

(2) The Secretary of State may by order-

    (a) exclude the application of sub-paragraph (1) in such cases as may be specified, or

    (b) provide that, in such cases as may be specified, the condition in sub-paragraph (1) is not to be regarded as satisfied unless such further conditions as may be specified in the order are also satisfied.

8.– (1) The processing is necessary for medical purposes and is undertaken by-

    (a) a health professional, or

    (b) a person who in the circumstances owes a duty of confidentiality which is equivalent to that which would arise if that person were a health professional.

(2) In this paragraph "medical purposes" includes the purposes of preventative medicine, medical diagnosis, medical research, the provision of care and treatment and the management of healthcare services.

> 8. *"Medical purposes": see sub-paragraph (2) for full definition.*
>
> *"health professional": see s.69.*

9.– (1) The processing-

    (a) is of sensitive personal data consisting of information as to racial or ethnic origin,

    (b) is necessary for the purpose of identifying or keeping under review the existence or absence of equality of opportunity or treatment between persons of different racial or ethnic origins, with a view to enabling such equality to be promoted or maintained, and

    (c) is carried out with appropriate safeguards for the rights and freedoms of data subjects.

(2) The Secretary of State may by order specify circumstances in which processing falling within sub-paragraph (1)(a) and (b) is, or is not, to be taken for the purposes of sub-paragraph (1)(c) to be carried out with appropriate safeguards for the rights and freedoms of data subjects.

> 9. *Ethnic monitoring exemption: this was proposed by Lord Dholakia, with the support of the Commission for Racial Equality and the CBI's equal opportunities forum. He commented that "equal opportunity has no meaning unless this process is adequately monitored"*[84]. *Data controllers should take care that this information is*
>
> ---
>
> 84   *House of Lords, 16 March 1998*

used for no other purpose than ethnic monitoring if they are to rely on the condition in this paragraph.

10. The personal data are processed in circumstances specified in an order made by the Secretary of State for the purposes of this paragraph.

10.   The Data Protection (Processing of Sensitive Personal Data) Order 2000 (SI 2000/417) specifies ten further circumstances in which the processing of certain categories of sensitive personal data will be fair. They cover processing:

- *for the purposes of prevention or detection of any unlawful act, where seeking the consent of the data subject to the processing would prejudice those purposes;*

- *required to discharge functions which protect members of the public from certain conduct which may not be unlawful (eg dishonesty or mismanagement);*

- *for journalistic, artistic or literary purposes relating to a wide range of conduct (eg unlawful acts, dishonesty, incompetence);*

- *required to discharge functions involving such services as confidential counselling and advice where the consent of the data subject is not obtained for one of the reasons set out in the paragraph;*

- *in certain insurance or occupational pension scheme contexts, where details of particular relatives of the insured or member are required (eg health details of relatives used to calculate the life expectancy of the insured). The data controller must not process the relatives' data in a way which relates to decisions or actions in respect of the relatives, and if the relatives object to the use of their data, no processing should take place;*

- *already under way as at 1 March 2000 in certain insurance and pension contexts. If the data subject objects to the processing, it should be discontinued. The data controller may dispense with the need to obtain explicit consent of the data subject if it is considered necessary so as not to prejudice the insurance or pension purposes;*

- *relating to monitoring of equality between persons with different religious beliefs or between persons of differing physical mental states or conditions;*

- *relating to political opinions by registered political parties, provided such processing does not cause anyone substantial damage or distress;*

- *necessary for research purposes, is unlikely to cause substantial damage or distress to anyone and does not support measures or decisions relating to the data subject without that person's consent;*

- *by the police in the exercise of their duties.*

SCHEDULE 4

CASES WHERE THE EIGHTH PRINCIPLE DOES NOT APPLY

This Schedule lists the cases where it is permissible to transfer data outside the EEA.

1. The data subject has given his consent to the transfer.

1.   As no mention of a requirement for explicit consent is made, it is assumed that implied consent will be sufficient. The Guidelines allude to the view that obtaining a blanket consent from data subjects is unlikely to be sufficient[85]. Therefore it would be wise for transferors of data to obtain consent from relevant data subjects to transfer their personal data to specified countries. As discussed in the Introduction (see "Processing personal data - the major provisions of the New Act"), such consent could be obtained contractually and perhaps via the use of a tick box. See the Commissioner's guidance notes "International Transfers of Personal Data" and "The Eighth Data Protection Principle and Transborder for Dataflows" for details about what will be likely to constitute valid consent. These notes provide useful guidance on the way in which Schedule 4 exemptions should be considered only as part of the assessment of adequacy for the protection of data when transferring overseas.

---

[85]   *Guidelines, Chapter 3, para 1.6 (via Chapter 3, para 8.4)*

2. The transfer is necessary-

   (a) for the performance of a contract between the data subject and the data controller, or

   (b) for the taking of steps at the request of the data subject with a view to his entering into a contract with the data controller.

3. The transfer is necessary-

   (a) for the conclusion of a contract between the data controller and a person other than the data subject which-

     (i) is entered into at the request of the data subject, or

     (ii) is in the interests of the data subject, or

(b) for the performance of such a contract.

4.– (1) The transfer is necessary for reasons of substantial public interest.

(2) The Secretary of State may by order specify-

    (a) circumstances in which a transfer is to be taken for the purposes of sub-paragraph (1) to be necessary for reasons of substantial public interest, and

    (b) circumstances in which a transfer which is not required by or under an enactment is not to be taken for the purpose of sub-paragraph (1) to be necessary for reasons of substantial public interest.

5. The transfer-

    (a) is necessary for the purpose of, or in connection with, any legal proceedings (including prospective legal proceedings),

    (b) is necessary for the purpose of obtaining legal advice, or

    (c) is otherwise necessary for the purposes of establishing, exercising or defending legal rights.

6. The transfer is necessary in order to protect the vital interests of the data subject.

7. The transfer is of part of the personal data on a public register and any conditions subject to which the register is open to inspection are complied with by any person to whom the data are or may be disclosed after the transfer.

8. The transfer is made on terms which are of a kind approved by the Commissioner as ensuring adequate safeguards for the rights and freedoms of data subjects.

8. The Confederation of British Industry and the International Chamber of Commerce have both produced a standard form contract suitable to be entered into by transferors and transferees of personal data. Both have been considered by the European Commission but, at the time of writing, have yet to be approved by either the European Commission or the Commissioner.

Both contracts substantially reproduce the requirements of the Act imposed upon data controllers so as to achieve the necessary level of protection for the rights and freedoms of individuals required by the eighth principle. As a result, they may appear onerous to companies in non-EEA countries. It may be that the contracts (if approved) are only suitable for inter-company transfers of personal data.

See also the Introduction, in which the European Commission's publication of model clauses is discussed.

9. The transfer has been authorised by the Commissioner as being made in such a manner as to ensure adequate safeguards for the rights and freedoms of data subjects.

9.   *See comments on adequacy of security and the "Safe harbour" provisions at Schedule 1, Part II, Paras 13 to 15.*

SCHEDULE 5

The Information Commissioner and the Data Protection Tribunal

Part I

The Commissioner

Status and capacity

1.– (1) The corporation sole by the name of the Data Protection Registrar established by the Data Protection Act 1984 shall continue in existence by the name of the Information Commissioner.

(2) The Commissioner and his officers and staff are not to be regarded as servants or agents of the Crown.

Tenure of office

2.– (1) Subject to the provisions of this paragraph, the Commissioner shall hold office for such term not exceeding five years as may be determined at the time of his appointment.

(2) The Commissioner may be relieved of his office by Her Majesty at his own request.

(3) The Commissioner may be removed from office by Her Majesty in pursuance of an Address from both Houses of Parliament.

(4) The Commissioner shall in any case vacate his office-

(a) on completing the year of service in which he attains the age of sixty-five years, or

(b) if earlier, on completing his fifteenth year of service.

(5) Subject to sub-paragraph (4), a person who ceases to be Commissioner on the expiration of his term of office shall be eligible for re-appointment, but a person may not be re-appointed for a third or subsequent term as Commissioner unless, by reason of special circumstances, the person's re-appointment for such a term is desirable in the public interest.

Salary etc.

3.– (1) There shall be paid-

(a) to the Commissioner such salary, and

(b) to or in respect of the Commissioner such pension,

as may be specified by a resolution of the House of Commons.

(2) A resolution for the purposes of this paragraph may-

(a) specify the salary or pension,

(b) provide that the salary or pension is to be the same as, or calculated on the same basis as, that payable to, or to or in respect of, a person employed in a specified office under, or in a specified capacity in the service of, the Crown, or

(c) specify the salary or pension and provide for it to be increased by reference to such variables as may be specified in the resolution.

(3) A resolution for the purposes of this paragraph may take effect from the date on which it is passed or from any earlier or later date specified in the resolution.

(4) A resolution for the purposes of this paragraph may make different provision in relation to the pension payable to or in respect of different holders of the office of Commissioner.

(5) Any salary or pension payable under this paragraph shall be charged on and issued out of the Consolidated Fund.

(6) In this paragraph "pension" includes an allowance or gratuity and any reference to the payment of a pension includes a reference to the making of payments towards the provision of a pension.

Officers and staff

4.– (1) The Commissioner-

(a) shall appoint a deputy commissioner, and

(b) may appoint such number of other officers and staff as he may determine.

(2) The remuneration and other conditions of service of the persons appointed under this paragraph shall be determined by the Commissioner.

(3) The Commissioner may pay such pensions, allowances or gratuities to or in respect of the persons appointed under this paragraph, or make such payments towards the provision of such pensions, allowances or gratuities, as he may determine.

(4) The references in sub-paragraph (3) to pensions, allowances or gratuities to or in respect of the persons appointed under this paragraph include references to pensions, allowances or gratuities by way of compensation to or in respect of any of those persons who suffer loss of office or employment.

(5) Any determination under sub-paragraph (1)(b), (2) or (3) shall require the approval of the Secretary of State.

(6) The Employers' Liability (Compulsory Insurance) Act 1969 shall not require insurance to be effected by the Commissioner.

5.– (1) The deputy commissioner shall perform the functions conferred by this Act on the Commissioner during any vacancy in that office or at any time when the Commissioner is for any reason unable to act.

(2) Without prejudice to sub-paragraph (1), any functions of the Commissioner under this Act may, to the extent authorised by him, be performed by any of his officers or staff.

Authentication of seal of the Commissioner

6. The application of the seal of the Commissioner shall be authenticated by his signature or by the signature of some other person authorised for the purpose.

Presumption of authenticity of documents issued by the Commissioner

7. Any document purporting to be an instrument issued by the Commissioner and to be duly executed under the Commissioner's seal or to be signed by or on behalf of the Commissioner shall be received in evidence and shall be deemed to be such an instrument unless the contrary is shown.

Money

8. The Secretary of State may make payments to the Commissioner out of money provided by Parliament.

9.– (1) All fees and other sums received by the Commissioner in the exercise of his functions under this Act or section 159 of the Consumer Credit Act 1974 shall be paid by him to the Secretary of State.

(2) Sub-paragraph (1) shall not apply where the Secretary of State, with the consent of the Treasury, otherwise directs.

(3) Any sums received by the Secretary of State under sub-paragraph (1) shall be paid into the Consolidated Fund.

Accounts

10.– (1) It shall be the duty of the Commissioner-

   (a) to keep proper accounts and other records in relation to the accounts,
   (b) to prepare in respect of each financial year a statement of account in such form as the Secretary of State may direct, and
   (c) to send copies of that statement to the Comptroller and Auditor General on or before 31st August next following the end of the year to which the statement relates or on or before such earlier date after the end of that year as the Treasury may direct.

(2) The Comptroller and Auditor General shall examine and certify any statement sent to him under this paragraph and lay copies of it together with his report thereon before each House of Parliament.

(3) In this paragraph "financial year" means a period of twelve months beginning with 1st April.

Application of Part I in Scotland

11. Paragraphs 1(1), 6 and 7 do not extend to Scotland.

PART II

THE TRIBUNAL

See above s.6 and s.28

Tenure of office

12.– (1) Subject to the following provisions of this paragraph, a member of the Tribunal shall hold and vacate his office in accordance with the terms of his appointment and shall, on ceasing to hold office, be eligible for re-appointment.

(2) Any member of the Tribunal may at any time resign his office by notice in writing to the Lord Chancellor (in the case of the chairman or a deputy chairman) or to the Secretary of State (in the case of any other member).

(3) A person who is the chairman or deputy chairman of the Tribunal shall vacate his office on the day on which he attains the age of seventy years; but this sub-paragraph is subject to section 26(4) to (6) of the Judicial Pensions and Retirement Act 1993 (power to authorise continuance in office up to the age of seventy-five years).

12. Members of the Tribunal must have been legally qualified for at least 7 years (see s.6(5)). The tribunal will consist of a chairman, deputy chairmen and other members (see s.6(4)).

Salary etc.

13. The Secretary of State shall pay to the members of the Tribunal out of money provided by Parliament such remuneration and allowances as he may determine.

Officers and staff

14. The Secretary of State may provide the Tribunal with such officers and staff as he thinks necessary for the proper discharge of its functions.

Expenses

15. Such expenses of the Tribunal as the Secretary of State may determine shall be defrayed by the Secretary of State out of money provided by Parliament.

Part III

Transitional provisions

16. Any reference in any enactment, instrument or other document to the Data Protection Registrar shall be construed, in relation to any time after the commencement of section 6(1), as a reference to the Commissioner.

17. Any reference in this Act or in any instrument under this Act to the Commissioner shall be construed, in relation to any time before the commencement of section 6(1), as a reference to the Data Protection Registrar.

SCHEDULE 6

Appeal proceedings

See s.48 and s.28(12).

Hearing of appeals

1. For the purpose of hearing and determining appeals or any matter preliminary or incidental to an appeal the Tribunal shall sit at such times and in such places as the chairman or a deputy chairman may direct and may sit in two or more divisions.

Constitution of Tribunal in national security cases

2.– (1) The Lord Chancellor shall from time to time designate, from among the chairman and deputy chairmen appointed by him under section 6(4)(a) and (b), those persons who are to be capable of hearing appeals under section 28(4) or (6).

2(1) The appeal panel in national security cases will be specially constituted.

A Minister of the Crown (see s.28(10)) may issue a certificate certifying that certain exemptions from the Act apply in relation to the processing of personal data where national security issues are at stake. Ss.28(4) and (6) concern appeals to the Tribunal either to overturn a decision to issue a certificate or for a determination that a certificate does not apply to the processing of particular personal data.

(2) A designation under sub-paragraph (1) may at any time be revoked by the Lord Chancellor.

3. In any case where the application of paragraph 6(1) is excluded by rules under paragraph 7, the Tribunal shall be duly constituted for an appeal under section 28(4) or (6) if it consists of three of the persons designated under paragraph 2(1), of whom one shall be designated by the Lord Chancellor to preside.

Constitution of Tribunal in other cases

4.– (1) Subject to any rules made under paragraph 7, the Tribunal shall be duly constituted for an appeal under section 48(1), (2) or (4) if it consists of-

(a) the chairman or a deputy chairman (who shall preside), and
(b) an equal number of the members appointed respectively in accordance with paragraphs (a) and (b) of section 6(6).

> *4(1) The references to s48(1), (2) or (4) are to the following:*
>
> *S.48(1): an appeal brought by a person served with an enforcement notice, information notice or special information notice;*
>
> *S.48(2): an appeal brought by a person served with an enforcement notice who has been refused an application to cancel or vary the notice under section 41(2);*
>
> *S.48(4): an appeal brought by a data controller who has received a determination concerning improper processing in relation to the special purposes under section 45.*

(2) The members who are to constitute the Tribunal in accordance with sub-paragraph (1) shall be nominated by the chairman or, if he is for any reason unable to act, by a deputy chairman.

Determination of questions by full Tribunal

5. The determination of any question before the Tribunal when constituted in accordance with paragraph 3 or 4 shall be according to the opinion of the majority of the members hearing the appeal.

> *5. The appeal will be decided by a majority.*

Ex parte proceedings

6.– (1) Subject to any rules made under paragraph 7, the jurisdiction of the Tribunal in respect of an appeal under section 28(4) or (6) shall be exercised ex parte by one or more persons designated under paragraph 2(1).

> 6. *Ex parte proceedings are those which are brought by one party without hearing from the other. They are likely to be reserved for urgent cases. This paragraph allows the Tribunal to hear such appeals.*
>
> *6(1): S.28(4) and (6): see note to para 2(1) above.*

(2) Subject to any rules made under paragraph 7, the jurisdiction of the Tribunal in respect of an appeal under section 48(3) shall be exercised ex parte by the chairman or a deputy chairman sitting alone.

> *6(2):S.48(3): an enforcement notice, information notice or special information notice may contain a statement requiring compliance with the notice as a matter of urgency. Reasons will be given for this in the statement. An appeal can be lodged against the statement and its effect, even if there is no appeal against the notice itself.*

Rules of procedure

7.– (1) The Secretary of State may make rules for regulating the exercise of the rights of appeal conferred by sections 28(4) or (6) and 48 and the practice and procedure of the Tribunal.

> *7(1):S.28(4) and (6): see note to para 2(1) above.*
>
> S.48: *this deals with the right of appeal against notices, statements and determinations under s.45.*

(2) Rules under this paragraph may in particular make provision-

   (a) with respect to the period within which an appeal can be brought and the burden of proof on an appeal,

   (b) for the summoning (or, in Scotland, citation) of witnesses and the administration of oaths,

(c) for securing the production of documents and material used for the processing of personal data,

(d) for the inspection, examination, operation and testing of any equipment or material used in connection with the processing of personal data,

(e) for the hearing of an appeal wholly or partly in camera,

(f) for hearing an appeal in the absence of the appellant or for determining an appeal without a hearing,

(g) for enabling an appeal under section 48(1) against an information notice to be determined by the chairman or a deputy chairman,

(h) for enabling any matter preliminary or incidental to an appeal to be dealt with by the chairman or a deputy chairman,

(i) for the awarding of costs or, in Scotland, expenses,

(j) for the publication of reports of the Tribunal's decisions, and

(k) for conferring on the Tribunal such ancillary powers as the Secretary of State thinks necessary for the proper discharge of its functions.

(3) In making rules under this paragraph which relate to appeals under section 28(4) or (6) the Secretary of State shall have regard, in particular, to the need to secure that information is not disclosed contrary to the public interest.

7(2) & (3)The rules referred to above are currently contained within two sets of rules, The Data Protection Tribunal (Enforcement Appeals) Rules 2000 (SI 2000/189) (referred to below as "The Appeals Rules") and The Data Protection Tribunal (National Security Appeals) Rules 2000 (SI 2000/206) (referred to below as "The National Security Appeals Rules").

The Appeals Rules - SI 2000/189
These rules regulate the exercise of rights of appeal against decisions of the Commissioner and the practice and procedure of the Information Commissioner in such cases.

Among other things, the rules:

- *require an appeal to be made by notice of appeal served on the Tribunal, stating the grounds of appeal and other specified particulars (rule 3);*

- *provide that the notice of appeal must be served within 28 days of the date on which the appellant received the Commissioner's decision (rule 4);*

- *allow the Commissioner to apply for the appeal to be struck out in limited circumstances (rule 7);*

- *allow parties to amend pleadings (rule 8);*

- *provide for the Tribunal to give directions (rule 11);*

- *allow the appeal to proceed without a hearing (rule 13);*

- *deal with issues such as the attendance of witnesses, the conduct of proceedings at a hearing, the powers of the chairman to act for the Tribunal, evidence, the determination of appeals and costs (rules 15, 20, 21, 23, 24 and 25).*

The National Security Appeals Rules - SI 2000/206
These rules regulate the exercise of the rights of appeal conferred by s.28 and the practice and procedure of the Data Protection Tribunal in such cases.

Many of the rules are similar to the Appeals Rules, although the National Security Appeals Rules provide certain powers and duties to the Minister responsible for certifying that the exemptions under s.28(2) would apply on grounds of national security. The Minister:

- *must provide a notice in reply to the notice of appeal (rule 7);*

- *may object, on national security grounds, to the disclosure of his notice of reply (rule 12);*

- *may apply, on national security grounds, for the Tribunal to reconsider proposals to exercise certain of its powers (rule 16).*

Obstruction etc.

8.– (1) If any person is guilty of any act or omission in relation to proceedings before the Tribunal which, if those proceedings were proceedings before a court having power to commit for contempt, would constitute contempt of court, the Tribunal may certify the offence to the High Court or, in Scotland, the Court of Session.

(2) Where an offence is so certified, the court may inquire into the matter and, after hearing any witness who may be produced against or on behalf of the person charged with the offence, and after hearing any statement that may be offered in defence, deal with him in any manner in which it could deal with him if he had committed the like offence in relation to the court.

SCHEDULE 7

Miscellaneous exemptions

Some of the exemptions available under the 1984 Act are no longer available: for example, there are no longer exemptions for payroll, pensions and accounts purposes, for unincorporated members' clubs, nor for certain types of mailing lists. For some of these, the transitional provisions will allow a breathing space before the entirety of the Act has to be applied. The Secretary of State may grant further exemptions under s.38.

Confidential references given by the data controller

1. Personal data are exempt from section 7 if they consist of a reference given or to be given in confidence by the data controller for the purposes of-

   (a) the education, training or employment, or prospective education, training or employment, of the data subject,

   (b) the appointment, or prospective appointment, of the data subject to any office, or

   (c) the provision, or prospective provision, by the data subject of any service.

1.   Confidential references: this exemption will not apply to confidential references prepared by a person who is not the data controller. For instance, if an employer holds on an employee's personnel file a confidential reference provided by that employee's former employer, the current employer cannot rely on this exemption to avoid making disclosure to the employee. What the current employer should do is firstly check with the individual who provided the reference that he or she has no objection to its being disclosed. If the referee does object, the current employer should see whether the reference could be disclosed without revealing the identity of the referee, or whether any information which indicates the identity of the referee can be blocked out. If, having addressed the problem in this way, the conclusion is drawn that the reference cannot be disclosed without revealing information which identifies the referee, the current employer is not obliged to comply with the request to disclose the reference (see s.7(4) to (6) for details).

1.   (c) this sub-paragraph covers those individuals and organisations which provide confidential references about data subjects who do business on their own account.

Armed forces

2. Personal data are exempt from the subject information provisions in any case to the extent to which the application of those provisions would be likely to prejudice the combat effectiveness of any of the armed forces of the Crown.

> *2. "subject information provisions": the exemption relates to paras 2 and 3 of the fair processing code, requiring data controllers to provide certain information to data subjects (Sch 1, Part II, paras 1 - 4) and subject access (s.7). A definition is provided in s.27(2). Those seeking to rely on this exemption will still have to demonstrate that the subject information provisions would be likely to prejudice the "combat effectiveness" of the armed forces.*

Judicial appointments and honours

3. Personal data processed for the purposes of-

   (a) assessing any person's suitability for judicial office or the office of Queen's Counsel, or
   (b) the conferring by the Crown of any honour,

are exempt from the subject information provisions.

Crown employment and Crown or Ministerial appointments

4. The Secretary of State may by order exempt from the subject information provisions personal data processed for the purposes of assessing any person's suitability for-

   (a) employment by or under the Crown, or
   (b) any office to which appointments are made by Her Majesty, by a Minister of the Crown or by a Northern Ireland department.

> *4. The Data Protection (Crown Appointments) Order 2000 (SI 2000/416) exempts from the subject information provisions (see s.27(2)) processing of personal data for the purposes of assessing any person's suitability for certain offices to which appointments are made by Her Majesty The Queen. Included in the schedule of offices are religious appointments, the Provost of Eton, the Poet Laureate and the Astronomer Royal.*

Management forecasts etc.

5. Personal data processed for the purposes of management forecasting or management planning to assist the data controller in the conduct of any business or other activity are exempt from the subject information provisions in any case to the extent to which the application of those provisions would be likely to prejudice the conduct of that business or other activity.

> *5.   Issues contemplated under this exemption include redundancies, long-term career prospects, company mergers and takeovers. The exemption only applies if providing subject information would be likely to prejudice the conduct of the business or activity of the data controller.*

Corporate finance

6.– (1) Where personal data are processed for the purposes of, or in connection with, a corporate finance service provided by a relevant person-

(a) the data are exempt from the subject information provisions in any case to the extent to which either-
  (i) the application of those provisions to the data could affect the price of any instrument which is already in existence or is to be or may be created, or
  (ii) the data controller reasonably believes that the application of those provisions to the data could affect the price of any such instrument, and
(b) to the extent that the data are not exempt from the subject information provisions by virtue of paragraph (a), they are exempt from those provisions if the exemption is required for the purpose of safeguarding an important economic or financial interest of the United Kingdom.

> *6.   The purpose of this exemption is to ensure that personal data in connection with corporate finance services can be processed without jeopardising the price or value of particular instruments such as stocks, futures or annuities (see sub-paragraph (3) below).*
>
> *6.(1) "corporate finance service": e.g. underwriting or issuing shares; advising on industrial strategy or providing services relating to mergers and acquisitions (see definition in (3) below).*
>
> *"relevant person": e.g. a person who is regulated under the Financial Services Act 1986 or an employee or partner who undertakes corporate finance work (see definition in (3) below).*

The exemption will not apply unless either the price of the instrument might be affected by applying the subject information provisions or an important economic or financial interest of the UK needs protecting. Also, the corporate finance service must be provided by a "relevant person" for the exemption to apply.

(2) For the purposes of sub-paragraph (1)(b) the Secretary of State may by order specify-

(a) matters to be taken into account in determining whether exemption from the subject information provisions is required for the purpose of safeguarding an important economic or financial interest of the United Kingdom, or

(b) circumstances in which exemption from those provisions is, or is not, to be taken to be required for that purpose.

6.(2) The Data Protection (Corporate Finance Exemption) Order 2000 (SI 2000/184) permits exemption from the subject information provisions (see s.27(2)) for the purpose of safeguarding "an important economic or financial interest of the United Kingdom".

Where:

- *the application of subject information provisions may have a prejudicial effect on the orderly functioning of financial markets or the efficient allocation of capital within the economy; and*

- *the data in question are data to which the application of the subject information provisions could, in the reasonable belief of the relevant person (as defined at sub-para (3)), affect decisions whether to deal in, subscribe for or issue instruments or decisions which are likely to affect any business activity*

the exemption to the subject information provisions applies.

(3) In this paragraph-

"corporate finance service" means a service consisting in-

(a) underwriting in respect of issues of, or the placing of issues of, any instrument,

(b) advice to undertakings on capital structure, industrial strategy and related matters and advice and service relating to mergers and the purchase of undertakings, or

(c) services relating to such underwriting as is mentioned in paragraph (a);

"instrument" means any instrument listed in section B of the Annex to the Council Directive on investment services in the securities field (93/22/EEC), as set out in Schedule 1 to the Investment Services Regulations 1995;

"price" includes value;

"relevant person" means-

(a) any person who is authorised under Chapter III of Part I of the Financial Services Act 1986 or is an exempted person under Chapter IV of Part I of that Act,

(b) any person who, but for Part III or IV of Schedule 1 to that Act, would require authorisation under that Act,

(c) any European investment firm within the meaning given by Regulation 3 of the Investment Services Regulations 1995,

(d) any person who, in the course of his employment, provides to his employer a service falling within paragraph (b) or (c) of the definition of "corporate finance service", or

(e) any partner who provides to other partners in the partnership a service falling within either of those paragraphs.

6.(3) "instrument": SI 1995/3275 - the Investment Services Regulations 1995: Schedule 1 Section B lists instruments, such as transferable securities and interest-rate, currency and equity swaps.

Negotiations

7. Personal data which consist of records of the intentions of the data controller in relation to any negotiations with the data subject are exempt from the subject information provisions in any case to the extent to which the application of those provisions would be likely to prejudice those negotiations.

7. Negotiations: e.g. negotiations over pay increases, severance packages, redundancy payments. If applying the subject information provisions would be unlikely to prejudice the negotiations, this exemption cannot be relied upon.

Possible future negotiations may also be protected under this paragraph. Geoff Hoon MP gave the example of an insurance company recording on the file of a customer the maximum at which it would be prepared to settle if a claim were made in future. Disclosure of that piece of information to the customer would frustrate any prospective negotiations. He added that "it would not matter that the negotiations had not yet started. It is sufficient for the prospect to exist of negotiation at some future time".[86]

---

[86]   *House of Commons, Standing Committee D, 4 June 1998*

Examination marks

8.– (1) Section 7 shall have effect subject to the provisions of sub-paragraphs (2) to (4) in the case of personal data consisting of marks or other information processed by a data controller-

(a) for the purpose of determining the results of an academic, professional or other examination or of enabling the results of any such examination to be determined, or

(b) in consequence of the determination of any such results.

---

8.   Examination marks: this paragraph extends the time limit for complying with a subject information request, as set out in s.7. It is not an exemption as such.

8.(1) "marks or other information": any commentary made by the examiner about the examinee's performance and the consequences of that performance will constitute "personal data".

---

(2) Where the relevant day falls before the day on which the results of the examination are announced, the period mentioned in section 7(8) shall be extended until-

(a) the end of five months beginning with the relevant day, or

(b) the end of forty days beginning with the date of the announcement,

whichever is the earlier.

8.(2) "relevant day": the day on which the request is made. It is often not practicable for an examination board to provide students with their results within a 40 day period.

8.(2)(b) Within 40 days of the results being announced (or within 5 months of the request, whichever is earlier), the data controller must provide other information, e.g. a commentary on that individual's performance or other personal data in connection with the examination.

(3) Where by virtue of sub-paragraph (2) a period longer than the prescribed period elapses after the relevant day before the request is complied with, the information to be supplied pursuant to the request shall be supplied both by reference to the data in question at the time when the request is received and (if different) by reference to the data as from time to time held in the period beginning when the request is received and ending when it is complied with.

> *8.(3) If more than 40 days pass between the date of the request and the provision of requested information, the data controller must provide further information, if the information which is the subject of the request has changed between the date of request and date of compliance. Subject to the script forming part of a "relevant filing system" (see s.1), an examination candidate will be entitled to be notified of any expressions of opinion recorded on the examination script. Candidates will not be entitled to an explanation about the marking system for an examination, because this will not constitute "personal data".*

(4) For the purposes of this paragraph the results of an examination shall be treated as announced when they are first published or (if not published) when they are first made available or communicated to the candidate in question.

(5) In this paragraph-

"examination" includes any process for determining the knowledge, intelligence, skill or ability of a candidate by reference to his performance in any test, work or other activity;

"the prescribed period" means forty days or such other period as is for the time being prescribed under section 7 in relation to the personal data in question;

"relevant day" has the same meaning as in section 7.

Examination scripts etc.

9.– (1) Personal data consisting of information recorded by candidates during an academic, professional or other examination are exempt from section 7.

(2) In this paragraph "examination" has the same meaning as in paragraph 8.

> *9.   Examination scripts etc: Candidates do not have the right to see their scripts once they have been handed in for marking. Nevertheless, they do have a right to certain information from the data controller, such as expressions of opinion about their performance if such opinions are recorded on the script and form part of a relevant filing system. See para 8(3).*

Legal professional privilege

10. Personal data are exempt from the subject information provisions if the data consist of information in respect of which a claim to legal professional privilege or, in Scotland, to confidentiality as between client and professional legal adviser, could be maintained in legàl proceedings.

> *10. Legal professional privilege: e.g. if a solicitor disclosed personal data relating to a third party in correspondence to a client, that third party would have no right to see that correspondence.*

Self-incrimination

11.– (1) A person need not comply with any request or order under section 7 to the extent that compliance would, by revealing evidence of the commission of any offence other than an offence under this Act, expose him to proceedings for that offence.

(2) Information disclosed by any person in compliance with any request or order under section 7 shall not be admissible against him in proceedings for an offence under this Act.

SCHEDULE 8

TRANSITIONAL RELIEF

PART I

INTERPRETATION OF SCHEDULE

> *There are two transitional periods: the first is up to but excluding 24 October 2001; the second from 24 October 2001 up to but excluding 24 October 2007. The first relates to certain types of automated and manual data; the second to certain types of manual data only.*
>
> *Given the difficulties of administering two regimes (one of which can take advantage of the transitional provisions and one of which cannot), data controllers may prefer to work on the assumption that the Act applies to all forms of processing.*
>
> *Data controllers should consider the provisions contained in this Schedule at the time of contemplating what to do about new and existing data.*

1.– (1) For the purposes of this Schedule, personal data are "eligible data" at any time if, and to the extent that, they are at that time subject to processing which was already under way immediately before 24th October 1998.

---

1.   (1) "subject to processing which was already under way": this is not specifically defined in the Act, although the meaning of this has been subjected to a great deal of parliamentary debate. Lord Williams of Mostyn (then Parliamentary Under-Secretary of State to the Home Office) wrote that the Government believed that this expression includes, among other things:

- *amendments to existing personal data;*

- *the addition of personal data on existing data subjects;*

- *the addition of personal data on new data subjects;*

- *essential program and software changes to enable such processing to continue.[87]*

The Guidelines recognise the wide definition of "processing" under the Act and the potential interpretation that any new action carried out on data after 24 October 1998 might fall outside the notion of "processing which was already under way". It provides the helpful guidance: "Where processing is different, but does not produce a new effect or result in terms of the data controller's overall processing operation, it is likely to be processing already under way".[88] This can be split into two questions: (a) is the processing different? (b) does it produce a new effect?

(a)   Is the processing different?

If data controllers are doing any of the following, it is likely that the processing will be different:

- *processing for a new purpose or purposes;*

- *changing the categories of data subject or recipient;*

- *changing the storage or destruction criteria.*

(b)   Does it produce a new effect?

If the processing is different, data controllers should consider its effect on the overall processing operation. For example, is the processing:

- *outside the data controller's normal range of activities?*

- *carried out in order to achieve a new objective?*

- *likely to produce a different effect on the data subject or result in a different application of the data?*

---

87   *House of Lords, 14 May 1998 - Written answers in response to a question put by Viscount Astor.*

88   *Guidelines, Chapter 6, para 2.2*

The Guidelines make it clear that the above list is not exhaustive and that other factors may need to be taken into account depending on the circumstances of the case.[89]

The Guidelines also recognise the difficulties which data controllers may encounter in trying to ascertain whether the data which they intend to process is "eligible" or not. If the Commissioner needs to decide upon this question, she will seek relevant information from the data controller and draw her own conclusions, which may differ from those of the data controller. Before taking enforcement action, the Commissioner will look at the question of the possible effect on individuals and whether damage or distress is likely to be or has been caused. Data controllers are nevertheless warned that a data subject is still free to pursue his/her own remedy through the courts.

"immediately before": this is not specifically defined. To take advantage of the transitional provisions, data controllers can only rely on processing in existence immediately before 24 October 1998; if the processing was carried out previously but had ceased on 24 October 1998, the transitional provisions are not available.

Except in relation to the second transitional period, the personal data which are subjected to the processing do not have to have been in existence prior to 24 October 1998. It is the processing which must have been already under way at that time.

---

89   *Guidelines, Chapter 6, para 2.2*

---

(2) In this Schedule-

"eligible automated data" means eligible data which fall within paragraph (a) or (b) of the definition of

"data" in section 1(1);

"eligible manual data" means eligible data which are not eligible automated data;

"the first transitional period" means the period beginning with the commencement of this Schedule and ending with 23rd October 2001;

"the second transitional period" means the period beginning with 24th October 2001 and ending with 23rd October 2007.

1.   (2) eligible automated or eligible manual data do not include data which are part of an "accessible record" as defined by s.68 (health record, educational record or accessible public record).

PART II

EXEMPTIONS AVAILABLE BEFORE 24TH OCTOBER 2001

Manual data

2.– (1) Eligible manual data, other than data forming part of an accessible record, are exempt from the data protection principles and Parts II and III of this Act during the first transitional period.

(2) This paragraph does not apply to eligible manual data to which paragraph 4 applies.

> 2.   (1) *The exemption relates to the data protection principles and Parts II and III of the Act. Parts II and III relate to the rights of data subjects and others and notification requirements; essentially, the Act does not apply to the processing of eligible manual data until 24 October 2001. Slightly different provisions apply with regard to certain eligible manual data processed by credit reference agencies (see sub-paragraph (4)).*

3.– (1) This paragraph applies to-

(a) eligible manual data forming part of an accessible record, and

(b) personal data which fall within paragraph (d) of the definition of "data" in section 1(1) but which, because they are not subject to processing which was already under way immediately before 24th October 1998, are not eligible data for the purposes of this Schedule.

(2) During the first transitional period, data to which this paragraph applies are exempt from-

(a) the data protection principles, except the sixth principle so far as relating to sections 7 and 12A,

(b) Part II of this Act, except-

(i) section 7 (as it has effect subject to section 8) and section 12A, and

(ii) section 15 so far as relating to those sections, and

(c) Part III of this Act.

> 3.   *Accessible records: Eligible manual data forming part of an accessible record, together with personal data (manual and automated) which are not eligible but which also form part of an accessible record, benefit from exemptions under this paragraph. The same exemptions are available as for other categories of eligible manual data except that the data controller must still comply with:*

> - *the data subject's access rights under s.7;*
> - *(prior to 24 October 2007) the data subject's rights to have inaccurate eligible manual data amended (etc) under s.12A (see Sch 13); and*
> - *s.15: where a court may require a data controller to disclose information to a court but not to the data subject or his representative, in a case requiring a court to determine whether a data subject is entitled to the information which he seeks.*

4.– (1) This paragraph applies to eligible manual data which consist of information relevant to the financial standing of the data subject and in respect of which the data controller is a credit reference agency.

(2) During the first transitional period, data to which this paragraph applies are exempt from-

(a) the data protection principles, except the sixth principle so far as relating to sections 7 and 12A,

(b) Part II of this Act, except-
(i) section 7 (as it has effect subject to sections 8 and 9) and section 12A, and
(ii) section 15 so far as relating to those sections, and

(c) Part III of this Act.

> *4.   Credit reference agencies: Eligible manual data relating to the financial standing of the data subject in cases where the data controller is a credit reference agency enjoy the same exemptions as under para 3 above.*

Processing otherwise than by reference to the data subject

5. During the first transitional period, for the purposes of this Act (apart from paragraph 1), eligible automated data are not to be regarded as being "processed" unless the processing is by reference to the data subject.

> *5.   The significance of this paragraph is that if eligible automated data are not processed by reference to the data subject, the Act does not apply until 24 October 2001. For example, if an employee's work performance is discussed at a management meeting and is stored under a computer file under the description "minutes of a meeting", the employee will have no rights of access because the processing has not been carried out by reference to him.*

Payrolls and accounts

> 6.   *Payroll and accounts: This is the first of the exemptions under the 1984 Act which will continue to enjoy an exemption but only until 23 October 2001. See also paras 7 to 12.*

6.– (1) Subject to sub-paragraph (2), eligible automated data processed by a data controller for one or more of the following purposes-

(a) calculating amounts payable by way of remuneration or pensions in respect of service in any employment or office or making payments of, or of sums deducted from, such remuneration or pensions, or

(b) keeping accounts relating to any business or other activity carried on by the data controller or keeping records of purchases, sales or other transactions for the purpose of ensuring that the requisite payments are made by or to him in respect of those transactions or for the purpose of making financial or management forecasts to assist him in the conduct of any such business or activity,

are exempt from the data protection principles and Parts II and III of this Act during the first transitional period.

> 6.   *(1) The data must only be processed for one or more of the following purposes:*
>
> *(a) Payroll:*
>
> - *calculating how much in the way of remuneration or pensions should be paid;*
>
> - *paying remuneration or pensions;*
>
> - *paying amounts deducted from remuneration or pensions.*
>
> *(b) Accounts:*
>
> - *keeping accounts;*
>
> - *keeping records of purchases, sales or other transactions (for specified purposes).*

(2) It shall be a condition of the exemption of any eligible automated data under this paragraph that the data are not processed for any other purpose, but the exemption is not lost by any processing of the eligible data for any other purpose if the data

controller shows that he had taken such care to prevent it as in all the circumstances was reasonably required.

(3) Data processed only for one or more of the purposes mentioned in sub-paragraph (1)(a) may be disclosed-

(a) to any person, other than the data controller, by whom the remuneration or pensions in question are payable,

(b) for the purpose of obtaining actuarial advice,

(c) for the purpose of giving information as to the persons in any employment or office for use in medical research into the health of, or injuries suffered by, persons engaged in particular occupations or working in particular places or areas,

(d) if the data subject (or a person acting on his behalf) has requested or consented to the disclosure of the data either generally or in the circumstances in which the disclosure in question is made, or

(e) if the person making the disclosure has reasonable grounds for believing that the disclosure falls within paragraph (d).

> 6.   (3) *Disclosure for solely payroll purposes can be made in the circumstances listed in (a) to (e).*

(4) Data processed for any of the purposes mentioned in sub-paragraph (1) may be disclosed-

(a) for the purpose of audit or where the disclosure is for the purpose only of giving information about the data controller's financial affairs, or

(b) in any case in which disclosure would be permitted by any other provision of this Part of this Act if sub-paragraph (2) were included among the non-disclosure provisions.

> 6.   (4) *Disclosure for payroll or accounts purposes can be made in the circumstances listed in (a) to (b).*

(5) In this paragraph "remuneration" includes remuneration in kind and "pensions" includes gratuities or similar benefits.

Unincorporated members' clubs and mailing lists

7.   Eligible automated data processed by an unincorporated members' club and relating only to the members of the club are exempt from the data protection principles and Parts II and III of this Act during the first transitional period.

> 7.   The Guidelines state that: "*An unincorporated members' club is a club whose members usually each contribute, by way of an entrance fee or subscription, to the club's funds. The property and funds of the club belong to the members, who manage the club and its property. The conduct of the club's business is usually delegated by the members to committees in accordance with the rules*".[90] *Essentially, eligible automated data under this paragraph are exempt from the Act until 24 October 2001. See Sch 8 para 1 for the definition of "eligible".*
>
> ---
>
> 90   *Guidelines Chapter 6, para 8 (C)*

8.   Eligible automated data processed by a data controller only for the purposes of distributing, or recording the distribution of, articles or information to the data subjects and consisting only of their names, addresses or other particulars necessary for effecting the distribution, are exempt from the data protection principles and Parts II and III of this Act during the first transitional period.

> 8.   *Computerised mailing lists which are "eligible" (see Sch 8 para 1) will largely be exempt from the Act until 24 October 2001. If the data controller obtains a list in order to sell it to another company, he will not benefit from the exemption. Similarly, if the data controller processes more information than is required for the act of distributing information to data subjects (e.g. if he holds details relating to their salary or occupation), the exemption does not apply.*

9.   Neither paragraph 7 nor paragraph 8 applies to personal data relating to any data subject unless he has been asked by the club or data controller whether he objects to the data relating to him being processed as mentioned in that paragraph and has not objected.

> 9.   *Data controllers would be well advised to make specific enquiries of the people on the list or club members to check that they are happy for their details to be processed and keep a record of that fact.*

10. It shall be a condition of the exemption of any data under paragraph 7 that the data are not disclosed except as permitted by paragraph 11 and of the exemption under paragraph 8 that the data are not processed for any purpose other than that mentioned in that paragraph or as permitted by paragraph 11, but-

(a) the exemption under paragraph 7 shall not be lost by any disclosure in breach of that condition, and

(b) the exemption under paragraph 8 shall not be lost by any processing in breach of that condition,

if the data controller shows that he had taken such care to prevent it as in all the circumstances was reasonably required.

> *10. All reasonable care must be taken to limit disclosure to those circumstances set out under para 11, otherwise the exemptions under para 7 and 8 will be lost.*

11. Data to which paragraph 10 applies may be disclosed-

(a) if the data subject (or a person acting on his behalf) has requested or consented to the disclosure of the data either generally or in the circumstances in which the disclosure in question is made,

(b) if the person making the disclosure has reasonable grounds for believing that the disclosure falls within paragraph (a), or

(c) in any case in which disclosure would be permitted by any other provision of this Part of this Act if paragraph 8 were included among the non-disclosure provisions.

Back-up data

12. Eligible automated data which are processed only for the purpose of replacing other data in the event of the latter being lost, destroyed or impaired are exempt from section 7 during the first transitional period.

> *12. Back-up data: "first transitional period": i.e. until 24 October 2001.*

Exemption of all eligible automated data from certain requirements

13.– (1) During the first transitional period, eligible automated data are exempt from the following provisions-

(a) the first data protection principle to the extent to which it requires compliance with-
(i) paragraph 2 of Part II of Schedule 1,
(ii) the conditions in Schedule 2, and
(iii) the conditions in Schedule 3,

(b) the seventh data protection principle to the extent to which it requires compliance with paragraph 12 of Part II of Schedule 1;

(c) the eighth data protection principle,

(d) in section 7(1), paragraphs (b), (c)(ii) and (d),

(e) sections 10 and 11,

(f) section 12, and

(g) section 13, except so far as relating to-

    (i) any contravention of the fourth data protection principle,

    (ii) any disclosure without the consent of the data controller,

    (iii) loss or destruction of data without the consent of the data controller, or

    (iv) processing for the special purposes.

Eligible automated data

13.(1) Processing which is not done by reference to the data subject will be exempt from the Act until 24 October 2001 (see Sch 8 para 5).

All eligible automated data are **subject to** *the following:*

- *1st principle: personal data should still be processed lawfully and fairly - see para 1 and 4 of Schedule 1 Part II. In particular, data controllers should ensure that the person from whom the personal data were obtained was not misled or deceived as to the purpose(s) for which data are to be processed;*

- *2nd-5th principle: (see Sch 1 Part I);*

- *6th principle: significantly, even where the automated data are eligible, certain subject access requirements still apply. The data controller has to supply information as to whether personal data (of which the individual making the request is the subject) are being processed by or on behalf of the data controller. If such personal data are being processed, the data subject is entitled to have that information constituting the personal data communicated to him;*

- *7th principle: most of the principle relating to security measures will apply, so data controllers must ensure a level of security appropriate to the type of data to be protected and to the harm that might be caused by a breach; reasonable steps must be taken to ensure the reliability of employees with access to personal data; and where the data controller uses the services of a data processor, sufficient guarantees must be provided (see Sch 1, Part II, paras 9 to 11).*

- *s.13: compensation for damage and distress is available in the limited circumstances set out in (g)(i) to (iv). The fourth principle relates to personal data being kept accurate and (where necessary) up to date.*

- *s.14: applications to the court for rectification, blocking, erasure or destruction of personal data.*

(2) The specific exemptions conferred by sub-paragraph (1)(a), (c) and (e) do not limit the data controller's general duty under the first data protection principle to ensure that processing is fair.

13.(2) Regardless of the exemptions which apply here, data controllers remain under a general duty to process fairly. Under the 1984 Act, criteria were developed for assessing the fair obtaining of personal data, and are likely to be adopted in respect of the Act.

PART III

EXEMPTIONS AVAILABLE AFTER 23RD OCTOBER 2001
BUT BEFORE 24TH OCTOBER 2007

Second transitional period
14. Eligible manual data.

The Guidelines suggest that in order to ascertain which data can benefit from the second transitional period, data controllers should put in place audit procedures to enable them to identify which data were held by them immediately prior to 24 October 1998.

14.– (1) This paragraph applies to-

(a) eligible manual data which were held immediately before 24th October 1998, and
(b) personal data which fall within paragraph (d) of the definition of "data" in section 1(1) but do not fall within paragraph (a) of this sub-paragraph,

but does not apply to eligible manual data to which the exemption in paragraph 16 applies.

The following categories of data can benefit from this second transitional period:

14. (1) (a) eligible manual data held immediately before 24 October 1998 (with the exception of data held for historical research): i.e. the data themselves must have been held prior to 24 October 1998, so the only data to enjoy this exemption will be data which are at least 3 years old at the start of the second transitional period.

14. (1) (b) accessible records (see s.68) containing personal data. Such records need not have been subject to processing already under way as at 24 October 1998, nor actually held at that time to enjoy this exemption.

14. (1) (b) The data to which this paragraph applies are therefore subject to:

- *the rest of the fair processing code (Sch 1 Pt II paras 1 and 4) and the Schedule 2 and Schedule 3 conditions;*

- *rights of data subjects, security measures, prohibition of transfer outside the EEA (principles 6, 7 and 8);*

- *s.14(4) to (6): data subjects who have suffered damage as a result of a breach of the Act may apply to court for an order for rectification, blocking, erasure or destruction of data.*

(2) During the second transitional period, data to which this paragraph applies are exempt from the following provisions-

(a) the first data protection principle except to the extent to which it requires compliance with paragraph 2 of Part II of Schedule 1,

(b) the second, third, fourth and fifth data protection principles, and

(c) section 14(1) to (3).

PART IV

EXEMPTIONS AFTER 23RD OCTOBER 2001 FOR HISTORICAL RESEARCH

15 to 18: Historical research exemptions: note that these exemptions start only after 23 October 2001 but will last indefinitely.

Prior to 24 October 2001, eligible manual and automated data processed for historical research will be governed by paras 2 and 13 of this Schedule.

See also the exemption under s.33 which may apply.

15. In this Part of this Schedule "the relevant conditions" has the same meaning as in section 33.

15. *"relevant conditions": in relation to any processing of personal data, means the conditions:*

- *that the data are not processed to support measures or decisions with respect to particular individuals, and*

- *that the data are not processed in such a way that substantial damage or substantial distress is, or is likely to be, caused to any data subject.*

16.– (1) Eligible manual data which are processed only for the purpose of historical research in compliance with the relevant conditions are exempt from the provisions specified in sub-paragraph (2) after 23rd October 2001.

(2) The provisions referred to in sub-paragraph (1) are-

    (a) the first data protection principle except in so far as it requires compliance with paragraph 2 of Part II of Schedule 1,

    (b) the second, third, fourth and fifth data protection principles, and

    (c) section 14(1) to (3).

16. *Historical research and eligible manual data:*

16. *(2) The data to which this paragraph applies are therefore* **subject to***:*

- *the rest of the fair processing code (Sch 1 Pt II paras 1 and 4) and the Sch 2 and Sch 3 conditions;*

- *rights of data subjects, security measures, prohibition of transfer outside the EEA (principles 6, 7 and 8);*

- *s.14(4) to (6): data subjects who have suffered damage as a result of a breach of the Act may apply to court for an order for rectification, blocking, erasure or destruction of data.*

17.– (1) After 23rd October 2001 eligible automated data which are processed only for the purpose of historical research in compliance with the relevant conditions are exempt from the first data protection principle to the extent to which it requires compliance with the conditions in Schedules 2 and 3.

(2) Eligible automated data which are processed-

    (a) only for the purpose of historical research,

    (b) in compliance with the relevant conditions, and

    (c) otherwise than by reference to the data subject,

are also exempt from the provisions referred to in sub-paragraph (3) after 23rd October 2001.

(3) The provisions referred to in sub-paragraph (2) are-

    (a) the first data protection principle except in so far as it requires compliance with paragraph 2 of Part II of Schedule 1,

    (b) the second, third, fourth and fifth data protection principles, and

    (c) section 14(1) to (3).

17. Historical research and eligible automated data:

17. (1) Eligible automated data which are processed only for historical research in compliance with the "relevant conditions" and processed by reference to the data subject are exempt from Schedule 2 and Schedule 3 conditions.

17. (2) Eligible automated data which are not processed by reference to the data subject are exempt from the same provisions as eligible manual data in para 16 above in addition to the Schedule 2 and Schedule 3 conditions.

18. For the purposes of this Part of this Schedule personal data are not to be treated as processed otherwise than for the purpose of historical research merely because the data are disclosed-

    (a) to any person, for the purpose of historical research only,

    (b) to the data subject or a person acting on his behalf,

    (c) at the request, or with the consent, of the data subject or a person acting on his behalf, or

    (d) in circumstances in which the person making the disclosure has reasonable grounds for believing that the disclosure falls within paragraph (a), (b) or (c).

18. This ties in with s.33(5). Disclosures limited to the above circumstances will not result in the loss of the exemption.

PART V

EXEMPTION FROM SECTION 22

19. Processing which was already under way immediately before 24th October 1998 is not assessable processing for the purposes of section 22.

Exemption from s.22

19.   Assessable processing:

Any processing which is particularly likely to cause substantial damage or distress to data subjects or significantly prejudice their rights and freedoms can be so specified by means of an order made by the Secretary of State. However, processing can only be "assessable" if it is new processing which began on or after 24 October 1998.

SCHEDULE 9

POWERS OF ENTRY AND INSPECTION

Issue of warrants

1.– (1) If a circuit judge is satisfied by information on oath supplied by the Commissioner that there are reasonable grounds for suspecting-

   (a) that a data controller has contravened or is contravening any of the data protection principles, or

   (b) that an offence under this Act has been or is being committed,

and that evidence of the contravention or of the commission of the offence is to be found on any premises specified in the information, he may, subject to sub-paragraph (2) and paragraph 2, grant a warrant to the Commissioner.

1(1) In Scotland warrants will be issued by the sheriff and in Northern Ireland by a county court judge (see Sch 9, para 14 & 15).

(2) A judge shall not issue a warrant under this Schedule in respect of any personal data processed for the special purposes unless a determination by the Commissioner under section 45 with respect to those data has taken effect.

1(2) s.45 covers the Commissioner's ability to determine whether data are being processed for one of the special purposes (i.e. journalism, artistic or literary purposes).

(3) A warrant issued under sub-paragraph (1) shall authorise the Commissioner or any of his officers or staff at any time within seven days of the date of the warrant to enter the premises, to search them, to inspect, examine, operate and test any equipment found there which is used or intended to be used for the processing of personal data and to inspect and seize any documents or other material found there which may be such evidence as is mentioned in that sub-paragraph.

> *1(3) Employees and agents of the Commissioner are under an obligation to keep confidential any information obtained pursuant to the Act relating to an individual or business (see s.59(1).) Should the Commissioner exercise her right to search premises, inspect, operate and/or test computer equipment, a business should evaluate whether the exceptions to this obligation of confidentiality are likely to apply (see s.59(2)). It would be wise to record precise details of any items which are seized.*
>
> *"Premises" is defined to include a vessel, vehicle, aircraft or hovercraft (see Sch 9, para 13).*

2.– (1) A judge shall not issue a warrant under this Schedule unless he is satisfied-

   (a) that the Commissioner has given seven days' notice in writing to the occupier of the premises in question demanding access to the premises, and
   (b) that either-
      (i) access was demanded at a reasonable hour and was unreasonably refused, or
      (ii) although entry to the premises was granted, the occupier unreasonably refused to comply with a request by the Commissioner or any of the Commissioner's officers or staff to permit the Commissioner or the officer or member of staff to do any of the things referred to in paragraph 1(3), and
   (c) that the occupier, has, after the refusal, been notified by the Commissioner of the application for the warrant and has had an opportunity of being heard by the judge on the question whether or not it should be issued.

(2) Sub-paragraph (1) shall not apply if the judge is satisfied that the case is one of urgency or that compliance with those provisions would defeat the object of the entry.

3. A judge who issues a warrant under this Schedule shall also issue two copies of it and certify them clearly as copies.

Execution of warrants

4. A person executing a warrant issued under this Schedule may use such reasonable force as may be necessary.

> *4   It is a criminal offence to intentionally obstruct or fail without reasonable excuse to assist anyone executing a warrant issued under the Act (see Sch 9, para 12). The offence is triable only in a Magistrates Court and conviction carries a maximum fine of £5,000.*

5. A warrant issued under this Schedule shall be executed at a reasonable hour unless it appears to the person executing it that there are grounds for suspecting that the evidence in question would not be found if it were so executed.

> *5   Presumably a reasonable hour would be normal working office hours.*

6. If the person who occupies the premises in respect of which a warrant is issued under this Schedule is present when the warrant is executed, he shall be shown the warrant and supplied with a copy of it; and if that person is not present a copy of the warrant shall be left in a prominent place on the premises.

7.– (1) A person seizing anything in pursuance of a warrant under this Schedule shall give a receipt for it if asked to do so.

(2) Anything so seized may be retained for so long as is necessary in all the circumstances but the person in occupation of the premises in question shall be given a copy of anything that is seized if he so requests and the person executing the warrant considers that it can be done without undue delay.

Matters exempt from inspection and seizure

8. The powers of inspection and seizure conferred by a warrant issued under this Schedule shall not be exercisable in respect of personal data which by virtue of section 28 are exempt from any of the provisions of this Act.

> *8   s.28 provides the national security exemption.*

9.– (1) Subject to the provisions of this paragraph, the powers of inspection and seizure conferred by a warrant issued under this Schedule shall not be exercisable in respect of-

(a) any communication between a professional legal adviser and his client in connection with the giving of legal advice to the client with respect to his obligations, liabilities or rights under this Act, or

(b) any communication between a professional legal adviser and his client, or between such an adviser or his client and any other person, made in connection with or in contemplation of proceedings under or arising out of this Act (including proceedings before the Tribunal) and for the purposes of such proceedings.

(2) Sub-paragraph (1) applies also to-

(a) any copy or other record of any such communication as is there mentioned, and

(b) any document or article enclosed with or referred to in any such communication if made in connection with the giving of any advice or, as the case may be, in connection with or in contemplation of and for the purposes of such proceedings as are there mentioned.

(3) This paragraph does not apply to anything in the possession of any person other than the professional legal adviser or his client or to anything held with the intention of furthering a criminal purpose.

(4) In this paragraph references to the client of a professional legal adviser include references to any person representing such a client.

10. If the person in occupation of any premises in respect of which a warrant is issued under this Schedule objects to the inspection or seizure under the warrant of any material on the grounds that it consists partly of matters in respect of which those powers are not exercisable, he shall, if the person executing the warrant so requests, furnish that person with a copy of so much of the material as is not exempt from those powers.

Return of warrants

11. A warrant issued under this Schedule shall be returned to the court from which it was issued-

(a) after being executed, or

(b) if not executed within the time authorised for its execution;

and the person by whom any such warrant is executed shall make an endorsement on it stating what powers have been exercised by him under the warrant.

Offences

12. Any person who-

(a) intentionally obstructs a person in the execution of a warrant issued under this Schedule, or

(b) fails without reasonable excuse to give any person executing such a warrant such assistance as he may reasonably require for the execution of the warrant,

is guilty of an offence.

12. The offence referred to here is punishable only as a summary offence (that is, a fine of no more than £5,000). All other offences in the Act are punishable in the Magistrates' or Crown Court. The maximum fine in the Magistrates' Court is £5,000 per offence. There is no upper limit in the Crown Court.

Vessels, vehicles etc.

13. In this Schedule "premises" includes any vessel, vehicle, aircraft or hovercraft, and references to the occupier of any premises include references to the person in charge of any vessel, vehicle, aircraft or hovercraft.

Scotland and Northern Ireland

14. In the application of this Schedule to Scotland-

    (a) for any reference to a circuit judge there is substituted a reference to the sheriff,

    (b) for any reference to information on oath there is substituted a reference to evidence on oath, and

    (c) for the reference to the court from which the warrant was issued there is substituted a reference to the sheriff clerk.

15. In the application of this Schedule to Northern Ireland-

    (a) for any reference to a circuit judge there is substituted a reference to a county court judge, and

    (b) for any reference to information on oath there is substituted a reference to a complaint on oath.

SCHEDULE 10

FURTHER PROVISIONS RELATING TO ASSISTANCE UNDER SECTION 53

If an individual applies to the Commissioner for assistance in relation to legal proceedings connected with processing for one of the special purposes (journalism, literary or artistic purposes) then the following types of assistance may be offered by the Commissioner. The aim is to ensure that cases of substantial public importance are decided upon and do not founder for lack of resources on the part of the claimant.

1. In this Schedule "applicant" and "proceedings" have the same meaning as in section 53.

2. The assistance provided under section 53 may include the making of arrangements for, or for the Commissioner to bear the costs of-

    (a) the giving of advice or assistance by a solicitor or counsel, and
    (b) the representation of the applicant, or the provision to him of such assistance as is usually given by a solicitor or counsel-
        (i) in steps preliminary or incidental to the proceedings, or
        (ii) in arriving at or giving effect to a compromise to avoid or bring an end to the proceedings.

3. Where assistance is provided with respect to the conduct of proceedings-

    (a) it shall include an agreement by the Commissioner to indemnify the applicant (subject only to any exceptions specified in the notification) in respect of any liability to pay costs or expenses arising by virtue of any judgment or order of the court in the proceedings,

> *3(a) "indemnify" means underwrite.*

    (b) it may include an agreement by the Commissioner to indemnify the applicant in respect of any liability to pay costs or expenses arising by virtue of any compromise or settlement arrived at in order to avoid the proceedings or bring the proceedings to an end, and
    (c) it may include an agreement by the Commissioner to indemnify the applicant in respect of any liability to pay damages pursuant to an undertaking given on the grant of interlocutory relief (in Scotland, an interim order) to the applicant.

4. Where the Commissioner provides assistance in relation to any proceedings, he shall do so on such terms, or make such other arrangements, as will secure that a person against whom the proceedings have been or are commenced is informed that assistance has been or is being provided by the Commissioner in relation to them.

5. In England and Wales or Northern Ireland, the recovery of expenses incurred by the Commissioner in providing an applicant with assistance (as taxed or assessed in such manner as may be prescribed by rules of court) shall constitute a first charge for the benefit of the Commissioner-

    (a) on any costs which, by virtue of any judgment or order of the court, are payable to the applicant by any other person in respect of the matter in connection with which the assistance is provided, and
    (b) on any sum payable to the applicant under a compromise or settlement arrived at in connection with that matter to avoid or bring to an end any proceedings.

> *5   The Commissioner is entitled to reimburse her expenditure made on behalf of a claimant from any damages or settlement moneys received by the claimant.*

6. In Scotland, the recovery of such expenses (as taxed or assessed in such manner as may be prescribed by rules of court) shall be paid to the Commissioner, in priority to other debts-

    (a) out of any expenses which, by virtue of any judgment or order of the court, are payable to the applicant by any other person in respect of the matter in connection with which the assistance is provided, and
    (b) out of any sum payable to the applicant under a compromise or settlement arrived at in connection with that matter to avoid or bring to an end any proceedings.

SCHEDULE 11

EDUCATIONAL RECORDS

Meaning of "educational record"

1. For the purposes of section 68 "educational record" means any record to which paragraph 2, 5 or 7 applies.

> *1   Such records will fall within the definition of data (assuming that they already do not do so by virtue of being processed by automatic equipment or forming part of a relevant filing system - see the definition of "data" s.1(1)) since they will be deemed to be an accessible record (see s.68(1)(c)).*

England and Wales

2. This paragraph applies to any record of information which-

    (a) is processed by or on behalf of the governing body of, or a teacher at, any school in England and Wales specified in paragraph 3,
    (b) relates to any person who is or has been a pupil at the school, and
    (c) originated from or was supplied by or on behalf of any of the persons specified in paragraph 4,

other than information which is processed by a teacher solely for the teacher's own use.

3. The schools referred to in paragraph 2(a) are-

(a) a school maintained by a local education authority, and

(b) a special school, as defined by section 6(2) of the Education Act 1996, which is not so maintained.

4. The persons referred to in paragraph 2(c) are-

(a) an employee of the local education authority which maintains the school,

(b) in the case of-

    (i) a voluntary aided, foundation or foundation special school (within the meaning of the School Standards and Framework Act 1998), or

    (ii) a special school which is not maintained by a local eduction authority,

a teacher or other employee at the school (including an educational psychologist engaged by the governing body under a contract for services),

(c) the pupil to whom the record relates, and

(d) a parent, as defined by section 576(1) of the Education Act 1996, of that pupil.

Scotland

5. This paragraph applies to any record of information which is processed-

(a) by an education authority in Scotland, and

(b) for the purpose of the relevant function of the authority,

other than information which is processed by a teacher solely for the teacher's own use.

6. For the purposes of paragraph 5-

(a) "education authority" means an education authority within the meaning of the Education (Scotland) Act 1980 ("the 1980 Act") or, in relation to a self-governing school, the board of management within the meaning of the Self-Governing Schools etc. (Scotland) Act 1989 ("the 1989 Act"),

(b) "the relevant function" means, in relation to each of those authorities, their function under section 1 of the 1980 Act and section 7(1) of the 1989 Act, and

(c) information processed by an education authority is processed for the purpose of the relevant function of the authority if the processing relates to the discharge of that function in respect of a person-

    (i) who is or has been a pupil in a school provided by the authority, or

    (ii) who receives, or has received, further education (within the meaning of the 1980 Act) so provided.

Northern Ireland

7.- (1) This paragraph applies to any record of information which-

(a) is processed by or on behalf of the Board of Governors of, or a teacher at, any grant-aided school in Northern Ireland,

(b) relates to any person who is or has been a pupil at the school, and

(c) originated from or was supplied by or on behalf of any of the persons specified

in paragraph 8, other than information which is processed by a teacher solely for the teacher's own use.

(2) In sub-paragraph (1) "grant-aided school" has the same meaning as in the Education and Libraries (Northern Ireland) Order 1986.

8. The persons referred to in paragraph 7(1) are-

   (a) a teacher at the school,
   (b) an employee of an education and library board, other than such a teacher,
   (c) the pupil to whom the record relates, and
   (d) a parent (as defined by Article 2(2) of the Education and Libraries (Northern Ireland) Order 1986) of that pupil.

England and Wales: transitory provisions

9.– (1) Until the appointed day within the meaning of section 20 of the School Standards and Framework Act 1998, this Schedule shall have effect subject to the following modifications.

(2) Paragraph 3 shall have effect as if for paragraph (b) and the "and" immediately preceding it there were substituted-

"(aa) a grant-maintained school, as defined by section 183(1) of the Education Act 1996,
(ab) a grant-maintained special school, as defined by section 337(4) of that Act, and
(b) a special school, as defined by section 6(2) of that Act, which is neither a maintained special school, as defined by section 337(3) of that Act, nor a grant-maintained special school."

(3) Paragraph 4(b)(i) shall have effect as if for the words from "foundation", in the first place where it occurs, to "1998)" there were substituted "or grant-maintained school".

SCHEDULE 12

ACCESSIBLE PUBLIC RECORDS

Meaning of "accessible public record"

1. For the purposes of section 68 "accessible public record" means any record which is kept by an authority specified-

   (a) as respects England and Wales, in the Table in paragraph 2,
   (b) as respects Scotland, in the Table in paragraph 4, or
   (c) as respects Northern Ireland, in the Table in paragraph 6,

and is a record of information of a description specified in that Table in relation to that authority.

> 1   *Like the records detailed in Schedule 11, these records will fall within the definition of data (assuming that they do not already do so by virtue of being processed by automatic equipment or forming part of a relevant filing system - see the definition of "data" s.1(1)) since they will be deemed to be an accessible record (see s.68(1)(c)).*

Housing and social services records: England and Wales

2. The following is the Table referred to in paragraph 1(a).

TABLE OF AUTHORITIES AND INFORMATION

The authorities	The accessible information
Housing Act local authority.	Information held for the purpose of any of the authority's tenancies.
Local social services authority.	Information held for any purpose of the authority's social services functions.

3.– (1) The following provisions apply for the interpretation of the Table in paragraph 2.

(2) Any authority which, by virtue of section 4(e) of the Housing Act 1985, is a local authority for the purpose of any provision of that Act is a "Housing Act local authority" for the purposes of this Schedule, and so is any housing action trust established under Part III of the Housing Act 1988.

(3) Information contained in records kept by a Housing Act local authority is "held for the purpose of any of the authority's tenancies" if it is held for any purpose of the relationship of landlord and tenant of a dwelling which subsists, has subsisted or may subsist between the authority and any individual who is, has been or, as the case may be, has applied to be, a tenant of the authority.

(4) Any authority which, by virtue of section 1 or 12 of the Local Authority Social Services Act 1970, is or is treated as a local authority for the purposes of that Act is a "local social services authority" for the purposes of this Schedule; and information contained in records kept by such an authority is "held for any purpose of the authority's social services functions" if it is held for the purpose of any past, current or proposed exercise of such a function in any case.

(5) Any expression used in paragraph 2 or this paragraph and in Part II of the Housing Act 1985 or the Local Authority Social Services Act 1970 has the same meaning as in that Act.

Housing and social services records: Scotland

4. The following is the Table referred to in paragraph 1(b).

TABLE OF AUTHORITIES AND INFORMATION

The authorities	The accessible information
Local authority. Scottish Homes.	Information held for the purpose of any of the body's tenancies.
Social work authority.	Information held for any purpose of the authority's functions under the Social Work (Scotland) Act 1968 and the enactments referred to in section 5(1B) of that Act.

5.– (1) The following provisions apply for the interpretation of the Table in paragraph 4.

(2) "Local authority" means-

(a) a council constituted under section 2 of the Local Government etc. (Scotland) Act 1994,

(b) a joint board or joint committee of two or more of those councils, or

(c) any trust under the control of such a council.

(3) Information contained in records kept by a local authority or Scottish Homes is held for the purpose of any of their tenancies if it is held for any purpose of the relationship of landlord and tenant of a dwelling-house which subsists, has subsisted or may subsist between the authority or, as the case may be, Scottish Homes and any individual who is, has been or, as the case may be, has applied to be a tenant of theirs.

(4) "Social work authority" means a local authority for the purposes of the Social Work (Scotland) Act 1968; and information contained in records kept by such an authority is held for any purpose of their functions if it is held for the purpose of any past, current or proposed exercise of such a function in any case.

Housing and social services records: Northern Ireland

6. The following is the Table referred to in paragraph 1(c).

TABLE OF AUTHORITIES AND INFORMATION

The authorities	The accessible information
The Northern Ireland Housing Executive.	Information held for the purpose of any of the Executive's tenancies.
A Health and Social Services Board.	Information held for the purpose of any past, current or proposed exercise by the Board of any function exercisable, by virtue of directions under Article 17(1) of the Health and Personal Social Services (Northern Ireland) Order 1972, by the Board on behalf of the Department of Health and Social Services with respect to the administration of personal social services under-
	(a) the Children and Young Persons Act (Northern Ireland) 1968; (b) the Health and Personal Social Services (Northern Ireland) Order 1972; (c) Article 47 of the Matrimonial Causes (Northern Ireland) Order 1978; (d) Article 11 of the Domestic Proceedings (Northern Ireland) Order 1980; (e) the Adoption (Northern Ireland) Order 1987; or (f) the Children (Northern Ireland) Order 1995.
An HSS trust	Information held for the purpose of any past, current or proposed exercise by the trust of any function exercisable, by virtue of an authorisation under Article 3(1) of the Health and Personal Social Services (Northern Ireland) Order 1994, by the trust on behalf of a Health and Social Services Board with respect to the administration of personal social services under any statutory provision mentioned in the last preceding entry.

7.– (1) This paragraph applies for the interpretation of the Table in paragraph 6.

(2) Information contained in records kept by the Northern Ireland Housing Executive is "held for the purpose of any of the Executive's tenancies" if it is held for any purpose of the relationship of landlord and tenant of a dwelling which subsists, has subsisted or may subsist between the Executive and any individual who is, has been or, as the case may be, has applied to be, a tenant of the Executive.

SCHEDULE 13

Modifications of Act having effect before 24th October 2007

1   The provisions of s.12A relate to rights of data subjects in relation to exempt manual data and apply until 23 October 2007. Without this section, data subjects would not have the right to rectify, block, or destroy certain manual records.

1. After section 12 there is inserted-

"**12A.–** (1)A data subject is entitled at any time by notice in writing-
  (a) to require the data controller to rectify, block, erase or destroy exempt manual data which are inaccurate or incomplete, or
  (b) to require the data controller to cease holding exempt manual data in a way incompatible with the legitimate purposes pursued by the data controller.
(2) A notice under subsection (1)(a) or (b) must state the data subject's reasons for believing that the data are inaccurate or incomplete or, as the case may be, his reasons for believing that they are held in a way incompatible with the legitimate purposes pursued by the data controller.
(3) If the court is satisfied, on the application of any person who has given a notice under subsection (1) which appears to the court to be justified (or to be justified to any extent) that the data controller in question has failed to comply with the notice, the court may order him to take such steps for complying with the notice (or for complying with it to that extent) as the court thinks fit.
(4) In this section "exempt manual data" means-
  (a) in relation to the first transitional period, as defined by paragraph 1(2) of Schedule 8, data to which paragraph 3 or 4 of that Schedule applies, and

1(4) (a) Exempt manual data are manual data forming part of an accessible record or eligible manual data relating to the financial standing of a data subject (see Sch 8, para 3 & 4)

    (b) in relation to the second transitional period, as so defined, data to which paragraph 14 of that Schedule applies.

> *1(4)(b) In relation to the second transitional period, exempt manual data are eligible manual data held before 24 October 1998 and accessible records (Sch 8, para 14).*

    (5) For the purposes of this section personal data are incomplete if, and only if, the data, although not inaccurate, are such that their incompleteness would constitute a contravention of the third or fourth data protection principles, if those principles applied to the data."

2. In section 32-

    (a) in subsection (2) after "section 12" there is inserted-
    "(dd) section 12A,", and
    (b) in subsection (4) after "12(8)" there is inserted ", 12A(3)".

3. In section 34 for "section 14(1) to (3)" there is substituted "sections 12A and 14(1) to (3)."

4. In section 53(1) after "12(8)" there is inserted ", 12A(3)".

5. In paragraph 8 of Part II of Schedule 1, the word "or" at the end of paragraph (c) is omitted and after paragraph (d) there is inserted "or

    (e) he contravenes section 12A by failing to comply with a notice given under subsection (1) of that section to the extent that the notice is justified."

SCHEDULE 14

TRANSITIONAL PROVISIONS AND SAVINGS

Interpretation

1. In this Schedule-

"the 1984 Act" means the Data Protection Act 1984;

"the old principles" means the data protection principles within the meaning of the 1984 Act;

"the new principles" means the data protection principles within the meaning of this Act.

Effect of registration under Part II of 1984 Act

2.– (1) Subject to sub-paragraphs (4) and (5) any person who, immediately before the commencement of Part III of this Act-

(a) is registered as a data user under Part II of the 1984 Act, or

(b) is treated by virtue of section 7(6) of the 1984 Act as so registered,

is exempt from section 17(1) of this Act until the end of the registration period or, if earlier, 24th October 2001.

2(1) See also the commentary at s.16(1).

---

(2) In sub-paragraph (1) "the registration period", in relation to a person, means-

(a) where there is a single entry in respect of that person as a data user, the period at the end of which, if section 8 of the 1984 Act had remained in force, that entry would have fallen to be removed unless renewed, and

(b) where there are two or more entries in respect of that person as a data user, the period at the end of which, if that section had remained in force, the last of those entries to expire would have fallen to be removed unless renewed.

(3) Any application for registration as a data user under Part II of the 1984 Act which is received by the Commissioner before the commencement of Part III of this Act (including any appeal against a refusal of registration) shall be determined in accordance with the old principles and the provisions of the 1984 Act.

(4) If a person falling within paragraph (b) of sub-paragraph (1) receives a notification under section 7(1) of the 1984 Act of the refusal of his application, sub-paragraph (1) shall cease to apply to him-

(a) if no appeal is brought, at the end of the period within which an appeal can be brought against the refusal, or

(b) on the withdrawal or dismissal of the appeal.

(5) If a data controller gives a notification under section 18(1) at a time when he is exempt from section 17(1) by virtue of sub-paragraph (1), he shall cease to be so exempt.

(6) The Commissioner shall include in the register maintained under section 19 an entry in respect of each person who is exempt from section 17(1) by virtue of sub-paragraph (1); and each entry shall consist of the particulars which, immediately before the commencement of Part III of this Act, were included (or treated as included) in respect of that person in the register maintained under section 4 of the 1984 Act.

(7) Notification regulations under Part III of this Act may make provision modifying the duty referred to in section 20(1) in its application to any person in respect of whom an entry in the register maintained under section 19 has been made under sub-paragraph (6).

(8) Notification regulations under Part III of this Act may make further transitional provision in connection with the substitution of Part III of this Act for Part II of the 1984 Act (registration), including provision modifying the application of provisions of Part III in transitional cases.

Rights of data subjects

3.– (1) The repeal of section 21 of the 1984 Act (right of access to personal data) does not affect the application of that section in any case in which the request (together with the information referred to in paragraph (a) of subsection (4) of that section and, in a case where it is required, the consent referred to in paragraph (b) of that subsection) was received before the day on which the repeal comes into force.

(2) Sub-paragraph (1) does not apply where the request is made by reference to this Act.

(3) Any fee paid for the purposes of section 21 of the 1984 Act before the commencement of section 7 in a case not falling within sub-paragraph (1) shall be taken to have been paid for the purposes of section 7.

4. The repeal of section 22 of the 1984 Act (compensation for inaccuracy) and the repeal of section 23 of that Act (compensation for loss or unauthorised disclosure) do not affect the application of those sections in relation to damage or distress suffered at any time by reason of anything done or omitted to be done before the commencement of the repeals.

5. The repeal of section 24 of the 1984 Act (rectification and erasure) does not affect any case in which the application to the court was made before the day on which the repeal comes into force.

6. Subsection (3)(b) of section 14 does not apply where the rectification, blocking, erasure or destruction occurred before the commencement of that section.

Enforcement and transfer prohibition notices served under Part V of 1984 Act

7.– (1) If, immediately before the commencement of section 40-

(a) an enforcement notice under section 10 of the 1984 Act has effect, and
(b) either the time for appealing against the notice has expired or any appeal has been determined,

then, after that commencement, to the extent mentioned in sub-paragraph (3), the notice shall have effect for the purposes of sections 41 and 47 as if it were an enforcement notice under section 40.

(2) Where an enforcement notice has been served under section 10 of the 1984 Act before the commencement of section 40 and immediately before that commencement either-

(a) the time for appealing against the notice has not expired, or
(b) an appeal has not been determined,

the appeal shall be determined in accordance with the provisions of the 1984 Act and the old principles and, unless the notice is quashed on appeal, to the extent mentioned in sub-paragraph (3) the notice shall have effect for the purposes of sections 41 and 47 as if it were an enforcement notice under section 40.

(3) An enforcement notice under section 10 of the 1984 Act has the effect described in sub-paragraph (1) or (2) only to the extent that the steps specified in the notice for complying with the old principle or principles in question are steps which the data controller could be required by an enforcement notice under section 40 to take for complying with the new principles or any of them.

8.– (1) If, immediately before the commencement of section 40-

(a) a transfer prohibition notice under section 12 of the 1984 Act has effect, and
(b) either the time for appealing against the notice has expired or any appeal has been determined,

then, on and after that commencement, to the extent specified in sub-paragraph (3), the notice shall have effect for the purposes of sections 41 and 47 as if it were an enforcement notice under section 40.

(2) Where a transfer prohibition notice has been served under section 12 of the 1984 Act and immediately before the commencement of section 40 either-

(a) the time for appealing against the notice has not expired, or
(b) an appeal has not been determined,

the appeal shall be determined in accordance with the provisions of the 1984 Act and the old principles and, unless the notice is quashed on appeal, to the extent mentioned in sub-paragraph (3) the notice shall have effect for the purposes of sections 41 and 47 as if it were an enforcement notice under section 40.

(3) A transfer prohibition notice under section 12 of the 1984 Act has the effect described in sub-paragraph (1) or (2) only to the extent that the prohibition imposed by the notice is one which could be imposed by an enforcement notice under section 40 for complying with the new principles or any of them.

Notices under new law relating to matters in relation to which 1984 Act had effect

9. The Commissioner may serve an enforcement notice under section 40 on or after the day on which that section comes into force if he is satisfied that, before that day, the data controller contravened the old principles by reason of any act or omission which would also have constituted a contravention of the new principles if they had applied before that day.

10. Subsection (5)(b) of section 40 does not apply where the rectification, blocking, erasure or destruction occurred before the commencement of that section.

11. The Commissioner may serve an information notice under section 43 on or after the day on which that section comes into force if he has reasonable grounds for

suspecting that, before that day, the data controller contravened the old principles by reason of any act or omission which would also have constituted a contravention of the new principles if they had applied before that day.

12. Where by virtue of paragraph 11 an information notice is served on the basis of anything done or omitted to be done before the day on which section 43 comes into force, subsection (2)(b) of that section shall have effect as if the reference to the data controller having complied, or complying, with the new principles were a reference to the data controller having contravened the old principles by reason of any such act or omission as is mentioned in paragraph 11.

Self-incrimination, etc.

13.– (1) In section 43(8), section 44(9) and paragraph 11 of Schedule 7, any reference to an offence under this Act includes a reference to an offence under the 1984 Act.

(2) In section 34(9) of the 1984 Act, any reference to an offence under that Act includes a reference to an offence under this Act.

Warrants issued under 1984 Act

14. The repeal of Schedule 4 to the 1984 Act does not affect the application of that Schedule in any case where a warrant was issued under that Schedule before the commencement of the repeal.

Complaints under section 36(2) of 1984 Act and requests for assessment under section 42

15. The repeal of section 36(2) of the 1984 Act does not affect the application of that provision in any case where the complaint was received by the Commissioner before the commencement of the repeal.

16. In dealing with a complaint under section 36(2) of the 1984 Act or a request for an assessment under section 42 of this Act, the Commissioner shall have regard to the provisions from time to time applicable to the processing, and accordingly-

  (a) in section 36(2) of the 1984 Act, the reference to the old principles and the provisions of that Act includes, in relation to any time when the new principles and the provisions of this Act have effect, those principles and provisions, and
  (b) in section 42 of this Act, the reference to the provisions of this Act includes, in relation to any time when the old principles and the provisions of the 1984 Act had effect, those principles and provisions.

Applications under Access to Health Records Act 1990 or corresponding Northern Ireland legislation

17.– (1) The repeal of any provision of the Access to Health Records Act 1990 does not affect-

(a) the application of section 3 or 6 of that Act in any case in which the application under that section was received before the day on which the repeal comes into force, or

(b) the application of section 8 of that Act in any case in which the application to the court was made before the day on which the repeal comes into force.

(2) Sub-paragraph (1)(a) does not apply in relation to an application for access to information which was made by reference to this Act.

18.– (1) The revocation of any provision of the Access to Health Records (Northern Ireland) Order 1993 does not affect-

(a) the application of Article 5 or 8 of that Order in any case in which the application under that Article was received before the day on which the repeal comes into force, or

(b) the application of Article 10 of that Order in any case in which the application to the court was made before the day on which the repeal comes into force.

(2) Sub-paragraph (1)(a) does not apply in relation to an application for access to information which was made by reference to this Act.

Applications under regulations under Access to Personal Files Act 1987 or corresponding Northern Ireland legislation

19.– (1) The repeal of the personal files enactments does not affect the application of regulations under those enactments in relation to-

(a) any request for information,
(b) any application for rectification or erasure, or
(c) any application for review of a decision,

which was made before the day on which the repeal comes into force.

(2) Sub-paragraph (1)(a) does not apply in relation to a request for information which was made by reference to this Act.

(3) In sub-paragraph (1) "the personal files enactments" means-

(a) in relation to Great Britain, the Access to Personal Files Act 1987, and
(b) in relation to Northern Ireland, Part II of the Access to Personal Files and Medical Reports (Northern Ireland) Order 1991.

Applications under section 158 of Consumer Credit Act 1974

20. Section 62 does not affect the application of section 158 of the (1974 c. 39.)Consumer Credit Act 1974 in any case where the request was received before the commencement of section 62, unless the request is made by reference to this Act.

SCHEDULE 15

MINOR AND CONSEQUENTIAL AMENDMENTS

Public Records Act 1958 (c. 51)

1.– (1) In Part II of the Table in paragraph 3 of Schedule 1 to the Public Records Act 1958 (definition of public records) for "the Data Protection Registrar" there is substituted "the Information Commissioner".

(2) That Schedule shall continue to have effect with the following amendment (originally made by paragraph 14 of Schedule 2 to the Data Protection Act 1984).

(3) After paragraph 4(1)(n) there is inserted-

"(nn)records of the Data Protection Tribunal".

Parliamentary Commissioner Act 1967 (c. 13)

2. In Schedule 2 to the Parliamentary Commissioner Act 1967 (departments etc. subject to investigation) for "Data Protection Registrar" there is substituted "Information Commissioner".

3. In Schedule 4 to that Act (tribunals exercising administrative functions), in the entry relating to the Data Protection Tribunal, for "section 3 of the Data Protection Act 1984" there is substituted "section 6 of the Data Protection Act 1998".

Superannuation Act 1972 (c. 11)

4. In Schedule 1 to the Superannuation Act 1972, for "Data Protection Registrar" there is substituted "Information Commissioner".

House of Commons Disqualification Act 1975 (c. 24)

5.– (1) Part II of Schedule 1 to the House of Commons Disqualification Act 1975 (bodies whose members are disqualified) shall continue to include the entry "The Data Protection Tribunal" (originally inserted by paragraph 12(1) of Schedule 2 to the Data Protection Act 1984).

(2) In Part III of that Schedule (disqualifying offices) for "The Data Protection Registrar" there is substituted "The Information Commissioner".

Northern Ireland Assembly Disqualification Act 1975 (c. 25)

6.– (1) Part II of Schedule 1 to the Northern Ireland Assembly Disqualification Act 1975 (bodies whose members are disqualified) shall continue to include the entry "The Data Protection Tribunal" (originally inserted by paragraph 12(3) of Schedule 2 to the Data Protection Act 1984).

(2) In Part III of that Schedule (disqualifying offices) for "The Data Protection Registrar" there is substituted "The Information Commissioner".

Representation of the People Act 1983 (c. 2)

7. In Schedule 2 of the Representation of the People Act 1983 (provisions which may be included in regulations as to registration etc), in paragraph 11A(2)-

    (a) for "data user" there is substituted "data controller", and
    (b) for "the Data Protection Act 1984" there is substituted "the Data Protection Act 1998".

Access to Medical Reports Act 1988 (c. 28)

8. In section 2(1) of the Access to Medical Reports Act 1988 (interpretation), in the definition of "health professional", for "the Data Protection (Subject Access Modification) Order 1987" there is substituted "the Data Protection Act 1998".

Football Spectators Act 1989 (c. 37)

9.– (1) Section 5 of the Football Spectators Act 1989 (national membership scheme: contents and penalties) is amended as follows.

(2) In subsection (5), for "paragraph 1(2) of Part II of Schedule 1 to the Data Protection Act 1984" there is substituted "paragraph 1(2) of Part II of Schedule 1 to the Data Protection Act 1998".

(3) In subsection (6), for "section 28(1) and (2) of the Data Protection Act 1984" there is substituted "section 29(1) and (2) of the Data Protection Act 1998".

Education (Student Loans) Act 1990 (c. 6)

10. Schedule 2 to the Education (Student Loans) Act 1990 (loans for students) so far as that Schedule continues in force shall have effect as if the reference in paragraph 4(2) to the Data Protection Act 1984 were a reference to this Act.

Access to Health Records Act 1990 (c. 23)

11. For section 2 of the Access to Health Records Act 1990 there is substituted-

    "Health professionals.
    2. In this Act "health professional" has the same meaning as in the Data Protection Act 1998."

12. In section 3(4) of that Act (cases where fee may be required) in paragraph (a), for "the maximum prescribed under section 21 of the Data Protection Act 1984" there is substituted "such maximum as may be prescribed for the purposes of this section by regulations under section 7 of the Data Protection Act 1998".

13. In section 5(3) of that Act (cases where right of access may be partially excluded) for the words from the beginning to "record" in the first place where it occurs there is substituted "Access shall not be given under section 3(2) to any part of a health record".

Access to Personal Files and Medical Reports (Northern Ireland) Order 1991 (1991/ 1707 (N.I. 14))

14. In Article 4 of the Access to Personal Files and Medical Reports (Northern Ireland) Order 1991 (obligation to give access), in paragraph (2) (exclusion of information to which individual entitled under section 21 of the Data Protection Act 1984) for "section 21 of the Data Protection Act 1984" there is substituted "section 7 of the Data Protection Act 1998".

15. In Article 6(1) of that Order (interpretation), in the definition of "health professional", for "the Data Protection (Subject Access Modification) (Health) Order 1987" there is substituted "the Data Protection Act 1998".

Tribunals and Inquiries Act 1992 (c. 53)

16. In Part 1 of Schedule 1 to the Tribunals and Inquiries Act 1992 (tribunals under direct supervision of Council on Tribunals), for paragraph 14 there is substituted-

"Data protection
14. (a) The Information Commissioner appointed under section 6 of the Data Protection Act 1998;
   (b) the Data Protection Tribunal constituted under that section, in respect of its jurisdiction under section 48 of that Act."

Access to Health Records (Northern Ireland) Order 1993 (1993/1250 (N.I. 4))

17. For paragraphs (1) and (2) of Article 4 of the Access to Health Records (Northern Ireland) Order 1993 there is substituted-

"(1) In this Order "health professional" has the same meaning as in the Data Protection Act 1998."

18. In Article 5(4) of that Order (cases where fee may be required) in sub-paragraph (a), for "the maximum prescribed under section 21 of the Data Protection Act 1984" there is substituted "such maximum as may be prescribed for the purposes of this Article by regulations under section 7 of the Data Protection Act 1998".

19. In Article 7 of that Order (cases where right of access may be partially excluded) for the words from the beginning to "record" in the first place where it occurs there is substituted "Access shall not be given under Article 5(2) to any part of a health record".

SCHEDULE 16

REPEALS AND REVOCATIONS

PART I

REPEALS

Chapter	Short title	Extent of repeal
1984 c. 35.	The Data Protection Act 1984.	The whole Act.
1986 c. 60.	The Financial Services Act Act 1986.	Section 190.
1987 c. 37.	The Access to Personal Files Act 1987.	The whole Act.
1988 c. 40.	The Education Reform Act 1988.	Section 223.
1988 c. 50.	The Housing Act 1988.	In Schedule 17, paragraph 80.
1990 c. 23.	The Access to Health Records Act 1990.	In section 1(1), the words from "but does not" to the end. In section 3, subsection (1)(a) to (e) and, in subsection (6)(a), the words "in the case of an application made otherwise than by the patient". Section 4(1) and (2). In section 5(1)(a)(i), the words "of the patient or" and the word "other". In section 10, in subsection (2) the words "or orders" and in subsection (3) the words "or an order under section 2(3) above". In section 11, the definitions of "child" and "parental responsibility".
1990 c. 37.	The Human Fertilisation and Embryology Act 1990.	Section 33(8).
1990 c. 41.	The Courts and Legal Services Act 1990.	In Schedule 10, paragraph 58.

Chapter	Short title	Extent of repeal
1992 c. 13.	The Further and Higher Education Act 1992.	Section 86.
1992 c. 37.	The Further and Higher Education (Scotland) Act 1992.	Section 59.
1993 c. 8.	The Judicial Pensions and Retirement Act 1993.	In Schedule 6, paragraph 50.
1993 c. 10.	The Charities Act 1993.	Section 12.
1993 c. 21.	The Osteopaths Act 1993.	Section 38.
1994 c. 17.	The Chiropractors Act 1994.	Section 38.
1994 c. 19.	The Local Government (Wales) Act 1994.	In Schedule 13, paragraph 30.
1994 c. 33.	The Criminal Justice and Public Order Act 1994.	Section 161.
1994 c. 39.	The Local Government etc. (Scotland) Act 1994.	In Schedule 13, paragraph 154.

PART II

REVOCATIONS

Number	Title	Extent of revocation
S.I. 1991/1142.	The Data Protection Registration Fee Order 1991.	The whole Order.
S.I. 1991/1707 (N.I. 14).	The Access to Personal Files and Medical Reports (Northern Ireland) Order 1991.	Part II. The Schedule.
S.I. 1992/3218.	The Banking Co-ordination (Second Council Directive) Regulations 1992.	In Schedule 10, paragraphs 15 and 40.
S.I. 1993/1250 (N.I. 4).	The Access to Health Records (Northern Ireland) Order 1993.	In Article 2(2), the definitions of "child" and "parental responsibility". In Article 3(1), the words from "but does not include" to the end.

Number	Title	Extent of revocation
		In Article 5, paragraph (1)(a) to (d) and, in paragraph (6)(a), the words "in the case of an application made otherwise than by the patient".
		Article 6(1) and (2).
		In Article 7(1)(a)(i), the words "of the patient or" and the word "other".
S.I. 1994/429 (N.I. 2).	The Health and Personal Social Services (Northern Ireland) Order 1994.	In Schedule 1, the entries relating to the Access to Personal Files and Medical Reports (Northern Ireland) Order 1991.
S.I. 1994/1696.	The Insurance Companies (Third Insurance Directives) Regulations 1994.	In Schedule 8, paragraph 8.
S.I. 1995/755 (N.I. 2).	The Children (Northern Ireland) Order 1995.	In Schedule 9, paragraphs 177 and 191.
S.I. 1995/3275.	The Investment Services Regulations 1995.	In Schedule 10, paragraphs 3 and 15.
S.I. 1996/2827.	The Open-Ended Investment Companies (Investment Companies with Variable Capital) Regulations 1996.	In Schedule 8, paragraphs 3 and 26.

Index

Index compiled by Terry Halliday,
Indexing Specialists, Hove.